Edward Harrison Barker

Wanderings by Southern Waters

Eastern Aquitaine

Edward Harrison Barker

Wanderings by Southern Waters
Eastern Aquitaine

ISBN/EAN: 9783337143749

Printed in Europe, USA, Canada, Australia, Japan

Cover: Foto ©Andreas Hilbeck / pixelio.de

More available books at **www.hansebooks.com**

A BIT OF OLD FIGEAC.

Frontispiece.

WANDERINGS
BY
SOUTHERN WATERS

EASTERN AQUITAINE

BY
EDWARD HARRISON BARKER
AUTHOR OF "WAYFARING IN FRANCE"

WITH ILLUSTRATIONS

LONDON
RICHARD BENTLEY AND SON
Publishers in Ordinary to Her Majesty the Queen
1893

CONTENTS

	PAGE
THE VALLEY OF THE OUYSSE AND ROC-AMADOUR	1
FROM THE ALZOU TO THE DORDOGNE	48
WAYFARING UNDERGROUND	91
IN THE VALLEY OF THE CÉLÉ	108
IN THE ALBIGEOIS	158
ACROSS THE ROUERGUE	209
THE BLACK CAUSSE	234
THE CAÑON OF THE TARN	248
IN THE VALLEY OF THE LOT	279

OAK CHIMNEY-PIECE AT THE SÉNÉCHAUSSÉE (NOW HÔTEL DE VILLE)
OF MARTEL.

LIST OF ILLUSTRATIONS

A BIT OF OLD FIGEAC - - - - *Frontispiece*

OAK CHIMNEY PIECE AT THE SÉNÉCHAUSSÉE (NOW HÔTEL DE
    VILLE) OF MARTEL - - - - *Page* vi

THE PONT VALENTRÉ AT CAHORS - - - ,, 1

ROC-AMADOUR - - - *To face page* 10

PORCH OF THE CATHEDRAL OF ALBI ,, 160

AMBIALET - - - - - ,, 182

CIGALA, THE SHOEBLACK - ,, 288

THE PONT VALENTRÉ AT CAHORS.

WANDERINGS BY SOUTHERN WATERS

THE VALLEY OF THE OUYSSE AND ROC-AMADOUR.

From the Old-English town of Martel, in Guyenne, I turned southward towards the Dordogne. For a few miles the road lay over a barren plateau; then it skirted a desolate gorge with barely a trace of vegetation upon its naked sides, save the desert-loving box clinging to the white stones. A little stream that flowed here led down into the rich valley of Creysse, blessed with abundance of fruit. Here I found the nightingales and the spring flowers that avoid the wind-blown hills. Patches of wayside took a yellow tinge from the cross-wort galium ; others, conquered by ground-ivy or veronica, were purple or blue. Presently the tiled roofs of the village of Creysse were seen through the poplars and walnuts. A delightful spot for a poetical angler is this, for the Dordogne runs close by in the shadow of prodigious rocks and overhanging trees. What a noble and stately river I thought it, as the old ferryman, with white cotton nightcap on his head, punted me across! I took the greater pleasure in its breadth and grandeur here because I had seen it an infant river in the Auvergne mountains, and had watched its growth as it rushed between walls of rock and forest towards the plains.

What witchery of romance and spell-bound fancy is in the song of the Dordogne as it breaks over its shallows under high rocky cliffs and ruined castles! Everything that can charm the poet and the artist is here. The grandeur of rugged nature combines with the most enticing beauty of water and meadow, and the voices of the past echo with a sweet sadness from cliff to cliff. It is said that several of these castles were built to prevent the English from coming up the river, but this may be treated as one of the many fanciful legends respecting the British period which are repeated throughout Aquitaine.

By cutting off a curve of the Dordogne I soon came to the river-side village of Meyronne, and here I stopped for a meal at a very pleasant little inn, where to my surprise I found that I had been preceded a few days before by another Englishman, who, accompanied by a Frenchman, had come up from Bordeaux in a boat. They must have found it very hard work rowing against the rapids. The hostess here was evidently a woman who treasured her household gods, but who liked also to show them. She gave me my coffee in a china cup that looked as if it had belonged to her great-grandmother; and in the bright little room where she served my lunch was a large walnut buffet elaborately and admirably carved, bearing the date 1676.

After Meyronne my road ran for a few miles beside the broad and curving river. The forms of the great cliffs on each side were ever changing. Over a sky intensely blue sailed the fleecy April clouds before the soft west wind, and whenever the sun shone out with unveiled splendour, the rays fell with summer warmth. While the tinkling of sheep-bells from the ledges of the rocks came down to me, the passionate warble of nightingales, that could not wait for the night, must have risen from the leafy valley to the ears of the listless shepherd-boy gathering feather-grass where goats would not dare to venture, or eating his dark bread in the sun on the edge of a precipice. Time flowed gently like the river, and I was surprised to find myself at Lacave so soon. This village is near the spot where the Ouysse falls into the Dordogne. A little beyond the clustering houses, upon the edge of a high rocky promontory overlooking the Ouysse, is the castle of Belcastel, still retaining its feudal keep and outer wall. In this fortress the English are said to have kept many of their prisoners.

I now left the Dordogne and ascended the valley of the Ouysse. This stream is one of the most remarkable of the natural phenomena of France. To judge from its breadth near the mouth, one would suppose that it had flowed fifty or a hundred miles, but its entire length is less than ten miles. It is already a river when it rises out of the depths of the earth. The narrow valley that it waters is a gorge 500 or 600 feet deep through the greater part of its distance. The traveller at the bottom supposes, or is ready to suppose, that he is in some ravine of the high mountains; in reality, it is simply a fissure of the plateau that was once the bed of the sea. There is no igneous, no metamorphic rock here; nothing but limestone of the jurassic formation. The convexities on one side of the fissure correspond with marked regularity to the concavities on the other.

For awhile I walked on the lush grass by the brimming river, where in the little creeks and bays the water-ranunculus floated its small white flowers that were to continue the race. Then I left the water and the green ribbon that followed its margin, and, taking a sheep-track, rose upon the arid steeps, where the thinly-scattered aromatic southernwood was putting forth its dusty leaves. The bare rocks, yellow, white, and gray, towered above me; they were beneath me; they faced me across the valley; wherever I looked they were shutting me off from the outer world. No nightingales were singing here, but I heard the melancholy scream of the hawk and the harsh croak of the raven. And yet, when I looked down into the bottom of this steep desert of stones, what soft and vernal beauty was there! Over the grass of living green was spread the gold of cowslips, just as if that strip of meadow, with its gently-gliding river, had been lifted out of an English dale and dropped into the midst of the sternest scenery of Southern France.

As I went on I soon found that the stony wastes had their flowers too. It would seem as if Nature had wished to console the desert by giving to it her loveliest and most enticing blossoms. I came upon colonies of the poet's narcissus, breathing over the rocks so sweet a fragrance that it was as if a miracle had been wrought to draw it out of the earth. I walked knee-deep through blooming asphodels, beautiful and strange, but only noticed here by the wild bee. I gathered sprays of the graceful alpine-tea, densely crowded with delicate white bloom, and marvelled at the wanton splendour of the iris colouring the gray and yellow stones with its gorgeous blue.

Still following the Ouysse, I came to a spot where the valley ended in an amphitheatre formed by steep hills more than 600 feet high, and covered for the most part with dwarf oak. In the hollow under the dark cliffs was a little lake or pool forty or fifty yards from shore to shore. The water showed no sign of trouble save where it overflowed its basin on the western side, and formed the river that I had been keeping in sight for hours. The pool filled the Gouffre de St. Sauveur. Until the Ouysse finds this opening in the earth it is a subterranean river, and it must flow at a great depth, probably at the base of the calcareous formation, inasmuch as it continues to rise from the gulf the whole year, although from the month of August until the autumn rains nearly every water-course in the country is marked by a curving line of dry pebbles. The funnel-shaped hole descends vertically to the depth of about ninety feet, but there is no means of knowing how far it descends obliquely. The tourist may occasionally catch sight of a shepherd boy or girl with goats or sheep upon the bare or wooded rocks, but his feeling will be one of deep loneliness. He will see ravens and hawks about the crags, and about the river half covered in summer with floating pond-weed, watercress, and the broad leaves of the yellow lily, he will notice many a water-ouzel bobbing with white breast, water-hens gliding from bank to bank, merry bands of divers, and the brilliant blue gleam of the passing kingfisher, which here is allowed to fish in peace, like the otter.

The Gouffre de St. Sauveur has its legend. It is said that when the church of St. Sauveur, on the neighbouring hill, was in imminent danger at the time of the Revolution, the bells were thrown into the pool so that they should not fall into the hands of the enemy. Imaginative people fancy that they can sometimes hear them ringing at the bottom of the water.

After leaving the pool—now very sombre in the shadow of the wooded hill—I crossed a ridge separating me from the Gouffre de Cabouy, out of which flows a tributary of the Ouysse. Thence I reached the deep and singularly savage gorge of the Alzou, which brought me to Roc-Amadour, when the afterlight of sunset was lingering rosily upon the naked crags.

*   *   *   *   *

Rocks reach far overhead, dazzlingly white where the sunbeams strike them, and below is a green line of narrow valley. A tinkling of bells comes from the stony sides of the gorge, where sheep are browsing the scant herbage and young shoots of southernwood; and from the curving fillet of meadow, where the grass seems to grow while the eye watches it, rises the shrill little song of the stream hurrying over its yellow bed, which may be dry again to-morrow. This Alzou is no more to be depended upon than a coquette. After a period of drought, a storm that has passed away hours ago will cause it suddenly to come hissing down over the dry stones; but the next day no trace of the flow may be found save a few pools. Or it may grow to a torrent, even a river, that in its wild career scoffs at banks, and spreads devastation through the valley.

It is April, and the nightingales, the swallows, the flowers, the bees, and the kids, whose trembling voices are heard all about the rocks, tell me that the spring has come. I cannot rest in my cottage on the side of the gorge, not even on the balcony that seems to hang in the air over the depth; the sounds from the valley, especially those that the imagination hears, are too enticing.

Upon a high ledge of rock to which I have climbed, not without some unpleasant qualms, I stretch myself out upon a strip of short turf sprinkled with the flowers of the white rock-rose and bordered with candytuft, and try to drive out of mind the only disagreeable thought I have at this moment— that of getting down to the path, where I was safe. The worst part of climbing precipitous places is not the going up, but the coming down. Not a human being or dwelling is in sight, so that I can contemplate the wildness of the scene to my mind's content. But a very hoarse voice not far above tells me that I am not alone. A raven perched upon a jutting piece of rock, that curiously resembles some monstrous animal, is watching me, and he looks a very crafty old bird who could speak either French or English if he liked. Presently he flaps heavily off to the opposite side of the gorge, and fetches his wife. They fly over me almost within gunshot, going round and round, expressing an opinion or sentiment with an occasional croak, but apparently quite willing to make their dinner-hour suit my convenience. Do they suppose that I have really taken the trouble to climb up here to die out of the world's way and the sight of my fellow-creatures, like that very unearthly poet whose story Shelley has written? Do they think that they are going to make a hearty meal upon me this evening or to-morrow morning? I remain quite still, pleased at the thought of cheating the greedy, croaking scavengers of Nature, and hoping that they will grow bold enough to settle at length somewhere near me. But they are too suspicious: perhaps with their superior sight they note the blinking of my eyes as I look upwards at the dazzling sky, or instinct may tell them that I am not lying down after the manner of a dying animal. Their patience is more than a match for mine, and so I come down from my ledge and make my way back to my cottage before the pink blush of evening has faded from the rocks.

When the angelus has sounded from the ancient sanctuary, and all the forms of the valley are dim in the dusk, the silence is broken again by a very quiet little bell, which might be called the fairies' angelus if it did not keep ringing all through the spring and summer nights. It is like a treble note of the piano softly touched. It steals up from amongst the flags, hyacinths, and box-bushes of the neglected little garden which I call mine, terraced upon the side of the gorge just beneath the balcony. Now, from all the terraced gardens planted with fruit-trees, comes the same sound of low, clear notes, some a little higher than others, but all in the treble, feebly struck by unseen musicians. How sweetly this tinkling rises from the earth, that trembles with the bursting of seeds and the shooting of stems in the first warm nights of spring! And to think that the musicians should be toads—yes, toads—the most despised and the most unjustly treated of creatures!

This cottage is at Roc-Amadour, and before writing about the place I cannot do better than go down to the level of the stream, and look up at the amazing cluster of buildings clinging to the rocks on one side of the gorge, while the old walls are whitened by the pale brilliancy of the moon. Above the roofs of all the houses is a mass of masonry, vast and heavy, pierced by narrow Romanesque windows — a building uncouth and monstrous, like the surrounding crags. It stands upon a ledge of the cliff, partly in the hollow of the rock, which, indeed, forms its innermost wall. Higher still a great cross shows against the sky, and near to it, upon the edge of the precipice, are the ramparts of a mediæval fortress, now combined with a modern building, which is the residence of the clergy attached to the sanctuary of Notre Dame de Roc-Amadour.

ROC-AMADOUR.

The sanctuary — it is inside the massive pile under the beetling rock, and over the roofs of the houses — explains why men in far-distant times had the strange notion of gathering together and constructing dwellings upon a spot where Nature must have offered the harshest opposition to such a project. The chosen site was not only precipitous, but lay in the midst of a calcareous desert, where no stream nor spring of water could be relied upon for six months in the year, and where the only soil that was not absolutely unproductive was covered with dense forest infested by wolves.* And yet, in course of time, there grew up upon these forbidding rocks, in the midst of this desert, a little town that obtained a wide celebrity, and was even fortified, as the five ruinous gateways, with towers along the line of the single street, prove even now, notwithstanding the deplorable recklessness with which the structures of the ancient burg have been degraded or demolished during the last half-century. Nothing is more certain than that the origin of Roc-Amadour, and the cause of its development, were religious. It was called into existence by pilgrims; it grew with the growth of pilgrimages, and if it were not for pilgrims at the present day half the houses now occupied would be allowed to fall into ruin. It is impossible to look

* Robert du Mont, in his supplement to Sigibert's Chronicles, wrote, more than five hundred years ago, of Roc-Amadour: 'Est locus in Cadurcensi pago montaneis et horribile solitudine circumdatus.'

at it without wonder, either in the daylight or the moonlight. It appears to have been wrenched out of the known order of human works—the result of common motives—and however often Roc-Amadour may suddenly meet the eye upon turning the gorge, the picture never fails to be surprising. It has really the air of a holy place, which many others famed for holiness have not.

The founder of the sanctuary was a hermit, whose contemplative spirit led him to this savage and uninhabited valley, whose name, in the early Christian ages, was *Vallis tenebrosa*, but in which Nature had fashioned numerous caverns, more or less tempting to an anchorite. He is called Amator—*Amator rupis*—by the Latin chroniclers—a name that, with the spread of the Romance language, would easily have become corrupted to Amadour by the people. According to the legend, however, which for an uncertain number of centuries has obtained general credence in the Quercy and the Bas-Limousin, and which in these days is much upheld by the clergy, although a learned Jesuit—the Père Caillau—who sifted all the annals relating to Roc-Amadour felt compelled to treat it as a pious invention, the hermit Amator or Amadour was no other than Zaccheus, who climbed into the sycamore. The legend further says that he was the husband of St. Veronica, and that, after the crucifixion, they left the Holy Land in a vessel which eventually landed them on the western coast of

Gaul, not far from the present city of Bordeaux. They became associated with the mission of St. Martial, the first Bishop of Limoges, and at a later period Zaccheus, hearing of a rocky solitude in Aquitania, a little to the south of the Dordogne, abandoned to wild beasts, proceeded thither, and chose a cavern in the escarped side of a cliff for his hermitage. Here, meditating upon the merits of the Mother of Christ, he became one of her most devoted servants in that age, and during his life he caused a small chapel to be raised to her upon the rock near his cavern, which was consecrated by St. Martial. All this is open to controversy, but what is undoubtedly true is that one of the earliest sanctuaries of Europe associated with the name of Mary was at Roc-Amadour.

It is recorded that Roland, passing through the Quercy in the year 778 with his uncle, Charlemagne, made a point of stopping at Roc-Amadour for the purpose of 'offering to the most holy Virgin a gift of silver of the same weight as his bracmar, or sword.' After his death, if Duplex and local tradition are to be trusted, this sword was brought to Roc-Amadour, and the curved rusty blade of crushing weight which is now to be seen hanging to a wall is said to be a faithful copy of the famous Durandel, which is supposed to have been stolen by the Huguenots when they pillaged the church and burnt the remains of St. Amadour.

That in the twelfth century the fame of Roc-

Amadour as a place of pilgrimage was established we have very good evidence in the fact that one of the pilgrims to the sanctuary in 1170 was Henry II. of England. He had fallen seriously ill at Mote-Gercei, and believing that he had been restored to health through the intercession of the Virgin, he set out for the 'Dark Valley' in fulfilment of a vow that he had made to her; but as this journey into the Quercy brought him very near the territory of his enemies, the annalists tell us that he was accompanied by a great multitude of infantry and cavalry, as though he were marching to battle. But he injured no one, and gave abundant alms to the poor. Thirteen years later, the King's rebellious son, Henry, Court Mantel, pillaged the sanctuary of its treasure in order to pay his ruffianly soldiers. This memorable sacrilege had much to do with the insurmountable antipathy of the Quercynois for the English.

I have before me an old and now exceedingly rare little book on Roc-Amadour, which was written by the Jesuit Odo de Gissey, and published at Tulle in 1666. In this, Court Mantel's exploit is spoken of as follows:

'Les guerres d'entre nos Rois très Chrétiens et les Anglais en ce Royaume de France guerroyant ruinèrent en quelque façon Roc-Amadour; mais plus que tous Henri III., Roi d'Angleterre, ingrat des grâces que son père Henri II. y avait reçues, en dépit de son père qui affectionnait cette Église, son avarice le poussant, pilla cet oratoire et enleva les plaques qui couvraient le corps de S. Amadour et emporta ce qui était de la Trésorerie ; mais Dieu qui ne laisse rien impuni châtia le sacrilege de cet impie Prince par une mort malheureuse. De quoi lise qui voudra Roger de Houedan, historien Anglais en la 2 partie de ses Annales.'

There are early records of miracles wrought at Roc-Amadour. Gauthier de Coinsy, a monk and poet born at Amiens in 1177, has left a poem telling how the troubadour, Pierre de Sygelard, singing the praises of the Virgin in her chapel at Roc-Amadour to the accompaniment of his *vielle* (hurdy-gurdy), begged of her as a miraculous sign to let one of her candles come down from her altar. According to the poem, the candle came down, and stood upon the musical instrument, to the horror and disgust of a monk who was looking on, and who saw no miracle in the matter, but wicked enchantment. He put the candle back indignantly, but when the minstrel sang and played it came down as before. The movement was repeated again before the monk would believe that the miracle was genuine. The poem, which is in the Northern dialect, and is marked throughout by a charming *naïveté*, commences with a eulogium of the Virgin :

'La douce mère du Créatour
À l'église à Rochemadour
Fait tants miracles, tants hauts faits,
C'uns moultes biax livres en est faits.'

The huge, inartistic, but imposing block of masonry that appears from a little distance to be clinging, after the manner of a swallow's nest, to the precipitous face of the rock, and which is reached from below by more than 200 steps in venerable dilapidation,* contains the church of St. Sauveur, the chapel of the Virgin, called the Miraculous Chapel, and the chapel of St. Amadour, all distinct. The last-named is a little crypt, and the Miraculous Chapel conveys the impression of being likewise one, for it is partly under the overleaning rock, the rugged surface of which, blackened by the smoke of the countless tapers which have been burnt there in the course of ages, is seen without any facing of masonry.

If by looking at certain details of this composite structure one could shut off the surroundings from the eye, the mind might feed without any hindrance upon the ideas of old piety and the fervour of souls who, when Europe was like a troubled and forlorn sea, sought the quietude and safety of these rocks, lifted far above the raging surf. But the hindrance is found on every side. The sense of artistic fitness is wounded by incongruities of architectural style, of ideas which meet but do not marry. The brazen altar in the Miraculous Chapel was well enough at the Paris Exhibition of 1889, where it could be admired as a piece of elaborate brass work, but at

* Since the foregoing was written the old slabs have been turned round, and the steps been made to look quite new.

Roc-Amadour it is a direct challenge to the spirit of the spot. Then again, late Gothic architecture has been grafted upon the early Romanesque. Those who restored the building after it had been reduced to a ruin by the Huguenots in 1562 set the example of bad taste. The revolutionists of 1793 having in their turn wrought their fury upon it, the work of restoration was again undertaken during the last half-century, but the opportunity of correcting the mistake of the previous renovators was lost. The piece of Romanesque architecture whose character has been best preserved is the detached chapel of St. Michael, raised like a pigeon-house against the rock; but even this has been carefully scraped on the outside to make it correspond as nearly as possible to some adjacent work of recent construction.

The ancient treasure of Roc-Amadour has been scattered or melted down, but the image of the Virgin and Child, which according to the local tradition was carved out of the trunk of a tree by St. Amadour himself, is still to be seen over the altar in the Miraculous Chapel. It is probably 800 years old, and it may be older. There is no record to help hypothesis with regard to its antiquity, for since the pilgrimage originated it appears to have been an object of veneration, and the commencement of the pilgrimage is lost in the dimness of the past. Like the statue of the Virgin at Le Puy, it is as black as ebony, but this is the effect of age, and the smoke of incense and candles.

The antiquity of the image is, moreover, proved by the artistic treatment. The Child is crowned and rests upon the Virgin's knee; she does not touch him with her hands. This is in accordance with the early Christian sentiment, which dwells upon the kingship of the Child as distinguished from the later mediæval feeling, which rests without fear upon the Virgin's maternal love and makes her clasp the Infant fondly to her breast.

The 'miraculous bell' of Roc-Amadour has not rung since 1551, but it may do so any day or night, for it is still suspended to the vault of the Miraculous Chapel. It is of iron, and was beaten into shape with the hammer—facts which, together with its form, are regarded as certain evidence of its antiquity. The first time that it is said to have rung by its own movement was in 1385, and three days afterwards, according to Odo de Gissey, the phenomenon was repeated during the celebration of the Mass. All those who were present bore testimony to the fact upon oath before the apostolic notary.

Very early in the Middle Ages the faith spread among mariners, and others exposed to the dangers of the sea, that the Lady of Roc-Amadour had great power to help them when in distress. Hugues Farsit, Canon of Laon, wrote a treatise in 1140, 'De miraculis Beatæ Virginis rupis Amatoris,' wherein he speaks of her as the 'Star of the Sea,' and the hymn 'Ave maris stella' is one of those most frequently sung in these days by the pilgrims at Roc-Amadour. A statement, written and signed by a Breton pilgrim in 1534, shows how widely this particular devotion had then spread among those who trusted their lives to the uncertain sea :

'I, Louis Le Baille, merchant of the town of Pontscorf, on the river Ellé, in the diocese of Vannes, declare with truth that, returning from a voyage to Scotland the 13th of the month of February, 1534, at about ten o'clock at night, we were overtaken by such a violent storm that the waves covered the vessel, in which were twenty-six persons, and we went to the bottom. During the voyage somebody said to me : " Let us recommend ourselves to God and to the Virgin Mary of Roc-Amadour. Let us put her name upon this spar and trust ourselves to the care of this good Lady." He who gave me this good counsel and myself fastened ourselves to the spar with a rope. The tempest carried us away, but in so fortunate a manner that the next day we found ourselves on the coast of Bayonne. Half dead, we landed by the grace of God and the aid of His pitiful mother, Notre Dame de Roc-Amadour. I have come here out of gratitude for this blessing, and have accomplished the journey in fulfilment of my vow to her, in proof of which I have signed here with my hand.— LOUIS BAILLE.'

Such streams of pilgrims crossed the country from various directions, moving towards the sanctuary in the Haut-Quercy, that inns or 'halts' were called into existence on the principal lines of route, and lanterns were set up at night for the guidance of the wanderers. The last halt was close to Roc-Amadour, at a spot still called the *Hospitalet*. Here were religious, who bound up the pilgrims' bleeding feet, and provided them with food before they descended to the burg and completed the last part of their pilgrimage—the ascent of the steps—upon their knees. The *sportelle*, or badge of Notre Dame de Roc-Amadour, ensured the wearer against interference or ill-treatment on his journey. It is acknowledged that the English respected it even in time of war. At the Great Pardon of Roc-Amadour, in 1546, so great was the crowd of pilgrims, who had come from all parts, that many persons were suffocated. The innkeepers' tents gave the surrounding country the appearance of a vast camp. Sixteen years later, when Roc-Amadour fell into the hands of the Huguenots, and the religious buildings were pillaged and partly destroyed, the pilgrimage received a blow from which it never quite recovered. It ceased completely at the Revolution, but has since been revived, and some thousand genuine pilgrims, chiefly of the peasant class, now visit Roc-Amadour every year.

For nearly 300 years the history of the Querey and Roc-Amadour was intimately associated with that of England. Henry II. did not at first claim the Querey as a part of Eleanor's actual possessions in Aquitaine; but he claimed homage from the Count of Toulouse, who was then suzerain of the Count of Quercy. Homage being refused, Henry invaded the county, captured Cahors, where he left Becket with a garrison, and thence proceeded to reduce the other strongholds. Roc-Amadour appears to have offered little if any resistance. The Quercy was formally made over to the English in 1191 by the treaty signed by Philip Augustus and Richard Cœur-de-Lion; but the aged Raymond V. of Toulouse protested, and the Quercynois still more loudly. These descendants of the Cadurci found it very difficult to submit to English rule. Unlike the Gascons, who became thoroughly English during those three centuries, and were so loath to change their rulers again that they fought for the King of England to the last, the Quercynois were never reconciled to the Plantagenets, but were ever ready to seize an opportunity of rebelling against them. It is well known that Richard Cœur-de-Lion lost his life at the hand of a nobleman of the Quercy. While Guyenne was distracted by the family quarrel of the first Plantagenets, the troubadour Bertrand de Born by his gift of words so stirred up the patriotic and martial ardour of the Aquitanians that a league was formed against the English, which included Talleyrand, Count of Périgord, Guilhem (or Fortanier) de Gourdon, a powerful lord of the Quercy, De Montfort, the Viscounts of Turenne and Ventadour. These nobles swore upon the

Gospels to remain united and faithful to the cause of Aquitaine; but Richard, partly by feats of war and partly by diplomacy, in which it is said the argument of money had no inconsiderable share, broke up the league, and Bertrand de Born, being abandoned, fell into the Plantagenet's hands. But he was pardoned, probably because Richard was a troubadour himself in his leisure moments, and had a fellow-feeling for all who loved the 'gai sçavoir.' Meanwhile, the Lord of Gourdon was not to be gained over by fair words or bribes, and Richard besieged his castle, some ruins of which may still be seen on the rock that overhangs the little town of Gourdon in the Quercy. The fortress was taken, and Richard in his fury caused the stern old man who defended it and two of his sons to be put to death. But there was a third son, Bertrand de Gourdon, who, seeking an opportunity of avenging his father and brothers, joined the garrison of the castle of Châlus in the Limousin, which Richard soon afterwards besieged. He aimed the bolt or the arrow which brought Richard's stormy life to a close. Although forgiven by the dying Cœur-de-Lion, Bertrand was flayed alive by the Brabançons who were in the English army. He left no descendants, but his collaterals long afterwards bore the name of Richard in memory of Bertrand's vengeance.

A member of a learned society at Cahors has sought to prove that Gourdon in the Quercy is the place where the family of General Gordon of Khartoum fame had its origin. It is true that the name of this town in all old charts is spelt Gordon; but, inasmuch as it is a compound of two Celtic words meaning raven's rock, it might as feasibly have been handed down by the Gaelic Scotch as by the Cadurcians.

The Plantagenets came to be termed 'the devil's race' by the people of Guyenne. This may have originated in a saying attributed to Richard himself in Aquitaine: 'It is customary in our family for the sons to hate their father. We come from the devil, and we shall return to the devil.'

In 1368 the English, having again to reduce the Quercy, laid siege to Roc-Amadour. The burghers held out only for a short time, and the place being surrendered, Perducas d'Albret was left as governor with a garrison of Gascons. Froissart quaintly describes this brief siege. Shortly before the army showed itself in the narrow valley of the Alzou, the towns of Fons and Gavache had capitulated, the inhabitants having sworn that they would remain English ever afterwards. 'But they lied,' observes Froissart. Arriving under the walls of Roc-Amadour, which were raised upon the lower rocks, the English advanced at once to the assault. 'Là eut je vous dy moult grant assaust et dur.' It lasted a whole day, with loss on both sides; but when the evening came the English entrenched themselves in the valley with the intention of renewing the assault on the morrow. That night, however, the consuls and burghers of Roc-Amadour took council of one another, and it was unanimously agreed that the English had shown great 'force and virtue' during the day. Then the wisest among them urged that the place could not hold out long against such an enemy, and that if it was taken by force they, the burghers, would be all hanged, and the town burnt without mercy. It was, therefore, decided to surrender the town the next day. This was accordingly done, and the burghers solemnly swore that they would be 'good English' ever afterwards. For their penance they undertook to send fifty mules laden with provisions to accompany the English army on its march for fifteen days. The fact that the burghers owned fifty mules in the fourteenth century shows how much richer they were then, for now they can scarcely boast half as many donkeys, although these beasts do most of the carrying, and even the ploughing.

It is difficult now to find a trace of the wall which defended the burg on the side of the valley; but here, not far above the bed of the Alzou, are some ruins of the castle where Henry II. stayed, and which the inhabitants still associate with his name. It is improbable that he built it; it is more reasonable to suppose that it existed before his marriage with Eleanor in 1152. His son, 'Short Mantle,' also used it when he came to Roc-Amadour, and behaved, as an old writer expresses it, 'like a ferocious beast.' Some ruined Gothic archways may still be seen from the valley, the upper stones yellow with rampant wallflowers in the early spring. The older inhabitants speak of the high walls, the finely-sculptured details, etc., which they remember; and, indeed, it is not very long ago that the ancient castle was sold for a paltry sum, to be used as building material. The only part of the interior preserved is what was once the chapel. It is vaulted and groined, and the old vats and casks heaped up in it show that it was long used for wine-making, before the phylloxera destroyed the vineyards that once covered the sides of the stony hills. A little below this castle is a well, with an extraordinary circumference, said to have been sunk by the English, and always called by the people 'Le puit des Anglais.' It is 100 feet deep, and those who made it had to work thirty feet through solid rock.

* * * * *

After wandering and loitering by rivers too well fed by the mountains to dry completely up like the perfidious little Alzou, I have returned to Roc-Amadour, my headquarters, the summer being far advanced. The wallflowers no longer deck the old towers and gateways with their yellow bloom, and scent the morning and evening air with their fragrance; the countless flags upon the rocky shelves no longer flaunt their splendid blue and purple, tempting the flower-gatherer to risk a broken neck; the poet's narcissus and the tall asphodel alike are gone; so are all the flowers of spring. The wild vine that clambers over the blackthorn, the maple and the hazel, all down the valley towards the Dordogne, shows here and there a crimson leaf; and the little path is fringed with high marjoram, whose blossoms revel amidst the hot stones, and seem to drink the wine of their life from the fiery sunbeams. Upon the burning banks of broken rock—gray wastes sprinkled with small spurges and tufts of the fragrant southernwood, now opening its mean little flowers—multitudes of flying grasshoppers flutter, most of them with scarlet wings, and one marvels how they can keep themselves from being baked quite dry where every stone is hot. The lizards, which spend most of their time in the grasshoppers' company, appear equally capable of resisting fire. In the bed of the Alzou a species of brassica has had time since the last flood to grow up from the seed, and to spread its dark verdure in broad patches over the dry sand and pebbles. The ravens are gone—to Auvergne, so it is said, because they do not like hot weather. The hawks are less difficult to please on the score of climate; they remain here all the year round, piercing the air with their melancholy cries.

I needed quiet for writing, and could not get it. Of all boons this is the most difficult to find in France. It can be had in Paris, where it is easy to live shut off from the world, hearing nothing save the monotonous rumble of life in the streets; but let no one talk to me about the blessed quietude of the country in France, unless it be that of the bare moor or mountain or desolate seashore. In villages there is no escape from the clatter of tongues until everybody, excepting yourself, is asleep. The houses are so built that wherever you may take refuge you are compelled to hear the conversation that is going on in any part of them. In the South the necessity of listening becomes really terrible. The men roar, and the women shriek, in their ordinary talk. A complete stranger to such ways might easily suppose that they were engaged in a wordy battle of alarming ferocity, when they are merely discussing the pig's measles, or the case of a cow that strayed into a field of lucern, and was found the next morning like a balloon. It is hard for a person who needs to be quiet at times to live with such people without giving the Recording Angel a great deal of disagreeable work.

I would not have believed that so small a place as Roc-Amadour, and such a holy one, could have been so noisy if my own experience had not informed me on this subject. Every morning at five the tailor who did duty as policeman and crier came with his drum, and, stationing himself by the town pump, which was just in front of my cottage, awoke the echoes of the gorge with a long and furious *tambourinade*. While the women, in answer to this signal, were coming from all directions, carrying buckets in their hands, or copper water-pots on their heads, he unchained the pump-handle. Now for the next two hours the strident cries of the exasperated pump, and the screaming gabble of many tongues, all refreshed by slumber and eager for exercise, made such a diabolic tumult and discord as to throw even the braying of the donkeys into the minor key. Of course, sleep under such circumstances would have been miraculous; but, then, no one had any right to sleep when the rocks were breaking again into flame, and the mists which filled the gorge by night were folding up their tents. I therefore accepted this noise as if it had been intended for my good, and the crowd in front of the pump was always an amusing picture of human life. It was at its best on Sunday, for then the tailor—who also did a little shaving between whiles—had put on his fine braided official coat, as well as his sword and best *képi*. (On very grand days he wore his cocked hat, and was then quite irresistibly beautiful.) He had to look after the women as well as the water. The latter was precious, and it was necessary to protect it in the interest of the community. Then the pump was parsimonious, and all the women being impatient to get their allowance and go, it was needful that someone in authority should stand by to decide questions of disputed priority, and to nip quarrels in the bud which might otherwise lead to a fight. Poor man! how those women worried him every morning with their *badinage*, and how glad he was to chain up the pump-handle and turn the key!

But this was only the opening act of the day's comedy, or rather the *lever de rideau*. The little square by the old gateway, whose immediate neighbourhood lent a mediaeval charm to my cottage, was the centre of gossip and idling. I did not think of this when I pitched my tent, so to speak, in the shadow of the old masonry. Knowing full well that the noise of tongues is one of the chief torments of my life, I am always leaving it out of my calculations, and paying the same bill for my folly over and over again. But then I know also that in provincial France, unless you live in an abandoned ruin upon a rock, it is well-nigh impossible to obtain the quietude which the literary man, when he has it not, imagines to be closely allied to the peace that passeth all understanding. The square served many purposes, except mine. The women used it as a convenient place for steaming their linen. This, fashioned into the shape of a huge sugar-loaf, with a hollow centre, stood in a great open caldron upon a tripod over a wood-fire. At night the lurid flames and the grouped figures, illuminated by the glare, were picturesque; but in the daytime the charm of these gatherings was chiefly conversational. Then the children made the square their playground, or were driven into it because it was the safest place for them, and every Sunday afternoon the young men of Roc-Amadour met there to play at skittles.

In quest of peace, I was driven at first into the loft of the inn, of which the cottage was a dependency. Here the vocal music of the inhabitants was somewhat muffled, but the opportunities for studying natural history were rather excessive. A swarm of bees had established themselves in a corner where they could not be dislodged, and they had a way of crawling over the floor that kept my expectations constantly raised. The maize grown upon the small farm having been stored here from time immemorial, the rats had learnt from tradition and experience to consider this loft as their Land of Goshen. When I took up my quarters among them they were annoyed, and also puzzled. They could not understand why I remained there so long and so quiet; but at length they lost patience and gave up the riddle. Then their impudence became unbounded; they helped themselves to the maize whenever they felt disposed to do so, and stared at me with the utmost effrontery as they sat upon their haunches nibbling; they ran races under the tiles and held pitched battles upon the rafters. Talking one day to the proprietor of the house about his rats and other live stock, I tried to excite and distress him by describing the depredation that went on day and night in the loft. But it was with a calm bordering on satisfaction that he listened to my story. Then he told me that the rats ate about two sacks of maize every year.

'And you do not put it elsewhere?'

'Non pas! I leave it here for them.'

'For the rats?'

'Certainly, for the rats. If I did not give them plenty of maize they would eat a hundred francs' worth of linen in a single winter. It is an economy to feed them.'

And there were about a dozen string-tailed cats about the place that never ventured into the loft. They must have been either afraid or too lazy to attack the rats in their stronghold. A man who could accept a plague of rodents in this philosophical spirit could not be otherwise than mild in his dealings with all animals, including men. My old friend liked to let every creature live and enjoy existence. He became so fond of his pigs that it grieved him sorely to have one killed. Much domestic diplomacy had to be used before the fatal order could be wrung from him. He would have gone on fattening the beast for ever had he been allowed, soothing his conscience over the waste with the vague hope that this pig of exceptional loveliness and vigour would grow to the size of a donkey if it were permitted to take its time. He never worried his *métayer* over money matters, or insisted upon seeing that everything was equally divided. Notwithstanding that he had been made to smart all his life for his trustfulness and indolent good-nature, experience had taught him nothing of this world's wisdom. No beggar, although known to be a worthless rascal, ever asked him for a piece of bread or a night's lodging in his barn without obtaining it. The old man would lock his ragged guest up for the night, and before letting him out in the morning would often carry some soup to him—stealthily, however, so as not to be observed. As he was always ready to give, and hated every harsh measure, it was to his wood that the unscrupulous went in winter, when they wanted fuel. Sometimes an informer would say to him: 'M—— So-and-so is cutting down your wood.' 'Oh, bast! *le pauvre*. It is cold weather!' was the reply that he would be most likely to make. His good qualities would have ruined him had not destiny with great discernment and charity nailed him to his little patrimony, where he was comparatively safe.

The bees in the loft were instructive and the rats amusing, but the fleas were neither the one nor the other—they were merely exciting. And so it came to pass that I forsook the place, and by climbing a little staircase cut in the rock, against which the house was built, reached a cavern far above the roof and found at last my ideal writing-place upon the ledge in front of it, where the mallow and the crane's-bill crept over a patch of turf. Here the voices of the noisy little world below were sufficiently toned down by distance. The noisiest creatures up here were the jackdaws, which were constantly flying in and out of the holes in the church wall that rose above me from another and wider ledge of rock. A pair of sooty-looking rock-swallows that had made their nest in the roof of the cavern were much irritated by my presence, but, like the rats, they became reconciled to it. The little martins, always trustful, never hesitated from the first to fly into the cave and drink from the dripping water. When the dusk came on, the bats, which had been hanging by their winged heels all day in dusky holes and corners, fluttered out one after another, and went zigzagging until they were lost to sight over the old stone roofs on which the moss had blackened.

A little before the bats came out was the time when to do aught else but let the sight feast upon the beauty of the rocky little world bounded by the walls of the narrow gorge would have been literally to waste the golden moments. Then it was that the naked crags, which caught the almost level rays of the setting sun, grew brighter and more brilliantly coruscating, until they seemed ready to melt from the intensity of their own heat; then this fiery golden colour would slowly fade and wane into misty purple tones, which lingered long when there was no more sun. Why did it linger? All the sky that I could see was blue, and of deepening tone. But the most wonderful sight was yet to come, when, while the valley was fast darkening, and along the banks of the Alzou's dry channel the walnut-trees stood like dark spectres of uncertain form, those rocks began to glow with fire again as if a wind had risen suddenly and had fanned their dying embers, and the luminous bloom that spread over them was not that of the earthly rose, but of the mystical rose of heaven. What I saw was the reflection of the after-glow, but the glow in the sky was hidden. Sometimes, as the rocks were fading again and a star was already glittering like steel against the dark blue, another flush arose in the dusk, and a faint redness still rested upon the high crags, when the owl flew forth with a shriek to hunt along the sides of the gorge.

One morning, as I climbed to my eyrie, I was shocked to see my oblong writing-table, which I had hoisted up there with considerable difficulty, in an attitude that my neighbour Decros's donkey endeavoured to strike in his most agitated moments — it was standing upon two legs, with the others in the air. The heavy branch of a large fig-tree that had been flourishing for many years upon the overhanging rock far above had come down upon the very spot where I was accustomed to sit, and thus the strange antics of the table were accounted for. From that day the thought of other things above, such as loose rocks, which might also have conceived an antipathy for the table, and might not be so considerate towards me as the fig-tree, weakened my attachment to my ideal writing-place, for the discovery of which I was indebted to the indefatigable tongues of the women of Roc-Amadour.

The mention of my neighbour's donkey recalls to mind an interesting religious ceremony in which that amiable but emotional beast figured with much distinction. Once every year all the animals at Roc-Amadour that are worth blessing are assembled on the plain near the Hospitalet to receive the benediction of the Church. The ceremony is called *La bénédiction des bêtes*. The animals are chiefly goats, sheep, donkeys, and mules. They are sprinkled with holy water, and prayers are said, so that they may increase and multiply or prosper in any other way that their owners may desire. As the meeting of the beasts took place very early in the morning, I reached the scene just as it was breaking up, and the congregation was dispersing in various directions. I met Decros coming down the hill with his donkey, and saw by the expression of his lantern jaws—he never laughed outright—that something had amused him very much.

'So you have been to the Blessing of the Beasts?' said I.

'*He* has been,' replied the man, pointing to the ass, and not wishing to be confounded with the *bêtes* himself.

The donkey stuck his long ears forward, which meant, 'Yes, I have,' and there was a deal of humour in the expression.

'And how did he behave?'

'Beautifully; he sang the whole time. The men laughed, but the women said, "Take the beast away!" "No, I won't," said I. "*Il chante la bénédiction.*"'

September brought the retreat, and the great pilgrimage, which lasts eight days. The first visitors to arrive were the beggars and small vendors of *objets de piété*. Some came in little carts, which looked as if they had been made at home out of grocers' boxes, and to which dogs were harnessed. At their approach all the Roc-Amadour dogs barked bravely, just as in the old days when the song was written of the 'beggars coming to town.' Others trudged in with their bundles upon their backs, hobbling, hungry and thirsty, but eager for the fray. Some in a larger way of business came in all sorts of vehicles, and a bazaar man arrived in a caravan of his own. Then followed the crowd of genuine pilgrims, nearly all of them peasants, humbly clad, but with money in their pockets which they were determined not to spend foolishly upon meat, drink, and lodging, for the good of their souls was uppermost in their minds, and the length of their stay would depend upon their success in making the money last. By far the greater number were women, and the many bent backs and withered faces among them were a pretty safe sign that they had not all come to implore the aid of the Virgin in that special form of domestic trouble from which so many thousands have sought relief century after century in her sanctuary of Roc-Amadour.

The plain white linen coif—very ugly, but delightfully primitive—worn by a large proportion of these peasants showed that they had crossed the Dordogne from the Bas-Limousin. Many had come all the way on foot, taking a couple of days or more for the journey, and a few had trudged over the hot roads and stony *causses** barefoot, just like pilgrims of the Middle Ages.

Indeed, these people were essentially the same in all social and mental characteristics as their predecessors of five or seven centuries ago; their faith was the same, their daily habits were the same, their language was the same, and their mode of dress, as far as the women were concerned, had scarcely changed. They came down the narrow street and under the old crumbling gateways in a continuous stream, holding their rosaries in their hands, together with their baskets and bundles, and praying aloud, even before they reached the foot of the steps. Arriving there, they dropped down upon their knees, and commenced the arduous ascent, interrupted by two hundred genuflexions, during which they repeated an *Ave Maria* and a special invocation to Notre Dame de Roc-Amadour. Although the stranger belonging to the outer world—so different in every way from that of these simple people—with his mind coloured by particular prejudices, habits of thought, religious or philosophical reasoning, may feel out of sympathy with such pilgrims,

---

* This Languedocian word, which has come to be generally used in describing the limestone uplands, as distinguished from the valleys and gorges of a very extensive district of Southern France, is said to be a corruption of *calx*.

he cannot but recognise their sincerity and the serene fulness of their faith.

Above all the pious murmuring rise the harsh voices of those who have come to sell, and who, putting no restraint upon their eagerness to get money, thrust their rosaries and medals almost in the pilgrims' faces. Beggars squatting or lying against the wall on either side of the steps exhibit the bare stump of a leg that wofully needs washing, a withered arm, or the ravages of some incurable and gnawing disease. Yet are they all terribly energetic, wailing forth prayers almost incessantly, or screaming spasmodically an appeal to charity, and adding to the dreadful din by jingling coppers in tin cups. In the immediate precincts of the church, where the hurly-burly of piety, traffic, and mendicity reaches its climax, are the vendors of candles for the chapel and of food for the pilgrims, whose diet is chiefly melon and bread. Creysse, by the Dordogne, produces melons in abundance, which are brought to Roc-Amadour by the cartload, and sold for two or three sous apiece. And to see these pilgrims devour the fragrant fruit in the month of September makes one think that if Notre Dame de Roc-Amadour were not very pitiful the consequences would be disastrous to many.

There was a humorous beggar on the steps who amused me much, for I watched him more closely than he supposed. He had something the matter with his legs—paralyzed, perhaps—but the upper part of his body was sound enough. With one hand he shook the tin cup, but the other, which held a short pipe, he kept steadfastly behind his back. Now and again he turned his face to the wall, as if to drop a tear unseen, but really to take a discreet pull at the pipe. I think he must have swallowed the smoke. Then he would face the crowd again, and repeat his doleful cry:

'De la charité! de la charité! Chrétiens, n'oubliez pas le pauvre estropié! Le bon Dieu vous bénira.'

After all, why should not a beggar smoke? If tobacco is a blessing, why should a man be debarred from it because his legs are paralyzed, and he is obliged to live on charity?

As one of the first thoughts of every genuine pilgrim to this ancient sanctuary is to get shrived, the chaplains, who, with their Superior, are ten in number, have something to do to listen to the story of sins that is poured into their ears almost in a continuous stream during the eight days of the retreat. The rush upon the confessionals begins at five in the morning, and goes on with little intermission all day. The penitents huddle together like sheep in a snowstorm around each confessional, so that the foremost who is telling his sins knows that there is another immediately behind him who, whenever he stops to reflect, would like to give him a nudge in the back. The peasants, whether it be that they have never cultivated the habit of whispering, or whether their zeal be such as to chase from their minds all considerations of worldly shame and human respect, say what they have to say without regard to the rows of ears behind them, and what takes place at these times is almost on a par with the public confessions of the primitive Church.

It is at night, however, during the retreat that the visitor to Roc-Amadour will see the strangest sight if he gives himself the trouble, for then the church of St. Sauveur becomes a *hospice* where the weary may find the sleep that refreshes and restores the faculties after the work of the day, as sung by St. Ambrose. The church is filled with pilgrims lying upon the chairs, upon the bare stones that the feet of other pilgrims have worn into hollows, sitting with their backs against the walls and piers, snoring also in the confessionals—the most comfortable quarters. Some remain awake most of the night praying silently or aloud. This is how the peasantry of the Quercy and the Limousin enter into the spirit of the September pilgrimage to Roc-Amadour. It is not because they need the money to pay for accommodation in the inns that they use the church by night as well as by day, but because they wish to go through their devotional programme thoroughly. And those who go to the inns often make one room serve for a family of three or four grown-up persons. If there is one person who does not belong to the family, the others see no harm in admitting him or her; indeed, they think that as Christians they are almost bound to do so.

On the night following the opening of the retreat, Roc-Amadour is illuminated, and the spectacle is one that renders the grandest illuminations in Paris mean and vulgar by comparison. It is not in the costliness of the display that its splendour lies; it is in what may almost be termed the zeal with which Nature works with art towards the same end. Without the rocks and precipices the spectacle would be commonplace; but the site being what it is, the scene has a strange and wonderful charm that may be called either fairylike or heavenly, as the imagination may prefer. The artistic means employed are simple enough—paper lanterns and little lamps of coloured glass; but what an effect is produced when chains of fire have been stretched across the gorge from the summits of the rocks on either side, when the long succession of zigzags reaching up the cliff, and forming the Way of the Cross, is also marked out with fire, when the ramparts on the brink of the precipice are ablaze with coloured lamps, recalling some old poetical picture of an enchanted castle, and a little to the right, on the summit of the cliff where the Via Crucis ends at Calvary, the great wooden cross which French pilgrims carried through the streets of Jerusalem stands against the calm starlit sky like a cross of blood-red flame!

A little below the summit of the cliff, from the

large cavern which has been fashioned to represent the Holy Sepulchre, there issues a brilliant light, together with the sound of many voices singing the 'Tantum ergo.' A faint odour of incense wanders here and there among the shrubs, and mingles with the fragrance of flowers upon the terraces. Presently the clergy and the pilgrims come forth, and, forming a long procession, descend the Way of the Cross; and as the burning tapers that they carry shine and flash amongst the foliage, these words, familiar to every pilgrim to Roc-Amadour, sung by hundreds of voices, may be heard afar off in the dark desolate gorge:

> 'Reine puissante,
> Mère d'Amour,
> Sois-nous compatissante,
> O Vierge d'Amadour?'

It is now the vigil of All Souls—the 'Day of the Dead.' No more pilgrims come to Roc-Amadour. A breeze would send the sapless walnut-leaves whirling through the air, but there is no breeze; Nature seems to hold her breath as she thinks of the dead whom she has gathered to her earthy breast. At sundown the people creep out of their houses silently and solemnly; they meet at the bottom of the steps, and when they are joined by the clergy and choir-boys, all move slowly upward, praying for the dead and kneeling upon each step. As their forms seen sideways show against the dusky sky, they look like shadows from the ghostly world, and still more so when the rocks on the other side of the gorge brighten again, as with the blood of the pomegranate made luminous, and through the air there spreads a beautiful solemn light that is tenderly yet deeply sad, and which adds something unearthly, something that cannot be named, to the ascending figures.

As the dusk deepens to darkness the funereal *glas* begins to moan from St. Saviour's Church. Two bells are rung together so as to make as nearly as possible one clash of sound. At first it is a moan, but it soon becomes a strident cry with a continuous under-wail. At the Hospitalet on the hill the bell of the mortuary chapel is also tolling. It is the bell of the dead who lie there in the stony burying-ground upon the edge of the wind-blown *causse*, calling upon the bells of Roc-Amadour to move the living to pity for those who have left the earth.

As I return to my cottage the dim street is quite deserted, and the arch of the ruined gateway, so often resounding with the voices that come from light hearts, is now as dark and silent as a grave. For two hours the bells continue to cry in the darkness, from the church overhead and from the chapel by the tombs. I can neither read nor write, but sit brooding over the fire on the hearth, piling on wood and sending tall flames and many sparks up the chimney; for that continuous undercry of the iron tongues, 'Pray for the dead! pray for the dead!'

fills the valley and seems to fill the world. No fireside feeling can be kindled; it is wasting wood to throw it upon the hearth to-night, for that doleful wail penetrates everywhere: even the demon that lurks at the bottom of Pomoyssin must shudder as he hears it. When at length the bells stop swinging and their vibrations die away, a screech-owl flies close by the open gallery of the house, which we call a balcony, and startles me with its ghostly scream.

The day comes again, fair and hopeful. I am waiting for the old truffle-hunter, with whom I made an appointment for this morning. Presently I see him coming up the bed of the stream, plodding over the yellow stones, which have been dry for four months. I recognise him by his pig, which walks by his side. They are both truffle-hunters, and have both an interest in the business, as will be seen. The man is gray and old, with a sharp prominent nose, suggestive of his chief occupation, and with a bent back—the effect, perhaps, of stooping to pull the pig's ear in the nick of time should the beast be tempted to snap up one of the savoury cryptogams. When it is added that he wears a short blouse and a low, broad-brimmed felt hat, I have described the appearance of the truffle-hunter. Now, inasmuch as the pig is about to play the most important part in the morning's work, its portrait should likewise be drawn. The animal is of a dirty-white colour, like all pigs in this part of France, and is utterly devoid of grace and elegance. It is, in fact, an extremely ugly beast, with an arched back and a very long turned-up nose; but it is four years old, and is accounted 'serious.' Like all other pigs used for truffle-hunting, it is of the female sex. The animal has been carefully educated; it wears a leather collar as a mark of distinction, and is allowed the same liberty as a dog.

We climb the rocky side of the gorge, which is hot work, for the south wind is blowing, and the sun is blazing in a blue sky. The walnuts by the line of the stream are changing colour, and the maples are already fiery; but otherwise there are few signs of autumn. On reaching the plateau we come at once to the truffle-ground. Here the soil is so thin, so stony, and withal so arid, that, were it not for the scant herbage upon which sheep and goats thrive, it would produce nothing but stunted oak, juniper, and truffles. Even the oaks only grow in patches where the rock is not close to the surface. The truffles are never found except very near these trees, or, in default of them, hazels. This is one of the mysteries of the cryptogamic kingdom, which no one has yet been able to explain. The truffle-hunters believe that it is the shade of the trees which produces the underground fruit, and the opinion is based upon experience. When an oak has been cut down, or even lopped, a spot near it that was rich in truffles year after year is soon scoffed at by the knowing pig.

Our work lies amongst the dwarf oaks, for there are no hazels here. At a sign from the old man, the pig sniffs about the roots of a little tree, then proceeds to dig with her nose, tossing up the larger stones which lie in the way as if they were feathers. The animal has smelt a truffle, and the man seizes her by the ear, for her manner is suspicious. This is the first time they have been out together since last season, and the beast has forgotten some of her education. She manages to get a truffle into her mouth; he tugs at her ear with one hand, and uses his stick upon her nose with the other. The brute screams with anger, but will not open her jaws wide enough for him to slip his stick in and hook the truffle out. The prize is swallowed, and the old man, forgetting all decorum, and only thinking of his loss, calls his companion a pig, which in France is always an insult. Our truffle-hunting to-day has opened badly, although one party thinks differently. In a few minutes, however, another truffle is found, and this time the old man delivers a whack on the nose at the right moment, and, seizing the fungus, hands it to me. Now he takes from his pocket a spike of maize, and, picking off a few grains, gives them to the pig to soothe her injured feelings, and encourage her to hunt again. This she is quite ready to do, for a pig has no *amour propre*. We move about in the dry open wood, keeping always near the trees, and truffle after truffle is turned up from the reddish light soil mixed with fragments of calcareous rock. The forgotten training soon comes back to our invaluable auxiliary: a mere twitch of the ear is a sufficient hint for her to retire at the right moment, and wait for the corn that is invariably given in exchange for the cryptogam. Indeed, before we leave the ground, the animal has got so well into work that when she finds a truffle she does not attempt to seize it, but points to it, and grunts for the equivalent in maize. The pig may be a correct emblem of depravity, but its intelligence is certainly of a superior order.

FROM THE ALZOU TO THE DORDOGNE.

ALTHOUGH the last days of May had come, the Alzou, usually dry at this time, was running with swift, strong current through the vale of Roc-Amadour. There had been so many thunderstorms that the channel was not large enough for the torrent that raced madly over its yellow pebbles. I lingered awhile in the meadow by the stream, looking at the rock-clinging sanctuary before wandering in search of the unknown up the narrow gorge.

In a garden terraced upon the lower flank of the rock, the labour of generations having combined to raise a soil there deep enough to support a few plum, almond, and other fruit trees, a figure all in black is hard at work transplanting young lettuces. It is that of a teaching Brother. He is a thin grizzled man of sixty, with an expression of melancholy benevolence in his rugged face. I have watched him sitting upon a bench with his arm round some little village urchin by his side, while the children from the outlying hamlets, sprawling upon a heap of stones in the sun, ate their mid-day meal of bread and cheese or buckwheat pancakes that their mothers had put into their baskets before they trudged off in the early morning. I have noticed by many signs that he is full of sympathy for the young peasants placed in his charge. Yet with all his kindness he is melancholy. So many years in one place, such a dull routine of duty, such a life of abnegation without the honour that sustains and encourages, such impossibility of being understood and appreciated by those for whose sake he has been breaking self upon the wheel of mortification since his youth, have made him old before the time and fixed that look of lurking sadness in his warmly human eyes.

There are few problems more profound than that of the courage with which men like him continue their self-imposed penal-servitude until they become too infirm to work and are sent to die in some refuge for aged *frères*. They have accepted celibacy and poverty, that they may the better devote their lives to the instruction of children. They have no sacerdotal state or ideal, no ecclesiastical nor social ambition to help them. They must be always humble; they must not even be learned, for much knowledge in their case would be considered a dangerous thing. Their minds must not rise above their work. They guide dirty little fists in the formation of pot-hooks, and when they have led the boys' intelligence up a few more steps of scholarship the end is achieved. The boy goes out into the world and refreshes his mind with new occupation;

but the poor Brother remains chained to his dreary task, which is always the same and is never done.

And what are the wages in return for such a life? Food that many a workman would consider insufficiently generous for his condition, a bed to lie upon and clothes which call down upon the wearer the sarcasms of the town-bred youth. What a land of contrast is France!

There are three Brothers here, but this one, the eldest, is the head. Others come and go, but he remains. Most of his spare time is given to the garden. When the eight o'clock bell begins to swing he will leave his lettuces and soon perch himself on the little platform behind his shabby old desk in the dingy schoolroom, which even in the holidays cannot get rid of its ancient redolence of boys. The school-house, now so much like a prison, was once a mansion, and the most modern part of it is of the period which we should call in England Tudor. A Gothic doorway leads into a hall arched and groined, the inner wall being the bare rock, as is the case with most of the houses at Roc-Amadour. A gutter cut in the stone floor to carry off the drippings formed by the condensation of the air upon the cold surface shows that these half-rock dwellings have their drawbacks.

I leave Roc-Amadour and take my way up the valley. Nature has now reached all that can be attained in vernal pride and beauty here. In a little while she will have put on the careworn look of the Southern summer. Many a plant now in splendid bloom, animated by the spirit of loveliness that presides over the law of reproduction, will soon be casting its seed and bringing its brief destiny to a close. Now all is coquetry, beauty, and ravishment. The rock-hiving bees, unconscious instruments of a great purpose, are yellow with pollen and laden with honey. They find more, infinitely more, nectar than they can carry away. The days are long, and every hour is full of joy. But already the tide is at the turn. The nightingale's rapturous song has become a lazy twitter; the bird has done with courtship; it has a family in immediate prospect, if not one already screaming for food, and the musician has half lost his passion for music. It will come again next year. How swiftly all this life and colour of spring passes away! So much to be looked at and so little time!

This narrow strip of meadow that winds along the bottom of the gorge is not the single tinted green ribbon it lately was. The light of its verdure has been dimmed by the light of flowers. The grass mounts high, but not higher than the oxeye daisies, the blue racemes of stachys, the mauve-coloured heads of scabious, the bladder-campions, the yellow buttercups and goat's-beard. The oxeyes are so numberless in one long reach of meadow that a white drapery, which every breeze folds or unfolds, seems to have been cast as light as sea-foam upon the illimitable forest of stems. The white butterflies that flutter above are like flecks of foam on the wing. Elsewhere it is the blue of the stachys and the spiked veronica that rules. Deeper in the herbage other races of flowers shine in the fair groves of this grassy paradise, and every blossom, however small, is a mystery, a miracle. Here is the star of Bethlehem, wide open in the sunshine and showing so purely white amidst the green, and yonder is the purple fringe-like tuft of the weird muscari. Along the banks of the stream tall lilac-purple, stock-like flowers rise proudly above the grasses. They belong to the hesperis or dame's violet, a common wild-flower in this valley. Upon my left is the abrupt stony slope of the gorge. Between it and the meadow are shrubs of yellow jessamine starred with blossom. But the stony steep that dazzles the eyes with the sun's reflected glare has its flowers too. Nature, in her great passion for beauty, even draws it out of the disintegrated fragments of time-worn rock, whose banks would otherwise be as stark and dry as the desert sand. Lightly as flakes of snow the frail blossoms of the white rock-rose lie upon the stones. Then there are patches of candytuft running from white into pink, crimson flowers of the little crane's-bill, and spurges whose floral leaves are now losing their golden green and taking a hue of fiery brown.

An open wood, chiefly of dwarf oak, and shrubs such as the wayfaring tree, the guelder-rose, and the fly-honeysuckle, now stretches along the opposite side of the gorge. Here scattered groups of columbine send forth a glow of dark blue from the shadowy places; the lily of the valley and its graceful ever-bowing cousin, the Solomon's seal, show their chaste and wax-like flowers amidst the cool green of their fresh leaves; and the monkey-orchis stands above the green moss and the creeping geraniums like a little rocket of pale purple fire just springing from the earth towards the lingering shreds of storm-cloud that are melting in the warm sky.

In a few weeks what will have become of all this greenness and beautiful colour of flowers? The torrid sun and the hot breath of summer will have burnt up the fair garment of spring, and laid bare the arid sternness of the South again. The nightingale still warbles fitfully in the green bushes, but the raven, perched up yonder upon the stark rock, croaks like a misanthrope at the quick passing away of youth and loveliness. What sad undertones, mournful murmurs of the deep that receives the drifted leaves, mingle with the spring's soft flutings and all the voices that proclaim the season of joy!

While listening and day-dreaming, I was overtaken by a man and his donkey, both old acquaintances. Every day, except Sundays and the great Church festivals, when the peasants of the Quercy abstain from work, like those of Brittany, this pair were in the habit of trudging together side by side to fetch and bring back wood from the slopes of the gorge. The ass did all the carrying, and his master the chopping and sawing. It was a monotonous life, but both seemed to think they were not worse off than the majority of men and donkeys. The man was contented with his daily soup of bread-and-water, with an onion or a leek thrown in, and a suspicion of bacon, and the beast with such herbage as he could find while his master was getting ready another load of wood. The man was an old soldier, who had seen some rough service, for he was at Sedan, and was afterwards engaged in the ghastly business of shooting down his own countrymen in Paris. But, with all this, he was as quiet a tempered creature as his donkey, which he treated as a friend. The army, he told me, was the best school for learning how to treat a beast with proper consideration.

I asked why.

'Because,' replied he, 'when a soldier is caught beating a horse, he has eight days of *salle de police*.'

Man and donkey having disappeared into a wood, my next companion was a small blue butterfly that kept a few yards in front of me, now stopping to look at a flower, now fluttering on again. Some insects, as well as certain birds, appear to derive much entertainment from watching the movements of that fantastic animal—man.

Arcadian leafiness; rocky desolation befitting the mouth of hell. Grass and flowers on which souls might tread in the paradise of the Florentine poet. Stony forms, monstrous, enigmatic, reared like symbolic tokens of defeated gods, or of the worn-out evil passions that troubled old creation before the coming of man, and the fresh order of spiritual and carnal bewilderment. Why should I go on and seek further amazement, while from the lowest to the highest I can read not one of the mystic figures of the solitude around me? What is my relation to them, and theirs to me? Why should that beetle in the grass, upon whose back all the colours of the prism change and glow like supernatural fire, trouble me with the cause and motive of its beauty? Why should yonder rock, standing like a spar of some ship wrecked in a cataclysm of the awful past, draw me to it as though it were the image of a grand, yet unattainable and blighted, longing of the human soul?

The gorge became so narrow and the rocks so high that there was a twilight under the trees, which still dripped with the rain-drops of last night's storm. Hesperis, columbine, and geranium contrasted their floral colours with the deep green of the young grass. Some spots of dark purple were on the ground where the light was most dim. They were the petals and calyxes of that strange flower, lathræa, of the broom-rape family. Each bloom seemed to be carried in the cup of another flower. The plant had no leaves, for it was a thief that drew its nutriment from the root of an honest little tree that had struggled upward in the shade of strong and greedy rivals, and had raised its head at length into the sunshine in spite of them.

After some difficulty in working round and over rocks that barred the passage, I came to a spot where it was impossible to follow the gorge any farther. The walls narrowed to an opening a few yards wide, where the stream fell in a cascade of some thirty feet. I took my mid-day meal like a forester in the midst of this beautiful desolation, and then, having found a spot where I could escape from the gorge of the Alzou, I climbed the steep towards the north.

Here there was a blinding glare of sunshine reflected by the naked stones. Goats looked down at me from the upper rocks near the line of the blue sky. When I reached the boy who tended them, I asked him the way to the road that I wished to strike upon the plateau. After staring at me for some time, he screwed up his mouth, and said : '*Je comprenais pas français, you.*' *You* did not apply to me, but to himself, for it means *I* in the Southern dialect.

Here was a boy unable to speak French, although all children in France are now supposed to be educated in the official language of the republic. Such cases are uncommon. In the Haut-Quercy, where *patois* is the language of everybody, even in the towns, one soon learns the advantage of asking the young for the information that one may need.

I found the road I wanted, and also the spot marked on the map as the Saut de la Pucelle. It is one of those numerous *gouffres* to be found in the Quercy, especially in the district of the Dordogne.

Here a stream plunges beneath the surface of the earth to join the subterranean Ouysse, or the Dordogne. A ravine, sinking rapidly, becomes a deep, dark, and gloomy gully, at the end of which is a wall of rock. The stream pours down a tunnel-like passage, at the base of the rock, with a melancholy wail. Where the sides are not too steep they are covered with trees and shrubs.

As I stood amidst the poisonous dog-mercury, under the hanging ivy and the hart's-tongue ferns, watching the stream glitter on the edge of everlasting darkness, and listening to its death-dirge, I pictured awful shadows issuing from the infernal passage and seizing the terror-stricken ghost of the guilty horseman, of whom I had heard from a local legend.

This legend, as it is commonly told, is briefly as follows: Centuries ago a virtuous young woman was persecuted by the lord of a neighbouring castle, who was not at all virtuous. One day, when she was mounted upon a mule, he gave chase to her on horseback. He was rapidly gaining upon her, and she, in agony of soul, had given herself up for lost, when, by one of those miracles which were frequent in those days, especially in the country of

Notre Dame de Roc-Amadour, the mule, by giving
a vigorous stamp with one of his hind-legs, kicked
a yawning gulf in the earth, which he, however,
lightly passed over with his burden, while the
wicked pursuer, unable to check his steed in time,
perished in the abyss.

Another legend of the Maiden's Leap is more
romantic, but less supernatural. It is a story of the
English occupation of Guyenne, and the revolt of
the Quercynois in 1368. Before the main body of
the British force that subdued Roc-Amadour as
related by Froissart arrived in the Haut-Quercy,
the castle of Prangères, near Gramat, was entered
by a troop of armed men in the English service
under Jéhan Péhautier, one of those brigand
captains of whom the mediaeval history and legends
of Guyenne speak only too eloquently. An orphan,
Bertheline de Castelnau, *châtelaine* of Prangères in
her own right, was in the fortress when it was thus
taken by surprise. Captivated by her beauty, Jéhan
Péhautier essayed to make Bertheline his prisoner;
but she made her escape from the castle by night,
and endeavoured to reach the sanctuary of Roc-
Amadour on foot. Her flight was discovered, and
Péhautier and a party of horsemen started in pursuit.
She would have been quickly captured had she not
met a mounted knight, who was no other than her
lover, Bertrand de Terride. She sprang upon his
horse, and away they both went through the oak
forest which then covered the greater part of the

causse; but the gleam of the knight's armour in the moonlight kept the pursuers constantly upon his track. Slowly but surely they gained upon the fugitives. Suddenly Bertheline, who knew the country, perceived that Bertrand was spurring his horse directly towards the precipice now called the Saut de la Pucelle. It was too late, however, to avoid the gulf; she had only time to murmur a brief prayer before the horse bounded over the edge of the rock. To the great wonder and joy of the lovers, the animal cleared the ravine, and alighted safely on the other side. But a very different fate awaited the pursuers. On they came, crashing through the wood, shouting exultantly, for they believed that the prey was now almost in their grasp, when suddenly the air was rent with cries of horror, mingled with the sound of crashing armour, and bodies falling upon the rocks and upon the bed of the stream. An awful silence followed. The dead men and horses were lying in the dark water. As Péhautier felt the solid earth leave him, he gave out his favourite oath, 'Mort de sang!' in a frightful shriek, and the words long afterwards rang in the ears of Bertheline and Bertrand.

As I returned to this spot some months later in order to explore the cavern, I may as well give an account of the adventure here. I was accompanied by my neighbour Decros, who gave his donkey on this occasion a half-holiday. Decros, although a native of the locality, could not tell me how far the cavern extended, for he had never been tempted to explore its depths himself, nor had he heard of anybody who knew more than himself about it. A story, however, was told of a shepherd-boy who long ago went down the opening, and was never seen again.

'Perhaps,' said I, 'we shall find his skeleton.'

This observation brought a peculiar expression to my companion's face, which meant that he had no ambition whatever to share the surprise of such a discovery. Although he had done his duty bravely in the war of 1870, he was by no means free from the awe with which these *gouffres* inspired the country-people, and his soldiering had still left him a Cadurcian Celt, with much of the superstition that he had drawn in with his native air. One morning he found that his donkey had nearly strangled himself over-night with the halter, and Decros could not shake off the impression that this accident was an omen intended to convey some message from the other world. He was ready to go with me into any cavern; but I am sure he would have much preferred scaling dangerous rocks in the broad sunlight, for there he would have felt at home.

There was not too much water to offer any danger, so we stooped down and entered the low vault after lighting candles. The roof soon rose, and we were in a spacious cavern, the sides of which had evidently been washed and worn away into hollows by the sea that rolled here long before the mysterious race raised its dolmens and tumuli upon the surrounding knolls. The passage was wide enough for us to walk on the margin of the stream, or where the water was very shallow; but had much rain fallen, the expedition would have been perilous, for the descending torrent would then have been strong enough to carry a man off his legs.

Stalactites hung from the rocks overhead, and as we proceeded they became more numerous, more fantastic, and more beautiful. They were just as the dropping water had slowly fashioned them in the darkness of ages, where day and night were the same, where nothing changed but themselves, save the voice of the stream, which grew louder or softer according to the play of winds and sunshine and clouds upon the upper world. Some tapered to a fine point, others were like pendant bunches of grapes; all were of the whiteness of loaf-sugar. No tourists stricken with that deplorable mania for taking home souvenirs of everything, and ready to spoil any beauty to gratify their vanity or their acquisitiveness, had cast stones into the midst of the fairy handicraft of the wizard water for the sake of a fragment; nor had the village boys amused themselves here at the expense of the stalactites, for happily they had been well trained in the horror of the supernatural. The cavern ran for a certain distance south-west; then the gallery turned at a sharp angle north-north-west, and continued in this direction. We followed the stream some three or four hundred yards, and then it entered a deep pool or lake under low rocks. We tried a side-passage to see if it led round this obstacle, but it soon came to an end. As I stood on the brink of the deep, black, silent pool, I had a great longing to know what lay beyond; but I had to content myself with imagining the unrevealed wonders of the cavern. It would be just possible, by crouching down in a little boat, to pass under the rock, which is probably no insuperable obstacle. The roof is just as likely to form a high vault on one side of it as on the other. The water is the serious obstacle; but it is safe to say, from the character of the formation, that the deep pool does not extend very far. A peculiarity of these underground streams of the *causses* is that they generally form a chain of pools.

If a shepherd-boy really lost his life in this cavern, he must have done so by trying to pass the pool, unless he was washed into it by a sudden rush of water after a heavy storm. It must be confessed that the spot is calculated to fill one with superstitious dread. The calm of the deep water into which the stream glides makes it quite easy to imagine, with the help of the surroundings, that there is an evil spirit lurking in it—perhaps that of the wicked Péhautier whom the demons dragged down here. I had another grim thought: Supposing this water, in obedience to some pressure elsewhere, should rise suddenly and flood the lower part of the cavern! There is no knowing what tricks water may play in this fantastic region, where the tendency of rivers is to flow underground, and where one gallery may be connected with a ramification of water-courses extending over many miles of country, and with reservoirs which empty themselves periodically by means of natural syphons. There is a world full of marvels under the *causses* of the Lot, the Aveyron, and the Lozère; but although much more will be known about it, a vast deal will remain for ever hidden from man.

I will now return to my wayfaring across the Causse de Gramat in the early summer.

I had passed through the village of Alvignac—a little watering-place that draws all the profit it can from a ferruginous spring which rises at Miers hard by, but otherwise uninteresting, and had left on my right the village of Thégra, where the troubadour Hugues de St. Cyr was born, when suddenly the landscape struck me with the sentiment of England. For some hours I had been walking chiefly over the stony *causse*, searching for a so-called castle that was not worth the trouble of finding. I had seen spurge and juniper, and ribs of rock rising everywhere above the short turf, until I grew weary of the sameness. Now, the sun, whose ardour was already melting into the tenderness of evening, shone upon a broad valley, where the grass stood high in rich meadows separated from other meadows and green cornfields by hedges, from the midst of which rose many a tall tree. The blackbird's low, flute-like note sounded above the shrilling of the grasshoppers.

The little village of Padirac was entered at sundown. The small inn where I chose my quarters for the night had a garden at the back, where vines in new leaf were trained over a trellis from end to end. There were also broad beans in flower, peas on sticks, currant-bushes, and pear-trees. It was a quiet, green spot, and as I strolled about it in the twilight, vague recollections of other gardens chased one another, but it would have been hard to say whether they were pleasant or sad. My dinner or supper was of sorrel soup and part of a goose that was killed the previous autumn, and, after being slightly salted, was preserved in grease.

Lean tortoiseshell cats, with staring eyes and tails like strings, kept near at hand, and seemed ready to commit any crime for the smallest particle of goose. String-tailed, goggle-eyed, meagre cats that seize your dinner if you do not keep watch over it, and when caressed promptly respond by scratching and swearing, appear to be held in high favour throughout this district. They are expected to live upon rats, and it is this that makes them so disagreeable, for although they kill rats for the pleasure of the chase, they do not like the flavour of them. On this subject there is a standing quarrel between them and society, which insists upon their eating the animals that they kill. In order that the cats shall have every facility for the chase, holes are often cut in the bottom of house-doors, so that at night they may go in and come out as the quarry moves them. Should any food have been left about, what with the rats and the cats, not a trace of it will be seen in the morning. This I know from experience.

Being within a mile or so of the Puit de Padirac —that gloomy hole in the earth which was supposed to be one of the devil's short-cuts between this world and his own, until M. Martel proved almost conclusively that it was not the way to the infernal city, but to a subterranean river, and a chain of lakes that could be followed for two miles—I set out the next morning to find it. I might have spent hours in vain casting about, but for the help of a peasant, who offered, quite disinterestedly, to be my guide. He was an old man, with a very Irish face, and eyes that laughed at life. But for his language he would have seemed a perfectly natural growth of Cork or Kerry.

Here may be the place to remark that the stock of the ancient Cadurci appears to have been much less impaired here in an ethnological sense by the mingling of races than in the country round Cahors. The peasants, generally, have nothing distinctively Southern in their appearance, although they speak a dialect which is in the main a Latin one, the Celtic words that have been retained being in a very small proportion. Gray or blue eyes are almost as frequent among them as they are with the English, and many of the village children have hair the colour of ripening maize.

We left the fertile valley and rose upon the stone-scattered *causse* where hellebore, spurges, and juniper were the only plants not cropped close to the earth by the flocks of sheep which thrive upon these wastes. All the sheep are belled, but the bells they wear are like big iron pots hanging upon their breasts. Each pot has a bone that swings inside of it and serves as a hammer. The chief use of these bells is to prevent the animal from leaving its best wool, that of the breast, upon the thorns of bushes.

We have now reached the brink of the pit, which is not bottomless, but looks so until the eye faintly distinguishes something solid at a depth that has been measured at 175 feet. The opening is almost circular, with a diameter at the orifice of 116 feet. This prodigious well, sunk in successive layers of secondary rock, looks as if it had been regularly quarried; but men could never have had the motive for giving themselves so much trouble. Did the rock fall in here? No explanation is satisfactory. How it fills one with awe to look into the depth while lying upon a slab of stone that stretches some distance beyond the side of the pit! Bushes with twisted and fantastic arms, growing, they or their ancestors, from time immemorial in the clefts of the rock, reach towards the light, and the elfish hart's-tongue fern, itself half in darkness, points down with frond that never moves in that eternal stillness which all the winds of heaven pass over, to a thicker darkness whence comes the everlasting wail and groan of hidden water.

This horrid gulf being in the open plain, with not even a foot of rough wall round it as a protection for the unwary, I asked the old man if people had never fallen into it.

'Yes,' he answered, 'but only those who have been pushed by evil spirits.'

He meant that only self-murderers had fallen into the Puit de Padirac. 'Pushed by evil spirits.' Perhaps this is the best of all explanations of the suicidal impulse. Strong thoughts are sometimes hidden under the simplicity of rustic expression. He told me the story of a man who, having gone by night to throw himself into the Puit de Padirac, came in contact with a tough old bush during his descent which held him up. By this time the would-be suicide disliked the feeling of falling so much that, so far from trying to free himself from the bush and begin again, he held on to it with all his might and shrieked for help. But as people who are not pushed by evil spirits give the Puit de Padirac a wide berth after sundown, the wretched man's cries were lost in the darkness. The next morning the shepherd children, as they led their flocks over the plain, heard a strange noise coming from the pit, but their horror was stronger than their curiosity, and they showed their sheep how to run. They went home and told their fathers what they had heard, and at length some persons were bold enough to look down the hole, from which the dismal sound the children had noticed continued to rise. Thus the cause of the mysterious noise was discovered, and the man was hauled up with a rope. He never allowed the evil spirits to push him into the Puit de Padirac again.

The people of these *causses* have a supernatural explanation for everything that they cannot account for by the light of reason and observation. They have their legend with regard to the Puit de Padirac, and it is as follows: St. Martin, before he became Bishop of Tours, was crossing one day this stony region of the Dordogne to visit a religious community on the banks of the Solane, whither he had been despatched by St. Hilary. He was mounted on a mule, and was ambling along over the desert plunged in pious contemplation, when he heard a little noise behind, and, looking round, he was surprised to see a gentleman close to him, who was also riding a mule. The stranger was richly dressed, and was altogether a very distinguished-looking person, but the excessive brilliancy of his eyes was a disfigurement. They shone in his head like two bits of burning charcoal. 'What do you want, cruel beast?' said St. Martin. This would scarcely have been saintly language had he not known with whom he had to deal. The gentleman thus impolitely addressed returned a soft answer, and forced his company upon the saint, who wished him at home. Presently Lucifer, for it was he, began to 'dare' St. Martin, after the manner of boys to-day. 'If I kick a hole in the ground I dare you to jump over it,' was the sort of language employed by the gentleman with the too-expressive eyes. 'Done!' said St. Martin, or something equivalent. 'Digging pits is quite in my line of business!' exclaimed the devil, in so disagreeable a voice that the saint's mule would have bolted had the holy rider not kept a tight rein upon her. At the same moment the ground over which the infernal mule had just passed fell in with a mighty rumble and crash, leaving a yawning gulf. 'Now,' said Lucifer, 'let me see you jump over that!' Whereupon, the bold St. Martin drove his spurs into his mule and lightly leapt over the abyss. And this was how the Puit de Padirac was made The peasants believe that they can still see on a stone the imprint left by the hoof of St. Martin's mule. This adventure did not cause the saint and the devil to part company. They rode on together as far as the valley of Medorium (Miers). 'Now,' said St. Martin, 'you jump over that!' pointing to a little stream that was seen to flow suddenly and miraculously out of the earth. Before challenging the arch enemy he had, however, taken the precaution to lay two small boughs in the form of a cross on the brink of the water. In vain the devil spurred his mule and used the worst language that he could think of to induce the beast to jump. The animal would not; but, as the spurring and swearing were continued, it at length went down on its knees before the cross. But this did not suit the devil's turn. On the contrary, the proximity of that emblem which St. Martin had placed unobserved on the ground made him writhe as though he had fallen into a font. Then with the speed of a lightning flash he returned to his own kingdom—possibly by the Puit de Padirac. A church dedicated to the saint was afterwards built near the scene of his triumph, and the healing spring where it comes out of the earth is still known by the name of *Lou Fount Sen Morti*—St. Martin's Fountain.

Having left the pit, we went in the direction of Loubressac, to which village my companion belonged. While still upon the *causse* a spot was reached where a small iron cross had been raised. The stone pedestal bore this inscription:

'SOUVENIR DE HÉLÈNE BONBÈGRE,
MORTE MARTYRE EN CE LIEU EN 1844.
VIEILLE-ESCAZE ET LAVAL ONT FAIT CONSTRUIRE CETTE CROIX.
PRIEZ POUR CES DEUX BIENFAITEURS.'

The old man knew Hélène Bonbègre when he was young, and he told me the tragic story of her death on this spot. She was going home in the evening, and her sweetheart the blacksmith accompanied her a part of the distance. They then separated, and she went on alone. They had been watched by the jealous and unsuccessful lover, whose heart was on fire. Where the cross stands the girl was found lying, a naked corpse. The murderer was soon captured, and most of the people in the district went to St. Céré to see him guillotined. It was a spectacle to be talked over for half a century. The blacksmith never forgave himself for having left the girl to go home alone, and it was he who forged the cross that marks the scene of the crime and sets the wayfarer conjecturing.

The peasant changed his ideas by filling his pipe. He smoked tobacco that he grew in a corner of his garden for his own use, and which he enjoyed all the more because it was *tabac de contrebande*. He gave me some, which I likewise smoked without any qualm of conscience, and thought it decidedly better than some tobacco of the *régie*. He lit his pipe with smuggled matches. Had I been an inspector in disguise, I should never have made matters unpleasant for him; he was such a cheery, good-natured companion. He had brought up his family, and had now just enough land to keep him without breaking his back over it. He was quite satisfied with things as they were. I did not ask him if he was a poacher, but took it for granted that he was whenever he saw a good chance. Almost every peasant in the Haut-Quercy who has something of the spirit of Nimrod in him is more or less a poacher. Those who like hare and partridge can eat it in all seasons by paying for it. Occasionally the gendarmes capture a young and over-zealous offender, but the old men, who have followed the business all their lives, are too wary for them. They are also too respectable to be interfered with.

At Loubressac I took leave of my entertaining friend, but not before we had emptied a bottle of white wine together. It was a *vin du pays*, this district having been less tried by the phylloxera than others farther south and west. I was surprised to find white wine there, the purple grape having been almost exclusively cultivated for centuries in what is now the department of the Lot.

In the room of the inn where I lunched there were four beds; two at one end and two at the other. There was plenty of space left, however, for the tables. The rafters were hidden by the heads of maize that hung from them. The host sat down at the same table with me, and when he had nearly finished his soup he poured wine into it, and, raising the plate to his lips, drank off the mixture. Objectionable as this manner of drinking wine seems to those who have not learnt to do it in their youth, it is very general throughout Guyenne. Those who have formed the habit would be most unhappy if they could not continue it. *Faire chabrou* is the expression used to describe this sin against good manners. The aubergiste was very friendly, and towards the close of the meal he brought out a bottle of his old red wine that he had treasured up 'behind the faggot.'

Before reaching this village I had heard of a retired captain who lived here in a rather dilapidated château, and who was very affable to visitors, whom he immediately invited to look through his telescope, which, although not a very large one, had a local celebrity, such instruments being about as rare as blue foxes in this part of the world. Conducted by the innkeeper, I called upon this gentleman. The house was one of those half-castellated manors which became scattered over France after the Renaissance, and of which the greater number were allowed to fall into complete or partial ruin when the territorial families who were interested in them were extinguished or impoverished by the Revolution. They are frequently to be found in Guyenne, but they are generally occupied by peasants either as tenant-farmers or proprietors; two or three of the better preserved rooms being inhabited by the family, the others being haunted by bats and swallows and used for the storage of farm produce. It suited the captain's humour, however, to live in his old dilapidated mansion, scarcely less cut off from the society that matched with his position in life than if he had exiled himself to some rock in the ocean.

The ceremony of knocking or ringing was dispensed with for the sufficient reason that there was neither bell nor knocker. We entered by the open door and walked along a paved passage, which was evidently not held as sacred as it should have been by the roving fowls; looked in at the great dark kitchen, where beside the Gothic arch of the broad chimney was some ruinous clockwork mechanism for turning the spit, which probably did turn to good purpose when powdered wigs were worn; then ascended the stone staircase, where there was room for four to walk abreast, but which had somewhat lost its dignity by the balusters being used for hanging maize upon. Presently we came to a door, which the aubergiste knocked sharply with his knuckles.

There was a sound of footsteps within, and then the door opened. I was standing before a rather florid man of about fifty, with close-cropped hair, a brush moustache, and a chin that seemed undecided on the score of shaving. He wore a flannel shirt open at the throat, and a knitted worsted *tricot*. This was the captain. He evidently did not like Sunday clothes. When he settled down here, it was to live at his ease, like a bachelor who had finished with vanities. But although no one would have supposed from his dress that he was superior to the people around him, his manners were those of a gentleman and an officer who had seen the world elsewhere than at Loubressac. The simple, easy courtesy with which he showed me his rooms, and pointed his telescope for me, was all that is worth attaining, as regards the outward polish of a man. This was so fixed upon him that his long association with peasants had taken none of it away. The few rooms that he inhabited were plainly furnished; in others were heaps of wheat, maize and beans. Passing along a passage I noticed a little altar in a recess, with a statue of the Virgin decked with roses and wild flowers. '*C'est le mois de Marie*,' said the captain. He lived with a sister, and she took care that religion was kept up in the house.

It being the *Fête-Dieu*, preparations were being made in the village for the procession that was to take place after vespers. Sheets were spread along the fronts of the houses, with flowers pinned to them, and *reposoirs* had been raised in the open air. I did not wait for the procession, as I expected to be in time for the one at the next village, Autoire. I took a path that led me up to the barren *causse*, from which the red roofs of Autoire soon became visible under an amphitheatre of high wooded hills.

As I approached the little village, the gleam of white sheets mingled with the picture of old houses huddled together, some half-timber, some with turrets and encorbelments, nearly all of them with very high-pitched roofs and small dormer windows. The procession was soon to start. I waited for it at the door of the crowded church, baking in the sun with others who could not get inside, one of whom was a woman with a moustache and beard, black and curly, such as a promising young man might be expected to have. The number of women in Southern France who are bearded like men shocks the feelings of the Northern wanderer, until he grows accustomed to the sight. The curé was preaching about the black bread, and all the other miseries of this life that had to be accepted with thankfulness. Presently the two bells in the tower began to dance, and the rapid ding-dong announced that the procession was forming. First appeared the beadle, extremely gaudy in scarlet and gold, then the cross-bearer, young men as chanters, little boys, most strangely attired in white satin knee-breeches and short lace skirts, scattering rose-leaves from open baskets at their sides; the curé came bearing the monstrance and Host, followed by Sisters with little girls in their charge; lastly was a mixed throng of parishioners. Most of the women held rosaries, and a few of them, bent with age, carried upon their heads the very cap that old Mother Hubbard wore, if tradition and English artists are to be trusted. As the last of the long procession passed out of sight between the walls of white linen, the wind brought the words clearly back:

'Genitori, Genitoque
Laus et jubilatio.'

Now I entered the little church that was quite empty, and where no sound would have been heard if the two voices in the tower had not continued to ring out over the dovecotes, where the white pigeons rested and wondered, and over the broad fields where the bending grasses and listening flowers stood in the afternoon sunshine, 'Laus et jubilatio,' in the language of the bells.

The church was Romanesque, probably of the twelfth century. The nave was flanked by narrow aisles. Upon the very tall bases of the columns were carved, together with foliage, fantastic heads of demons, or satyrs of such expressive ugliness that they held me fascinated. Some were bearded, others were beardless, some were grinning and showing frightful teeth, others had thick-lipped, pouting mouths hideously debased. A few were really *bons diables*, who seemed determined to be gay, and to joke under the most trying circumstances; but the greater number had morose faces, puckered by the long agony of bearing up the church. Such variety of expression in ugliness was a triumph of art in the far-off age, when the chisel of an unremembered man with a teeming imagination made these heads take life from the inanimate stone.

The road from Autoire to St. Céré soon led me into the valley of the Bave, a beautiful trout-stream, galloping towards the Dordogne through flowery meadows, on this last day of May, and under leaning trees, whose imaged leaves danced upon the ripples in the green shade. As I had no need to hurry, I loitered to pick ragged-robins upon the banks, flowers dear to me from old associations. Very common in England, they are comparatively rare in France.

New pleasures await the wayfarer every hour, almost every minute, in the day, and however long he may continue to wander over this wonderful world of inexhaustible variety, if he will only stop to look at everything, and so learn to feel the charm of little things.

I met a beggar, and fell into conversation with him. He asked me for nothing, and was surprised when I gave him two sous. He was a ragged old man, with a canvas bag, half filled with crusts, slung upon his side. I had already met many such beggars in this part of France. They travel about from village to village, filling their bags with pieces of bread that are given them, and selling afterwards what they cannot eat as food for pigs. As they rarely receive charity in the form of money, they do not expect it. This kind of mendicant is distinctly rural, and belongs to old times.

The bold front of an early Renaissance castle, with round towers at the angles, capped with pointed roofs, drew me from the highroad. It was the Château de Montal, in connection with which I had already heard the story of one Rose de Montal, a young lady of some three centuries ago, who had given her heart to a nobleman of the country, Roger de Castelnau. By-and-by the charms of another lady caused him to neglect the fair Rose de Montal. She remained almost constantly at a window of one of the towers, scanning the country, and longing to catch sight of the faithless Roger. One day he came down the valley of the Bave, and she sang from the height of her tower a plaintive love-song, hoping that he would stop and make some sign; but he passed on, unmoved by the tender appeal of the noble damsel. As he disappeared, she cried, 'Rose, plus d'espoir!' and threw herself from the window.

The *métayer*, now placed in charge of the castle, showed me over it. It was a sad spectacle. The building, one of the best preserved and most elaborately decorated works of the Renaissance in this part of Guyenne until a few years ago, then fell into the hands of a vulgar speculator, who detached all the carvings that could be removed without difficulty, and sold them in Paris. The noble staircase and all its delicate sculpture remain, but these only add to the regret that one feels for what is no longer there. Had the Commission of Historic Monuments placed the Château de Montal upon its list, it would probably have escaped spoliation, although, in the case of private property, the State has no power to prevent destruction, however grievous the national loss.

I entered St. Céré at sundown. This bright little town lies in the midst of fertility. It is on the banks of the Bave, and at the foot of a hill that rises abruptly from the plain, and is capped by two towers of a ruined feudal stronghold, which show against the horizon far into the Quercy, the Corrèze, and the Cantal. Some of the old streets have quite a mediæval air, with their half-wood houses with stories projecting upon the floor-joists, and others of a grander origin with turrets resting on encorbelments. I had the luck to find a good old-fashioned inn here, and to pass the evening in very pleasant company.

The next morning I climbed to the top of the neighbouring hill to have a closer view of those towers which had been my landmarks on the previous day, passing through the little village of St. Laurent-les-Tours, which lies immediately under the old fortress after the manner of so many others of feudal origin. The towers are rectangular *donjons* of the twelfth and fourteenth centuries, one being nearly a hundred and fifty feet high. The castle was raised upon a table of calcareous rock; but only the towers, a portion of the outer wall built of enormous blocks of stone, and a ruined archway marking the spot where the drawbridge once hung, remain to tell the tale of the past.

That the Romans had fortified this height there is the strongest evidence in the fact that the substructure of the rampart that once surrounded the castle is of cubic stones laid together according to the method so much practised by the Romans, and known as *opus reticulatum*. Moreover, the coins, pottery, and arms found here seem to afford conclusive proof that this remarkable hill was one of the fortified positions of the Romans in Gaul.

The spot has its Christian legend, which is briefly

this: In the castle that crowned the height in the time of the Visigoth kings was born St. Espérie, daughter of a Duke of Aquitaine. Being pressed to marry, notwithstanding the vow she had made to consecrate her life to God, she hid herself in a neighbouring forest for three months. She was at length discovered by her enraged brother and lover, who cut off her head. Like St. Denis, St. Espérie picked up her head, to the unspeakable astonishment and dismay of her persecutors. They fled from her, but she followed them as far as a little stream that flows into the Bave at St. Céré. Espérie is a saint much venerated in the Haut-Quercy. The church of St. Céré is dedicated to her, and the name given to the town is supposed to be a corruption of Espérie.

From St. Céré I took the road to Castelnau-de-Bretenoux, returning for some distance by the way I came. Inns being now very scarce in the district, I decided to take my chance of lunch in a small village called St. Jean-Lespinasse. Another saint! The map of France is still covered with the names of saints, in spite of all the efforts of revolutionists and pagan reformers to make the people abandon their 'Christian superstitions.' Those who in the 'ages of faith' built up this association of saints and places could have had no conception of the power that these names would have in binding Christianity to the soil in the faithless or doubting ages to come. The only inn at St. Jean-Lespinasse was kept by a blacksmith, and the room where I had my meal was over the forge. Bread and cheese and eggs were, as I expected, the utmost that such a hostelry could offer in the way of food for a wayfarer's entertainment. Before leaving the village I found the church—a curious old structure of the Transition period, with a large open porch covered with mossy tiles, held up by rough pillars. There were stone benches inside, on which generations of villagers had sat and gossiped in their turn. In the interior were columns engaged in the wall of the nave, with the capitals elaborately and heavily foliated with pendent bunches of flowers and fruit, much more in accordance with English than French taste.

I crossed the Bave, and followed a road bordered with hedgerows of quince that presently skirted sunny slopes covered with lately-planted vines. Thunder was moaning and growling in the distance when I reached the much-embowered village of Castelnau, upon a height immediately under the reddish walls and towers of the immense feudal stronghold, the fame of which went far and wide in the Middle Ages. Its name in the Southern dialect means 'new castle,' but it dates from the eleventh or twelfth century. Extensive additions were made in subsequent ages, notably a wing in the Renaissance style, which was inhabited until the middle of the present century, when all but the walls was destroyed by fire.

The feudal castle was built upon the plan of a triangle, with a tower at each angle, the one at the apex being the *donjon*. The form of this lofty keep is rectangular, and the machicolations and embattlements which were added in the fifteenth century are in a perfect state of preservation. Upon the platform, which I was able to reach by means of ladders and the half-ruinous spiral staircase, viper's bugloss spread its brilliant blue flowers over the dark stones, and enticed the high-soaring bees. The view of the wide and beautiful Dordogne Valley from these old battlements was not less grand because more than one-half of the sky was of a bluish-black—a mysterious canopy that concealed the genius of the storm, but from the turbulent folds of which there darted every minute a dazzling line of light. The tower on which I stood, although the highest of the three, had never been struck by lightning, but one of the others had been repeatedly struck, and the ruined masonry showed abundant signs of the scorching it had undergone in this way. Lightning is capricious and incomprehensible in its preferences.

This castle was besieged by Henry Plantagenet in 1159, but without success. Subsequently he made another effort, and then reduced it. His son Henry made it his headquarters for some time after he had revolted. In 1369 Thomas de Walkaffera, the English seneschal who held Réalville on behalf of his sovereign, was besieged there by a Lord of

Castelnau, assisted by other barons. The garrison was overcome and massacred. Another Lord of Castelnau, John, Bishop of Cahors, convened a meeting of the States of the Quercy in his fortress, at which a rising against the English was decided upon. It resulted in their temporary expulsion from the Quercy.

Besides the towers and exterior walls, there are some chambers of the old castle in good preservation. The chapel is still roofed, and the altar-stone is in its place. In an elevated chamber at the lower end, the dead were laid while awaiting burial.

Descending to the village, I entered the parish church—a Gothic building of the fourteenth century, containing many interesting details. The oak stalls, each with a quaint human figure carved upon it, are exceedingly curious. Outside the church little girls were playing, in the charge of a Sister who had a beautiful sweet face. She showed me the way to the next village, where I hoped to find shelter from the gathering storm. I have a pleasant picture in the mind of Castelnau—a bowery, ancient, mossy place, with vines climbing about the houses or on trellises in the little steep gardens, and a golden bloom of stonecrop upon the rough walls.

I reached the village of Prudhomat just as the storm burst over it, and took shelter in a small inn, which, like most of those in the country, had its room for the public upstairs. Two women who were there made the sign of the cross each time the lightning flashed—a widespread custom of the French peasantry; but a couple of men who were eating salad and bread paid no heed to the furious cannonade that was kept up by the darkened heavens. It was four o'clock, and they were having their *goûter*. The peasants of the Quercy do not live on the fat of the land; but they generally have five meals a day, two more than the middle-class French. They begin with soup at a very early hour in the morning; then they have their dinner about ten, which is chiefly soup; at three or four they have a *goûter* of bread and cheese, salad or fruit; and at six or seven they have their supper, which is soup again.

The old woman who sat near the window worked diligently with her distaff laden with hemp, except when the flashing lightning made her stop to raise her thin hand to her forehead. She was twisting the thread from which the sheets of the country are made. They are coarse, but they last longer than the hands that work the hemp, and descend from mother to daughter.

More than two hours I waited in this auberge while the rain fell in torrents, the lightning blazed, and the thunder crashed. The whole sky was the colour of slate. When at length a line of bright light appeared in the western sky, I could curb my impatience no longer, and, hoisting my pack, I was soon on the road to Carennac.

A little beyond the village I passed a gipsy encampment ranged along the side of the highway on a strip of waste land. There were no tents; but there were four or five miserable little caravans, roofed over with tattered and dirty canvas. They were tents on wheels. Some thin and ascetic-looking old mules and wizen donkeys had been taken out of the shafts, and were now nibbling the short wayside grass, the young burdocks and mulleins, which, but for the rain, would have filled their mouths with dust. Small portable stoves—alas! not the traditional fire with three stakes set in the ground and tied at the top, with the pot swinging therefrom—had been lighted outside the caravans, and gipsy women were making the evening soup. Bright-eyed, shock-headed, uncombed, unwashed, but exceedingly happy gipsy children were tumbling over one another on the wet turf, showing so much of their brown skin between their rags that they would have been more comfortable and quite as decent had they been naked. A hideous old man, merely skin and bones, sitting nose and knees together upon a sack, did not take my curiosity in good part, but glared at me morosely. The younger men of this interesting community were elsewhere

perhaps mending saucepans, or reassuring ducks alarmed by the thunderstorm. A musician of the party must have been kept in by the bad weather, for from one of the caravans came the diabolic screech of a wheezing concertina that had got rid of all its ideals and dreams of distinction.

The bright line in the west moved very slowly upwards, and the rain continued to fall, although less drenchingly than before. The setting sun strove with the cloud-rack and coloured the veil of vapour that its rays could not pierce. The nightingales and thrushes in the shrubs, and the finches amidst the later blossoms of the may, took heart again, and the song rose from so many throats near and far that the whole valley of the Dordogne was filled with warbling. As the birds grew drowsy the frogs came out to spend a happy night on the margins of the pools and the brooks, until their joyful screaming and croaking was a universal chorus. I was by the side of the broad river that flowed calmly through the fairest meadows. The face of the stream, the pools in the road, the grass and the leaves, were brightened with the orange glow of a veiled light as of some sacred fire shining in the dusk through clouds of incense. It grew warmer and warmer until it purpled and died away in grayness and mournful shadow. The beauty of nature at such moments, when the colours brighten and fade like the powers of the mind as the human day is closing, takes a solemnity that is unearthly, and it is good to be alone with the mystery.

It was dark when I reached Carennac. I did not realize how wet I was until I sat down in an auberge and tried to make myself comfortable for the night. It is not easy, however, to be happy under such circumstances. When the fire on the hearth was stirred up and fed with fresh wood to cook my dinner of barbel that had just had time to die after being pulled out of the Dordogne, I placed myself in the chimney-corner to dry before the welcome blaze. How cheering is a fire, even in June and in Southern France, on a rainy night, when the sound of sighing trees comes down the chimney and the tired wayfarer's clothes are sticking to his legs and back! How cheering, too, at such a time is a dinner, however modest, in the light and warmth of the fire. A humble barbel has then a more delicate flavour than a salmon-trout cooked with consummate art for people who never know what it is to be hungry.

The next morning I was in the cloisters belonging to the Benedictine priory of Carennac, of which Fénélon was the titular prior. Hither he came for quietude, and here he wrote his 'Télémaque,' a historical trace of which is found in a little island of the Dordogne, which is called 'L'Ile de Calypso.' It is recorded that the mother of the great Churchman and writer, when she feared that she would be childless, went on a pilgrimage to Roc-Amadour, and that Fénélon was the consequence of that act of devotion.

The cloisters of Carennac, built from plans furnished by that fountain of ecclesiastical art in the Middle Ages, the monastery of Cluny, must, judging from the remnants of tracery in the arcades, and the delicately carved bosses of the vaults, have been once a spot where the spirit of Gothic archi-

tecture found delight. Now the spirit of ruin dwells
there, leading the bramble and the celandine to
conquer, year after year, some fresh territory upon
the ancient quadrangle's crumbling wall. Above,
where the sunbeam strikes upon the wrinkled stone,
the lizard basks and the bee fresh from its hive
hums as blithely among the yellow flowers of the
celandine as if the blocks raised by men in their
reaching towards Heaven were nothing more than
the rocks that cast their shadows upon the Dordogne.
Upon the ground, man, by using no rein of respect
to curb the lower needs of life, has desecrated the
spot with pigsties! Some inhabitant of Carennac,
into whose hands the cloisters passed in recent times,
thought that a place which was good enough for
Benedictine monks to walk in might, with a little
fresh masonry, be made fit for pigs to feed and
sleep in. But an end had come to this idyllic state
of things. The cloisters of Carennac had just been
placed on the list of historic monuments. The
adjoining church had been 'classed' long before.

This church, a small Gothic edifice of the twelfth
century, has a far-projecting porch enriched with a
specimen of mediæval carving which is a long
delight to the few archæologists who find their way
to the almost forgotten village of Carennac. The
composition, which fills the tympan of the scarcely-
pointed arch, represents Christ surrounded by the
twelve Apostles. The influence of Byzantine art is
perceptible in the treatment. Very few such master-

pieces of twelfth-century carving have been so well preserved as this. The seated figure of Christ in the act of blessing His Apostles, the right hand upraised, the left resting upon a clasped book, impresses the beholder by its majesty and serenity. Very different are the figures of the Apostles: these are men, and of a very common type too, such as the Benedictines were accustomed to see in their own cloisters, or among their dependents at Carennac. But how animated are the forms, and how expressive the faces! The mouldings which serve as a border to the composition are much more Romanesque or Byzantine than Gothic, and the columns that support it have capitals which are purely Romanesque. In the interior of the church is a fifteenth-century group of seven figures, representing the scene of the Holy Sepulchre; an admirable composition, showing to what a high degree of excellence French sculpture had attained even at the dawn of the Renaissance.

Upon the stony plateau above Roc-Amadour is a cavern well known in the district as the Gouffre de Révaillon. It had for me a peculiar attraction on account of the gloomy grandeur of the scene at the entrance. When I saw it for the first time I understood at once the supernatural horror in which the peasant has learnt to hold such places. It responds to impressions left on the mind of the 'Stygian cave forlorn,' the entrance to Dante's 'City of Sorrow,' and that other cave where Æneas witnessed in cold terror the prophetic fury of the Sibyl.

This effect of gloom, horror and sublimity is the result of geological conditions and the action of water, which together have produced many similar phenomena in the region of the *causses*, but in no other case, I believe, with such power in composing the picturesque. Imagine an open plain which in the truly Dark Ages whereof man has had no experience, but of whose convulsions he has learnt to read a little from the book whose leaves are the rocks, cracked along a part of its surface as a drying ball of clay might do, the fissure finishing abruptly and where it is deepest in front of a mass of rock that refused to split. This was apparently the beginning of the Gouffre de Révaillon. Then came another submersion which greatly modified the appearance of things. There was evidently a deluge here after the land had dried and cracked, and it must have lasted a very long time for the waves to have hollowed, smoothed and polished the rocks inside the caverns and elsewhere as we now see them. Those who have observed with a little attention a rugged coast will, without being geologists, recognise the distinctly marine character of the greater number of these orifices in the calcareous district of the *causses*. The washing and smoothing action of the sea along the sides of the gorges which cut up the surface of the country in such an astonishing manner is not so easy to distinguish. But the reason is obvious. This limestone rock is by its nature disintegrating wherever it is exposed to the air and frost, and the foundations of the bastions which support the *causses* are being continually sapped by water which carries away the lime in solution and deposits a part of it elsewhere in the form of stalactite and stalagmite in the deep galleries where subterranean rivers often run, and which probably descend to the lowest part of the formation. Thus by the dislodgment of huge masses of rock which have rolled down from their original positions, and the breaking away of the surfaces of others, the most convincing traces of the sea's action here have nearly disappeared. In the gorge of the Alzou, however, near Roc-Amadour, about 100 feet above the channel of the stream, there is a considerable reach of hard rock approaching marble, the polished and undulating surface of which tells the story of the ocean, just as the sides of the caverns in much more elevated positions tell it.

In the rock where the fissure ends at Révaillon is an opening like a vast yawning mouth, the roof of which forms an almost perfect dome. Adown this a stream trickles towards the end of summer, but plunges madly and with a frightful roar in winter and spring. The steep sides of the narrow ravine are densely wooded, and the light is very dim at the bottom when the sun is not overhead. I made my first attempt to descend the dark passage in the early summer, but there was too much water, and I was soon obliged to retreat. One afternoon in October I returned with a companion, and we took with us a rope and plenty of candles. We carried the rope in view of possible difficulties in the shape of rocks inside the cavern, for it should be borne in mind that in *gouffres* of this character the stream frequently descends by a series of cascades. The weather was very sultry, and the sky towards the west was of a slaty blue. A fierce storm was threatening, but we paid no attention to it—a mistake which others bent on exploring caverns where streams still flow should be warned against. There is probably no force in nature more terrible, or which makes a man's helplessness more miserably felt, than water suddenly rushing towards him when he is underground.

The sun was still shining, however, when we reached the Gouffre de Révaillon and descended into the ravine over roots of trees coiling upon the moss like snakes, some arching upward as if about to spring at the throat of those who disturbed the elfish solitude. At our coming there rose from the great rock such a multitude of jackdaws that for some seconds they darkened the air. With harsh screams the birds soared higher and higher above their fortress, which they had possessed for ages in perfect security. We reached the bed of the stream, where scattered threads of water tinkled as they fell over huge blocks into little pools below, and then went whispering on their way towards the darkness. At the bottom of a long slant of greenish slimy stone, patched here and there with moss, I stopped a few minutes, feeling that I could not grasp without an effort the deep gloom and grandeur of my surroundings. The jackdaws had all flown away, and there was no sound now but the tinkle and gurgle of the water. Great snails crawled upon the tufts of rank grass wet with the autumnal dews that the sun had failed to dry, and upon the glistening hart's-tongue ferns, and they looked just the kind of snails that witches would collect to make a hell-broth. Dark ivy hung down from the rocks, and under the vaulted entrance of the cavern was a clump of elders, very sinister-looking, and giving forth when touched an evil narcotic odour. Near these forlorn shrubs was a solitary plant of angelica, now woebegone, its fringed leaves drooping, waiting for the rising water to wash it into the darkness. There were willow-herbs still in bloom, but the crane's-bill struggled with the gloom farther than any other flowering plant, and its bright little purple lamps shone in the very mouth of Night. Gnats there were too, spinning in the semi-darkness, now sinking, now rising, keeping together, a merry band of musicians, each with a small flute, piping perhaps to the little goblins that swung on spiders' webs, and slept upon the fronds of the ferns.

Candles were now lighted, and we left the glimmer of day behind us. A little beyond the great dome the roof became so low that we had to creep along almost on hands and knees, but it presently rose again, and to a great height. The first obstacle— the one that sent me back a few months before— was a steep rock down which the water then fell in such a cascade that there was no getting a foothold upon it. Now the water scarcely covered it, and there was no difficulty in reaching the bottom. Here, however, was a pool through which we had to wade knee-deep. The cavern continued, and the stalagmite became interesting by its fantastic shapes. Here was a mass like an immense sponge, even to the colour, and there, descending from the roof down the side of the rock, was the waved hair of an undine that had been changed into white and glistening stone. The stalactites were less remarkable. The sound of dropping water told us that another cascade was near. This we left behind by climbing along the side of the gallery, clinging to the rock, and in the same way four more obstacles of precisely the same character were overcome. All the distance the slope was rapid, but at intervals there was a sudden fall of from ten to fifteen feet, with a black-looking pool at the foot of the rock, hollowed out by the action of the tumbling torrent. The last of these falls was the worst to cross. To this point the cavern had been already explored, but no farther apparently, the local impression being that it ended just beyond. It was an ugly place. The rock over which the water fell was almost perpendicular, and the pool at the bottom was larger and deeper than the others. Seen by the light of day, any schoolboy might have scoffed at the difficulty of getting beyond it, but when you are descending into the bowels of the earth, where the light of two candles can only dissolve the darkness a few yards around you, every form becomes fantastic and awful, and the effect of water of unknown depth upon the imagination is peculiarly disturbing. But we made up our minds to go on if it were possible. The passage was very narrow, and the sides offered few salient points to which one could cling. We moved along a very narrow ledge in a sitting posture, and then, when we had gone as far as we could in this way, and there was nothing beyond to sit upon, we made a spring. My companion, being the more agile, nearly cleared the pool, but I went in with a great splash, as I expected, and thought myself lucky in being only wetted to the waist. The water was not very cold, the temperature of the cavern being much higher than that of the outer air.

We reckoned that we had by this time travelled underground about half a mile, and as we had been descending rapidly all the way, the distance beneath the surface must have been considerable. My theory with regard to this stream was that it was a tributary of the subterranean Ouysse; but the fact that the cavern ran north-west made me change my opinion, and conclude that this water-course took an independent line towards the Dordogne.

A little beyond the last pool the running water suddenly vanished. We looked around to see if it had taken any side passage; but no: it simply disappeared into the earth, although no hole was perceptible in its stony channel. It passed by infiltration into some lower gallery, where the light of a candle had never shone, and is never likely to shine. But we had not reached the end of the cavern, although the passage became so low that we had now really to go down on all-fours in order to proceed. We had not to keep this posture long, for again the roof rose, although to no great height. We walked on about fifty yards or more, and then came to the end. There was no opening anywhere except by the way we entered. We were like flies that had crawled into a bottle, and a very unpleasant bottle it might have proved to us. We noticed—at first with some surprise—that, although there was not a drop of water now in this *cul-de-sac*, our feet sank into damp sand that had evidently been carried there by water. Sticks were also lying about, and the walls up to the roof were covered with a muddy slime. It was evident that this hole had been filled with water, and not very long ago; probably the last thunderstorm accounted for the signs of recent moisture. While we were talking about this, a strange, muffled, moaning sound reached our ears. We looked at one another over the tops of two candles. 'Thunder,' said my companion. In a few minutes the same dismal moan, long drawn out, came down the cavern, which acted like a speaking-tube between us and the outer world, and conveyed a timely warning. Was it in time? We were not quite sure of this, for as we issued from the *cul-de-sac* we heard the water coming down the rocks with a very different voice from that which it had not many minutes before. It was clear that the storm was beginning to tell upon the stream, and if the rain had been falling for half an hour, as I had already seen it fall in the Quercy, we might find the work of recrossing those pools and climbing up the cascades anything but cheerful. Already where we had been able to walk on dry stones the water was now up to our ankles. The first cascade to surmount was the worst. We decided to try it on the side opposite to the one by which we descended, for we observed a jutting and highly-polished piece of stalagmite, which promised to help the manœuvre. One went first, and the other waited, holding the candle. I was in the rear. When my companion had reached the top of the cascade, I threw him the coil of rope — a useless encumbrance, as it happened — and in so doing put out the candle. Before I was sure that I had a dry match upon me, I failed to seize the humour, although I felt the novelty of the situation. During those seconds of uncertainty, the sound of the water — really fast increasing — seemed to become a deafening roar. However, we both had dry matches, and were able to relight our candles; but it might have been otherwise, wet as we were. Without light we should have been as helpless beneath those rocks as mice in a pitcher. The first cascade conquered, we felt much more comfortable, for the picture of being washed into that *cul-de-sac* had flashed upon the mind of each.

As the next and the next cascade were passed, our spirits rose still more; and when we saw the gray daylight in the distance, our gaiety was quite genuine, and we no longer 'laughed yellow,' as the French phrase it. The stream was rapidly becoming a frantic torrent, but we were not afraid of it now.

On reaching the dome, we saw the water pouring over rocks that were dry when we entered, and the clouds seemed to be emptying their rain in frenzy.

An hour later the stream that was lisping so innocently as it threaded its way amongst the stones, and dropped from rock to rock before the storm, sent up a wild roar from the bottom of the valley, and shrieked like a tormented fiend, as it leaped into the black mouth of the Gouffre de Révaillon. Tons of water had probably collected there at the bottom of the gulf. And I, in my shortsightedness, had hoped that the cavern was two or three miles long! I had great reason to be thankful that it ended where it did, for the excitement of adventure would have carried us on, and we might have gone too deep into the earth to hear the thunder.

On emerging from the darkness, we made all the haste we could to reach the nearest inn. The storm was still at its height; the thunder was an almost continuous roar; and the quick lightning-flashes lit up the streaming country. We were quite drenched on reaching a little wayside auberge. Water was soon boiling upon the wood-fire, and having set rheumatism at defiance with steaming glasses of grog, we left for Roc-Amadour, where, on our arrival, we found our friends about to start with lanterns to look for us in the Gouffre de Révaillon.

Noticing one day a low cavern in the rocks

beside the Ouysse, I asked if anyone had ever entered it, and was told that a man had done so; that he had found a long, low gallery, which he followed for two or three hundred yards, and then gave up the attempt to reach the end. It was well known that the hole, being on a level with the water, was much used by otters. The desire to explore this cavern becoming strong, I spoke to Decros about the adventure. He was ready to go with me ; and so we started, taking with us enough candles to light a ball-room.

On our way over the hills from Roc-Amadour, we passed two dolmens, one of which was in good preservation. There are several hundred of them in the Quercy ; and the peasants, who call them *pierros levados* (raised stones), also 'tombs of the giants' and *caïrous*, in which last name the Celtic word *cairn* has been almost preserved, treat them now with indifference, although it is recorded of one of the early bishops of Cahors that he caused a menhir to be broken to pieces because it was an object of idolatrous worship. Those who have been to the trouble of excavating have almost invariably found in each dolmen a *cella* containing human bones. In some of them flint implements have been discovered ; in others iron implements and turquoise ornaments, showing that the tombs, although all alike, belong to different periods. Tumuli are also numerous, but only a few menhirs and traces of cromlechs are to be seen.

Close to the Gouffre de Cabouy, whose outflow forms a tributary of the Ouysse, is a cottage where a man lives whose destiny I have often envied. When he is tired of fishing or shooting, he works in his thriving little vineyard, which he increases every year. The river is as much his own as if it belonged to him; he gets all he wants by giving himself very little trouble, and has no cares. We needed this man's boat for our expedition, and we found it drawn into a little cove beside the ruined mill, long since abandoned. It was a somewhat porous old punt, with small fish swimming about in the bottom; but it was well enough for our purpose. In the warm sunshine of the October afternoon we glided gently down the quiet stream, which is very deep, but so clear that you can see all the water-plants which revel in it, down to the sand and pebbles. Near the banks we passed over masses of water-cress, and what might be likened to floating fields of lilies and pond-weed.

It needed no little reflection and expenditure of art to insert the prow of the boat into the mouth of the cavern. What an ugly and uninteresting hole I then thought it! Having run the punt as far as we could into the opening, there still remained about six feet of water to cross before reaching the sandy mud beyond. A plank, however, that we brought with us served as a bridge. The story of the otters was no fable, for here were the footprints of the beasts all over the mud. We lighted candles and looked into the hole. The ground rose and the roof descended, so that to enter it was necessary to lie perfectly flat, and to crawl along by a movement very like that of swimming; then the passage became so small that there was only room for one to go at a time. Neither of us was ambitious to go first, for there was just a chance of an otter seizing the invader by the nose; but neither liked to show the white feather. Each in turn went in a few yards, planted a lighted candle in the mud, and then found some pretext for returning. The hot air of the cavern was almost suffocating, and one felt so helpless flattened against the earth, with the rock pressing so tight upon the back that even to wriggle along was difficult. 'Decros is a native,' thought I, 'and he ought to be used to this kind of work. I will let him understand that he is expected now to do his duty.' In he went again, and planted another candle about a yard in front of the last one. Then he stopped and fired a shot from the revolver that we carried in turn for the otters, and the sound of the detonation seemed to echo in a muffled fashion from the bowels of the earth.

'How many otters have you killed?' I shouted.

'None,' he replied. 'I just fired to let them know that we are here.'

I then asked him if he was going on, and I fancied that he tried to shrug his shoulders, but found the rock in the way. His practical reply, however, was to slowly back out. When he was able to stand up again, he said he believed he had seen the end of the cavern, and would like me to take another look. I now realized that if the secrets of the fantastic realm which my fancy had pictured were to be revealed to me, there must be no more shirking. When I flattened myself out again upon the mud, it was with the determination to go right through the neck of the bottle, for such the passage figuratively was. At one moment I felt tightly wedged, unable to move forward or backward, in a hot steamy atmosphere that was not made any pleasanter by the smoke of the burnt powder; but the sight of the now rising roof encouraged me to further efforts, and presently I was able to stand upright—in fact, I was in a cavern where a giant of the first magnitude could have walked about with ease, but where he might have been a prisoner for life. I was resolved, however, that Decros should not escape his share of the adventure, so I called to him to come on, and he quickly joined me. To my great disappointment, the cavern soon came to an end. Where, we asked, could the otters be hiding themselves? Examining the place more carefully, we found a passage going under the rock at the farther extremity, but nearly filled with sand which the river had washed up in time of flood. Here, then, was the continuation of the cavern. The passage had been made by water, for a subterranean stream must at one time have found an exit here into the Ouysse, and now water was reversing the process by filling up the ancient conduit. But for the otters that kept it open, we should probably have seen no trace of it; and it was for this that we had wriggled our way into the hideous hole like serpents! I left with the impression that there was much vanity in searching for the wonders of the subterranean world.

Having brought back the boat, we stopped at the cottage by the vineyard and tried the juice of the grapes which three weeks before were basking in the sun. It was now a fragrant wine of a rich purple, with a certain flavour of the soil that made it the more agreeable. The fisherman's wife also placed upon the table a loaf of home-made bread, of an honest brown colour, some of the little Roc-Amadour cheeses made from goat's milk, and a plate of walnuts. The window looked out upon the sunny vines, whose leaves were now flaming gold or ruddy brown; the blue river shone in the hollow below, and through the open door there came the tinkling of bells from the rocky wastes where the small long-tailed sheep were moving slowly homeward, nibbling the stunted herbage as they went.

This sound reminded us that the sun would soon drop behind the hill, and that the Pomoyssin, to which we intended to pay a visit on our way home, was not a spot that gained attractiveness from the shades of night. I had heard the country-people speak of it as a peculiarly horrible and treacherous *gouffre*, and its name, which means 'unwholesome hole,' corresponds to the local opinion of it. The shepherd children would suffer torture from thirst rather than descend into the gloomy hollow and dip out a drop of the dark water which is said to draw the gazer towards it, and then into its mysterious depths under the rock, by the spell of some wicked power. Some years ago a woman, supposed to have been drawn there by the evil spirit, was found drowned, and since then the spot has been avoided even more than it was before.

It was to this place, then, that we went when the sun was setting. The way led up a deep little valley which was an absolute desert of stones. A dead walnut-tree, struck apparently by lightning, with its old and gnarled branches stretching out on one side like weird arms, was just the object that the imagination would place in a valley blighted by the influence of evil spirits, in proximity to a passage communicating from their world to this one. Presently, as we drew near some high rocks, Decros, pointing to a dark hollow in the shadow of them said, 'There it is.' We went down into the basin to the edge of the water that lay there, black and still, Decros showing evident reluctance and restlessness the while, so strongly was his mind affected by all the stories he had heard about the pool. Moreover, it was rapidly growing dusk. In this half-light the funnel in which we were standing certainly did look a very diabolic and sinister hole. The fancy aiding, everything partook of the supernatural: the dark masses of brambles hanging from the rocks, the wild vines clinging to them with leaves like flakes of deep-glowing crimson fire, and especially the intermittent sound of gurgling water.

I was glad to have seen the Pomoyssin under circumstances so favourable, but it was with relief that I left it and began to climb the side of the gorge from this valley of dreadful shadows towards the pure sky that reddened as the brown dusk deepened below.

IN THE VALLEY OF THE CÉLÉ.

It was a burning afternoon of late summer when I walked across the stony hills which separate the valley of the Lot from that of its tributary the Célé, between Capdenac and Figeac. I did not take the road, but climbed the cliffs, trusting myself to chance and the torrid *causse*. I wished that I had not done so when it was too late to act differently. There was nothing new for me upon the bare hills, where all vegetation was parched up except the juniper bushes and the spurge. At length I found the road that went down with many a flourish into the valley of the Célé, and I reached Figeac in the evening, covered with dust, and as thirsty as a hunted stag. Here I took up my quarters for awhile.

Figeac is not a beautiful town from the Haussmannesque point of view—the one that is destined to prevail in all municipal councils; but it is full of charm to the archæologist and the lover of the picturesque. There are few places even in France which have undergone so little change during the last five or six hundred years. Elsewhere, thirteenth and fourteenth century houses are becoming rare;

here they are numerous. There are streets almost entirely composed of them. These streets are in reality narrow crooked lanes paved with pebbles, slanting towards the gutter in the centre. Some are only three or four yards wide, and the walls half shut out the light of day. You look up and see a mere strip of blue sky, but trailing plants reaching far downward from window-sills, one above the other, light up the gloom with many a patch of vivid green. You venture down some dim passage and come suddenly upon a little court where an old Gothic portal with quaint sculptures, or a Renaissance doorway with armorial bearings carved over the lintel, bears testimony to the grandeur and wealth of those who once lived in the now grimy, dilapidated, poverty-stricken mansion. Pretentious dwellings of bygone days have long since been abandoned to the humble.

Here is a typical house in the Rue Abel, which is scarcely wide enough for two to walk abreast. The oak door is elaborately carved with heads and leaves, flowers and line ornament, all in strong relief. One grimacing puckered head has a movable tongue that once lifted a latch on being touched. Near the ground the oak has been half devoured by the damp. This door would have been sold long ago to antiquaries or speculators if the house since the Revolution had not become the property of several persons all equally suspicious of one another, and with the Cadurcian bump of obstinacy equally developed. They had no respect for the carving, and they were eager to 'touch' the money; but their interests in the house not being the same, they could never come to an understanding over the door; consequently, in spite of very tempting offers, the piece of massive oak continues to hang upon its rusty hinges. So much the better for the student of antiquities, for, without denying that museums are eminently useful, it is certain that they deprive objects of a great deal of their interest and their power of suggesting ideas by detaching them from their surroundings. Moreover, it is not at all sure that these things, when they have been bought up and carried away, will ever be put in a place where anybody can see them who may have the wish to do so. And then, when a thing has been put into a museum, it becomes such labour and painfulness to look for it; and most of us are so lazy by nature. I will make a frank confession. For my own part, I should scarcely look at this old door if it were in the Cluny or any other museum; but here, in ancient Figeac, I see it where it was many lustres ago, and the pleasure of finding it in the midst of the sordidness and squalor that follow upon the decay of grandeur and the evaporation of human hopes makes me feel much that I should not feel otherwise, and calls up ideas as a February sunbeam calls gnats out of the dead earth and sets them spinning.

I venture up the stone staircase, although most of the finely carved balusters are gone, and the arch-stones have so slipped out of place that they seem to cling together by the will of Providence rather than by any physical law. The stairs themselves, although of fine stone that has almost the polish of marble, are cracked as if an earthquake had tormented them, and worn by the tread of innumerable feet into deep hollows. I reach a landing where a long corridor stretches away into semi-darkness. The floor is black with dirt, and so are the doors which once opened into rooms where luxury waited upon some who were born, and upon others (perchance the same) who died. A sound reaches me from the far-end of the corridor that makes me feel like a coward. It is the raving of a madman. How he seems to be contending with all the fiends of hell! Sometimes his voice is so low, and the words crowd one upon another so fast, that the muttering is like the prolonged growl of a wild beast; then the mood changes, and the unseen man seems to be addressing an invisible audience in grand sonorous sentences as though he were a Cicero; and perhaps he may be, but as he speaks in *patois* his eloquence is lost upon me. What a terrible excitement is in his voice! How it thrills and horrifies! And he is alone, quite alone in this dismal old house with the fiends who harass him. This I learn from a young girl whom I meet at the bottom of the staircase. She tells me that the man is only mad at the time of the new or the full moon (I forget which), and that his raving lasts but two or three days. Then nobody ventures near him; but at other times he is quite rational and harmless. He has left, however, upon me an impression more lasting perhaps than that of the old tottering staircase that threatens to close up every moment like a toy snake that has been stretched out.

Most of the old houses are entered by Gothic doorways, and the oak doors are studded with large nail-heads. The locks and bolts are of mediæval workmanship. Sometimes you see an iron ring hanging to a string that has been passed through a hole in the door. It is just such a string as Little Red Riding-hood (an old French fable, by-the-bye) pulled to lift the latch at the summons of the wicked wolf. And what a variety of ancient knockers have we here! Many are mere bars of iron hanging to a ring; but others are much more artistic, showing heads coifed in the style of the fifteenth and sixteenth centuries, serpents biting their own tails, and all manner of fanciful ideas wrought into iron. In wandering about the dim old streets, paved with cobble stones, architectural details of singular interest strike one at every turn. Now it is the encorbelment of a turret at the angle of a fifteenth or sixteenth century mansion that has lost all its importance; now a dark archway with fantastic heads grimacing from the wall; now an arcade of Gothic windows, with graceful columns and delicate carvings—a beautiful fragment in the midst of ruin.

What helps much to render these dingy streets, passages, and courts of Figeac so delightfully picturesque is the vegetation which, growing with southern luxuriance in places seemingly least favourable to it, clings to the ancient masonry, or brightens it by the strong contrast of its immediate neighbourhood in some little garden or balustraded terrace. Wherever there are a few feet of ground some rough poles support a luxuriant vine-trellis, and grapes ripen where one might suppose scarcely a gleam of sunshine could fall. The vine clambers over everything, and sometimes reaches to the top of a house two stories high. The old walls of Figeac are likewise tapestried with pellitory and ivy-linaria, with here and there a fern pushing its deep-green frond farther into the shadow, or an orpine sedum lifting its head of purple flowers into the sunshine that changes it to a flame.

There is much in the life of this place that matches perfectly with the surroundings. Enter by a Gothic doorway, and you will come upon a nail-maker's forge, and see a dog turning the wheel that keeps the bellows continually blowing. The wheel is about a foot broad, and stands some three feet high. The dog jumps into it at a sign from his master, and as the wheel turns the sparks from the forge fall about the animal in showers. Each dog is expected to work five or six hours; then, when his task is done, he is allowed to amuse himself as he pleases, while a comrade takes his turn at the wheel. The nailmakers discovered long ago that dog labour was cheaper than boy labour, and not so troublesome. Nevertheless, these wheels belong to an order of things that has nearly passed away.

The crier or *tambourineur*, as he is generally called, because he carries a drum, which he beats most lustily to awaken the curiosity of the inhabitants, is making the round of the town with an ox, which is introduced to the public as ' le bœuf ici présent.' The crier's business is to announce to all whom it may concern that the animal is to be killed this very evening, and that its flesh will be sold to-morrow at 1 franc 25 centimes the kilo. It will all go at a uniform price, for this is the local custom. Those who want the *aloyau*, or sirloin, only have to be quick. The ox, notwithstanding that he has a rope tied round his nose and horns, and is led by the butcher, evidently thinks it a great distinction to be *tambouriné*; his expression indicating that this is the proudest day of his life. Every time the drum begins to rattle he flourishes his tail, and when each little ceremony is over he moves on to a fresh place with a jaunty air, as if he were aware that all this drumming and fuss were especially intended for his entertainment. No condemned wretch ever made his last appearance in public with a better grace.

Another day I see this crier going round the town accompanied by a boy every available part of whose person is decked with ribbons, and all kinds of things ordinarily sold by drapers and haberdashers. Over each shoulder is slung a pair of women's boots. The boy is a walking advertisement of an exceptional sale, which a tradesman announces with the help of the crier and his drum.

A band of women and girls come up from the riverside, walking in Indian file, and each with a glittering copper water-pot on her head. What beautiful water-pots these are! They have the antique curve that has not changed in the course of ages. They swell out at the bottom and the top, and fall gracefully in towards the middle. As the women quit the sunshine and enter the deep shadow of the street the shine of their water-pots is darkened suddenly, like the sparks of burnt paper which follow one upon another and go out.

The sound of solemn music draws me into a church. A requiem Mass is being chanted. In the middle of the nave, nearer the main door than the altar, is a deal coffin with gable-shaped lid, barely covered by a pall. A choir-boy comes out of the sacristy, carrying a pan of live embers, which he places at the head of the coffin. Then he sprinkles incense upon the fire, and immediately the smoke rises like a snow-white cloud towards the vaulting; but, meeting the sunbeams on its way, it moves up their sloping golden path, and seems to pass through the clerestory window into the boundless blue.

Now the procession moves towards the cemetery. It is a boy's funeral, and four youths of about the same age as the one who lies in darkness hold the four corners of each pall, two of which are carried in front of the coffin. After the hearse come members of the confraternity of Blue Penitents, one of whom carries a great wooden cross upon his shoulder. Others carry staves with small crosses at the top, or emblems of the trades that they follow. The dead boy's father is a Penitent, and this is why the confraternity has come out to-day. They now wear their *cagoules* raised; but on Good Friday, when they go in procession to a high spot called the Calvary, the leader walking barefoot and carrying the cross on his shoulder in imitation of Christ, they wear these dreadful-looking flaps over their faces. Their appearance then is terrible enough; but what must that of the Red Penitents, who accompanied condemned wretches to execution, have been? In a few years there will be no Blue Penitents at Figeac. As the old members of the confraternity die, there are no postulants to fill their places. Already they feel, when they put on their 'sacks,' that they are masquerading, and that the eye of ridicule is upon them. This state of mind is fatal to the conservation of all old customs. The political spirit of the times is, moreover, opposed to these religious processions in France. That of the *fête-Dieu* at Figeac would have been suppressed some years ago by the Municipal Council had it not been for the outcry of the tradespeople. All the new dresses, new hats, and new boots that are bought for this occasion cause money to be spent that might otherwise be saved, and those who are interested in the sale of such things wish the procession through the streets to be kept up, although in heart they may be among the scoffers at religion.

The religious confraternities in Aquitaine date from the appearance of the *routiers* at the close of the twelfth century. These *routiers* were then chiefly Brabançons, Aragonese, and Germans. According to an ecclesiastical author and local historian, the Abbé Debon, the lawless bands spread such terror through the country that they stopped the pilgrims from going to Figeac, Conques, and other places that had obtained a reputation for holiness. A canon of Le Puy in Auvergne, much distressed by the desertion of the sanctuary of Notre Dame de Puy, which rivals that of Roc-Amadour in antiquity, formed the design of instituting a confraternity to wage war against the *routiers* and destroy them. A 'pious fraud' was adopted. A young man, having been dressed so as to impersonate Notre Dame du Puy, appeared to a carpenter who was in the habit of praying every night in the cathedral, and gave him the mission of revealing that it was the will of the Holy Virgin that a confraternity should be formed to put down the brigands and establish peace in the country. Hundreds of men enrolled themselves at once. The confrères, from the fact that they wore hoods of white linen, obtained the name of Chaperons Blancs. Upon their breasts hung a piece of lead with this inscription : 'Agnus Dei qui tollis peccata mundi dona nobis pacem.' The confraternity spread into Aquitaine, and the *routiers* were defeated in pitched battles with great slaughter ; but the *chaperons* in course of time became lawless fanatics, and were almost as great a nuisance to society as those whom they had undertaken to exterminate. They were nevertheless the ancestors in a sense of the confraternities of penitents who, at a later period, became so general in Europe.

The monthly fair at Figeac offers some curious pictures of rural life. The peasants crowd in from the valleys and the surrounding *causses*. Racial differences, or those produced by the influences of soil and food—especially water—for a long series of generations, are very strongly marked. There is the florid, robust, blue-eyed, sanguine type, and there is the leaden-coloured, black-haired, lantern-jawed, sloping-shouldered, and hollow-chested type. Then there are the intermediates. Considered generally, these peasants of the Haut-Quercy are not fine specimens of the human animal. They are dwarfed, and very often deformed. Their almost exclusively vegetable diet, their excessive toil, and the habit of drinking half-putrid rain-water from cisterns which they very rarely clean, may possibly explain this physical degeneration of the Cadurci. Their character is honest in the main, but distrustful and superficially insincere by nature or the force of circumstance. Their worst qualities are shown at a fair, where they cheat as much as they can, and place no limit to lying. Their canon of morality there is that everyone must look after himself. I have been assured by a priest that they never think of confessing the lies that they tell in bartering, because they maintain that every man who buys ought to understand his business. I much wondered why, at a Figeac fair, when there was a question of buying a bullock, the animal's tail was pulled as though all his virtue were concentrated in this appendage. I learnt that the reason of the tugging was this: Cattle are liable to a disease that causes the tail to drop off, but the people here have discovered a very artful trick of fastening it on again, and it needs a vigorous pull to expose the fraud. Among other tricks of the country is that of drenching an ill-tempered and unmanageable horse with two *litres* of wine before taking him to the fair. He then becomes as quiet as a lamb. I heard the story of a *curé*, who was thus imposed upon by one of his own parishioners. He wanted a very quiet horse, and he found one at the fair; but the next day, when he went near the animal, it appeared to be possessed of the devil. All this is bad; but there is satisfaction to the student of old manners in knowing that everything takes place as it did centuries ago. The cattle-dealers and peasants here actually transact their business in *pistoles* and *écus*. A *pistole* now represents 10 francs, and an *écu* 3 francs.

The summer is glorious here, and as the climate is influenced by that of Auvergne, it is less enervating by the Célé than in the neighbouring valley of the Lot. There, some twenty miles farther south, the grapes ripen two or three weeks sooner than they do upon these hillsides. But the *vent d'autan* —the wind from the south-east—is now blowing, and, although there is too much air, one gasps for breath. The brilliant blue fades out of the sky, and the sun just glimmers through layers of dun-coloured vapour. It is a sky that makes one ill-tempered and restless by its sameness and indecision. But the wind is a worse trial. It blows hot, as if it issued from the infernal cavern. It sets the nerves altogether wrong, and disposes one to commit evil deeds from mere wantonness and the feeling that some violent reaction from this influence is what nature insists upon. It is a wind that does not blow a steady honest gale, but goes to work in a treacherously intermittent fashion now lulled to a complete calm, now springing at you like a tiger from the jungle. Then your eyes are filled with dust, unless you close them quickly, or turn your back to the enemy in the nick of time. The night comes, and brings other trouble. You try to sleep with closed windows, so that you may hear less of the racket that the wind makes outside, but it is impossible: you stifle. You get up and open a window—perhaps two windows. The wind rushes in, but it is like the hot breath of a panting dog. The noise of swinging *persiennes* that have got loose, and are banged now against the wall, now against the window-frame, mingles with a woful confusion of sounds within, as though a most unruly troop of ghosts were dancing the *farandole* all through the house. If any door has been left open, it worries you more by its banging at intervals of a minute than if it went on without stopping to consider. Therefore you are compelled to rise again, and go and look for it—anything but a cheerful expedition if you cannot find the matches. When this south wind falls, the rain generally comes, bringing great refreshment to the parched earth, and all the animals that live upon it.

As I have referred to the house in which I live, I may as well say something more with regard to it and the things which it contains. It is not one of the ancient houses of Figeac, but it is old-fashioned and provincial. The rooms are rather large, the floors are venerably black, and the boarded ceilings supported by rafters have never had their structural secrets or the grain of the timber concealed by a layer of plaster. What you see over-head is simply the floor of the room or the loft above. And yet this is not considered a poor kind of house; it is as good as most good people hereabouts live in. The furniture is simple, but solid; it was made to last, and most of it has long outlasted the first owners.

In every room, the kitchen excepted, there is a bed, according to the very general custom of the country. The character of the people is distinctly utilitarian, notwithstanding the blood of the troubadours. There is even a bed in the *salle à manger*. A piece of furniture, however, from which my eye takes more pleasure is one of those old clocks which reach from the ceiling to the floor, and conceal all the mystery and solemnity of pendulum and weights from the vulgar gaze. It has a very loud and self-asserting tick, and a still more arrogant strike, for such an old clock; but, then, everybody here has a voice that is much stronger than is needed, and it is the habit to scream in ordinary conversation. A clock, therefore, could not make itself heard by such people as these Quercynois, unless it had a voice matching in some sort with their own. Another piece of furniture that pleases me, because it is of shining copper, which always throws a homely warmth into a room, is a large basin fixed upon a stand against the wall, with a little cistern above it, also of copper. It is intended for washing the hands by means of a fillet of water that is set running by turning the tap. In this dry part of the world water has to be used sparingly, and, indeed, there is very little wasted upon the body. Everybody who has travelled in Guyenne must be familiar with the article of household furniture just described. Every young wife piously provides herself with one, together with a warming-pan; for the old domestic ideas are religiously handed down here from mother to daughter. But I must shorten this 'journey round my room,' so little in the manner of Le Maistre.

Most of the furniture was once the property of a priest, and would be still if he were alive. The good man is gone where even the voices of the Figeacois cannot reach him; but he has left abundant traces of his piety behind him. The walls of these rooms are almost covered by them. I cannot help being edified, for I am unable to look upon anything that approaches the profane.

When I grow thoughtful over all these works of art and *objets de piété*—engravings, lithographs, statuettes, crucifixes, crosses worked in wool, stables of Bethlehem, little holy-water stoops, and the faded photographs belonging to the early period of the art (portraits, no doubt, of brothers, sisters, nephews, and nieces, all revealing that air of rusticity in Sunday clothes which is not to be mistaken)—I have before me the whole story of a simple life, surrounding itself year after year with fresh emblems and tokens of the hope that reaches beyond the grave, and the affections of nature that become woven on this side of it, and which mingle joy and sorrow even in the cup of a village priest.

It is in these quiet, provincial places, where existence goes on in the old-fashioned, humdrum way, that people take care of their household property, and respect the sentiment that years lay up in it; they hand it down to the next generation as they received it. Little objects of common ornament, of religious or intellectual pleasure, thus preserved, throw in course of time a vivid light on human changes.

And it is this vivid light that I am now feeling in these dim rooms. I am aware that nearly everything here is the record of an epoch to which I do not belong—that the world's mind has undergone a great change even in the provinces since the influence that comes forth from these silent traces of past thought were in harmony with it. What interests me more than anything else here is an allegorical or mystical map, designed, drawn, and coloured with all the patience and much of the artistic skill of an illuminating monk of the thirteenth century. I doubt if in any presbytery far out in the marshes or on the mountains a priest could now be found with the motive to undertake such a task. It belongs to the same order of ideas as the 'Pilgrim's Progress.' In this map one sees the 'States of Charity,' the 'Province of Fervour,' the 'Empire of Self-Contempt,' and other countries belonging to a vast continent, of which the centre is the 'Kingdom of the Love of God,' connected to a smaller continent—that of the world—by a narrow neck of land called the 'Isthmus of Charity.' In the continent of the world are shown the 'Mountain of Ingratitude,' the 'Hills of Frivolity,' the territory of

'Ennui,' of 'Vanity,' of 'Melancholy,' and of all the evil moods and vices to which men are liable. Separated from the mainland, and washed by the 'Torrent of Bitterness,' are the 'Rocks of Remorse.' Among the allegorical emblems in various parts of the chart is a very remarkable tree with blue trunk and rose-coloured leaves called the 'Tree of Illusions.' Far above it lies the 'Peninsula of Perfection,' and near to this, under a mediæval drum-tower, is the gateway of the 'City of Happiness.'

There is a little garden at the back of the house, where flowers and vegetables are mixed up in the way I like. The jessamine has become a thicket. Vines ramble over the trellis and the old wall, and from the window I see many other vines showing their lustrous leaves against tiled roofs of every shade, from bright-red to black. In the next garden is my friend the *aumônier*, an octogenarian priest, who is still nearly as sprightly of body as he is of mind. He lives alone, surrounded by books, in the collection of which he has shown the broad judgment and impartiality of the genuine lover of literature. There is a delicious disorder in his den, because there is no one to interfere with him. He is now much excited against the birds because they will not leave his figs alone, and someone has just lent him a blunderbuss wherewith to slay them. Perhaps he will show them the deadly weapon, and hope that they will take the hint; but there is too much kindness underneath his wrath for him to be capable of murdering even a thievish sparrow. He likes to make others believe, however, that he is desperately in earnest. His keen sense of the comic and the grotesque in human nature makes him one of the raciest of story-tellers; but although he does not put his tongue in traces, he is none the less a worthy priest. There are many such as he in France—men who are really devout, but never sanctimonious, whose candour is a cause of constant astonishment, who are good-natured to excess, and who are more open-hearted than many children. Their friendship goes out readily to meet the stranger, and, speaking from my own experience, I can say that it wears well.

In the street, on the other side of the house, six women have perched themselves in a row. They have come out to talk and enjoy the coolness of the evening, and, in order that their tender consciences may not prick them for being idle, they are paring potatoes, and getting ready other vegetables for the morrow. They all scream together in Languedocian, which, by-the-bye, is anything but melodious here when spoken by the common people. It becomes much less twangy and harsh a little farther South. How these six charmers on chairs can all listen and talk at the same time is not easy to understand. The truth is, very little listening is done in this part of the world. The saying *On se grise en parlant* is quite applicable here. People often get drunk on nothing stronger than the flow of their own words.

All the women being now on their way to the land of dreams, and consequently quiet for a few hours, and all the sounds of the earth being hushed save the song of the crickets among the vine-leaves, and in the fruit-trees of the moonlit garden, I will try to see Figeac up the vista of the ages, and if I succeed, perhaps the reader may be helped at the same time to gather interest in this queer old place, whose name, having been made familiar to the English who followed Henry II. to France in the twelfth century, is perhaps a reason why their descendants will not 'skip' at first sight these few pages of local history.

The early history of Figeac, or what has long passed as such, is based upon an ingenious stratification of fraud, arising out of a very old quarrel between the monks of Figeac and the monks of Conques, and the determination of the former to prove at all costs that their monastery was the more ancient of the two This would be a matter of indifference to me had I not been myself entrapped by the snares laid by certain abbots of Figeac for their contemporaries and posterity, and been obliged to throw away much that I had written, and which was far more interesting than the truth. If I had only suspected the fraud, I might have been tempted to keep suspicion down in order to spare the picture of the Carlovingian age which I had elaborated; but it is known at the École des Chartres, and the Abbé B. Massabie of Figeac has, moreover, written a book that removes all doubt as to the spuriousness of the charters upon which the abbots of Figeac, when their jealousy of Conques reached its climax in the eleventh century, based their pretensions to priority. The most important of these charters, and the one that has sent various local historians on a voyage into the airy realms of fiction, is attributed to Pepin le Bref, and bears the date 755. Another is a Bull attributed to Pope Stephanus II., also dated 755, in which is described the ceremony of consecrating the church of St. Sauveur, attached to the abbey, which in the first-mentioned document Pepin is said to have founded. Here it is related that when the Pontiff approached the church strains of mysterious music were heard issuing from the edifice, and such a cloud stood before it that the procession waited for hours before entering. Then, when the Pope walked up to the altar-stone, he found that it had been miraculously consecrated, crosses being marked upon it in oil still wet. Now, the charter attributed to Pepin contains many passages copied verbatim from one preserved at Rodez, and signed by Pippinus, or Pepin I., King of Aquitaine. Its date is 838, and it enriches the monastery of Conques, already existing, with certain lands at Fiacus (Figeac), which is thenceforward to be called New Conques; the motive of this gift being to extend to the monks those material advantages which a rich valley is able to afford, but which are not to be found in a stony gorge surrounded by barren hills. There would have been less scandal to Christianity if Pepin had put a curb on his pious generosity, and had left the monks of Conques to contend with the desert. The charter, moreover, sanctions the building of a monastery at Figeac, which is to remain under the rule and governance of the abbots of Conques. In the eleventh century, the discord between the two monasteries had reached such a pass that popes and councils were appealed to to settle the question of priority. In 1096 the Council of Nimes laid down a *modus vivendi* without pronouncing upon the principle. It was decreed that the abbots of Figeac should thenceforth be independent of the abbots of Conques.

The monks of Conques appear to have followed originally the rule of St. Martin, and to have adopted that of St. Benedict soon after its introduction into France. The abbey of Figeac was therefore always Benedictine. About the year 900 the monks began to cultivate learning, their labour having previously been devoted almost exclusively to the soil. A certain Abbot Adhelard set them to copy manuscripts, and in course of time Figeac possessed a valuable library, of which the religious wars of the sixteenth century and the Revolution have left very few traces.

The first half of the eleventh century was full of turmoil, trouble, and torment. The 'blood-rain' that fell all over Aquitaine, and which made people watch in terror for what might come next, was followed by a three years' famine, which drove men in their hunger to prey upon one another. The inns were man-traps; solitary travellers who ventured inside of them were killed and devoured. Those were not good wayfaring days. A man actually offered human flesh for sale in the market of Tournus; but he was burnt alive. During this frightful period, the Abbot of Figeac distinguished himself by his charity, and, in order to find work for the unemployed, built a wall round the burg; but the monastery was much impoverished in consequence.

Towards the close of the eleventh century four slender obelisks—called 'needles' in the country were set up on the hills around Figeac apparently to mark the boundaries of the *sauveté*; for the abbey enjoyed the right of sanctuary. Two of these needles still exist. According to an absurd story, which has been repeated by various writers, misled by the forgeries already mentioned, the monks, when they came to this part of the valley of the Célé, found it an uninhabited wilderness without a name, and somebody exclaimed, 'Fige acus!' ('Set up needles!'), when the question of marking the boundary was being discussed. This ingenious explanation of the word Figeac will not bear examination.

Every traveller in Aquitaine must have been struck by the remarkable number of places there whose names end in *ac*. It is commonly supposed that the termination is derived from *aqua*, and refers to the river or stream near which the town or village was built.

Ac, however, does not at all correspond to the well-known corruptions of *aqua* still found in the names of places in France where the Romans constructed baths. We are on much surer ground in assuming it to be of Celtic origin, and to have belonged in a special manner to the dialect spoken by the Cadurci, Ruteni and other Southern tribes. It nevertheless occurs at Carnac that spot of Brittany where is to be seen the most remarkable of all monuments, commonly attributed to the Celts. The word probably meant town. It is unreasonable to suppose that the monks found the valley of the Célé a desert, considering how densely populated was the whole of this part of Gaul at the time of Cæsar's invasion. So inhabited was it that the surplus population spread all over the known world, just as the English do to-day. The popular notion with regard to the needles is that they were intended to carry lanterns to guide the pilgrims by night either to Figeac or to Roc-Amadour. Such lanterns were set up in Aquitaine, and some examples may still be seen; but they are very different in character from these obelisks, which in all probability were used to mark the boundary of the *salvamentum*. It is true that in the Middle Ages the right of asylum was, as a rule, confined to the sanctuary itself or its immediate precincts; but there were exceptions,

especially in the South of France, where this sacred
zone, which in the Romance language was termed
the *sauvetat*, often extended a considerable distance
beyond the walls of a monastic town. Within these
bounds persons fleeing from pursuers had the right
of asylum; but, on the other hand, there are documents to show that those who committed crimes
inside the limit were held guilty of sacrilege.

Early in the Middle Ages the town of Figeac
enjoyed the privileges of a royal borough under the
protection of the kings of France, who in course of
time came to be represented there by their *viguier*
(vicar). The civic administration was in the hands
of consuls as early as the year 1001. They rendered
justice and even passed sentence of death. The
burghers were exempt from all taxation and servitude. The municipality had the right of coining
money for the king, and the ruined mint can still
be seen. Such was the state of things down to the
time when the English appeared in the country.
Henry II., having taken Cahors in 1154, left his chancellor, Becket, there as governor. The Figeacois,
who at first looked upon Becket as an enemy, after
he was murdered at Canterbury, and when the fame
of his saintliness began to spread through France,
dedicated a church to him. This edifice has disappeared; but the part of the town where it was
situated, or where, to speak more correctly, it was
afterwards rebuilt, is still called the Quartier St.
Thomas. So little were the English loved, how-

ever, as a nation by the Quercynois, that, after
St. Louis had been canonized, they refused to
observe his festival, because they found it impossible
to forgive him for having, by the treaty of Abbe-
ville, passed them over to England without their
consent.

Figeac was less troubled than some other towns
in the Quercy by the English, because in different
treaties the kings of France managed to keep a grip
upon it as a royal borough.

The gates of the town were, however, thrown
open to the English without a struggle about the
middle of the fourteenth century, and to punish the
consuls, when they again became French, King
John took away their right to coin money; but the
privilege was restored in consideration of the ardour
they had shown in freeing themselves from the
British yoke.

The victory of the Black Prince at Poitiers, followed by the treaty of Brétigny, made the King
of England absolute master of the Quercy. The
Prince of Wales came in person to take possession
of Cahors in 1364, and despatched his seneschal,
Thomas de Walkaffara, to Figeac to receive from
the inhabitants the oath of fealty. They swore
obedience, but with much soreness of soul. They
afterwards got released from their oath by the Pope,
and joined a fresh league formed against the English.
After enjoying the sweets of French nationality again
for a brief period, they were made English once

more by the treaty of Troyes. But the British domination in Guyenne was now approaching its close. The maid of Domrémy was about to change her distaff for an oriflamme. The year 1453 saw the English power completely broken in Aquitaine; a collapse which an old rhymer records with more relish than inspiration:

> 'Par Charles Septième à grande peine
> Furent chassés en durs détroits
> Les Anglais de toute Aquitaine,
> Mil quatre cent cinquante trois.'

Figeac escaped the horrors which were spread through the South of France by the religious wars of the twelfth and thirteenth centuries; but it was not similarly spared by those of the sixteenth century. The Huguenots laid siege to the town in 1576, and entered it by the treasonable help of a woman—the wife of one of the consuls. There was the usual massacre that followed victory, whether on the side of Protestants or Catholics, and the people became Calvinists for the same reason that they had centuries before become English. In less than fifty years afterwards they were all Catholics again. During this unsettled period, however, there was great domestic dissension in the town, owing to the circumstance that many women belonging to the old Catholic stock had married Protestants who had come into the place. As they could not agree with their husbands, and as many of these refused to be converted for their sake (they may have been thankful for an opportunity of getting rid of them), a refuge called 'L'hospice des mal-mariées' was built for the unhappy wives. When the need for this very singular institution no longer existed it was pulled down.

The Church of St. Sauveur, as we see it to-day, is disappointing. It has been so much rebuilt after different convulsions, and pulled about when there has been less excuse, that many a church in an obscure village gives more pleasure as a whole to the eye that seeks unity of design and inspiration in a work of art. Nevertheless, there are details here that no archæologist will despise. In the nave are the piers and Romanesque capitals of an early, but not the earliest, church on the spot. They are certainly not later than the twelfth century. Baptismal fonts, now used as holy-water stoups, are probably of anterior workmanship. Cut out of solid blocks of stone, their carving shows all the interlacing lines and exquisite finish of detail, purely ornamental, that marks the pre-Gothic period in the South of France, when the artistic spirit of Christianity was still confined to the close imitation of Roman and Byzantine art.

The Church of Notre Dame du Puy, built upon a height, as the word *puy* implies, is likewise interesting only in respect of details, such as the sculptured archivolts of the portal and the fourteenth-century rose-window. It, however, contains a very remarkable example of sixteenth-century wood-carving in its massive and elaborate reredos, a portion of which, having been destroyed by fire, has been repaired with plaster, but so skilfully that it is very difficult to perceive where the artistic fraud begins and where it ends.

The extraordinary interest of Figeac to the archæologist lies, however, in its civic and domestic architecture. This has been preserved simply because the inhabitants have for centuries played no part in the political history of the country, and their pursuits or interests having remained constantly agricultural, they have been equally cut off from the commercial movement. But every year will diminish the charm of this dirty old town to the antiquary. It will be observed that all the old streets are not accidentally crooked, but that they have been carefully laid out on curved or zigzag lines, which turn now in one direction and now in another. The motive was a defensive one in view of street-fighting, which was often so terrible and so prolonged in the Middle Ages. Each curve of a street formed an obstacle to the onward rush of an enemy, and only allowed those burghers who were actually engaged to be exposed to arrows and bolts. The townsmen could dispute the ground inch by inch and for days, as they did at Cahors when they were surprised by Henry of Navarre, although fire-arms had then come into use.

Wine-growing, until some eight or ten years ago, was the chief source of revenue to the people of

Figeac, as well as to those in the neighbouring valley of the Lot. Middle-aged people here can recollect the days when wine was so cheap that the inn-keepers did not take the trouble to measure it out to their customers, but charged them a uniform price of two sous for stopping and drinking as much as they pleased. But all this has been changed by the phylloxera. From being exceptionally prosperous, the people of the district have become poor. Very few have now any money to lay out in replanting their vineyards. Land has so fallen in value that it can be bought at a price that seems scarcely credible. With £100 one might become the proprietor of a large vineyard. Higher up the hills, where the chestnut and juniper thrive, half the money would buy quite a considerable estate. Here and elsewhere in France thousands of acres lie uncultivated and unproductive, except as regards that which nature unaided renders to man. Not all, but a very large portion, of this waste-land would well repay cultivation if the capital needed for clearing and working it were obtainable. That the lands suitable for wine-growing could be rendered remunerative is absolutely certain if those who undertook the task had the money necessary for the first outlay of planting and could afford to wait for the return.

The valley of the Célé between Figeac and the junction of the little river with the Lot contains some of the most picturesque scenery to be found in the Quercy. About ten miles below Figeac it becomes a gorge, which until past the middle of the present century was almost cut off from communication with neighbouring towns. All the carrying was done on the backs of mules and donkeys; but since the road was made along the right bank of the Célé, these animals have been used less and less. It is no uncommon thing, however, to see now a heavily-laden pack-mule coming up the valley to the Figeac fair. It was in their rock-fortresses by the Célé that the English companies in Guyenne are said to have made their final resistance. The long and sustained efforts which were needed to dislodge them from their almost inaccessible fastnesses will be understood by anyone who may go wayfaring like myself along the banks of this tributary of the Lot.

For the first two hours the walk was unexciting, for the valley was too wide and too cultivated to give much pleasure to the eye that looks for character in nature. At the village of Corn there was a decided change. Here lofty honeycombed rocks rose behind the houses that were built not very far above the stream, whose swiftness is supposed to have been the origin of its name. Not one of the several caverns extends far into the cliff. Their chief interest lies in the traditions with which they are associated. In one of them the inhabitants of the little burg are said to have assembled in the

Middle Ages to elect their consuls freely, and to
escape possible annoyance from their lord, whose
castle was on the opposite hill. Another, still called
the Citadel, was that in which they took refuge from
the enemy, especially from the roving bands of
armed men who made common cause with England.
In 1380 Bertrand de Bassoran, captain of an English
company, captured Corn, and using this place as his
point d'appui, he placed garrisons in the neighbouring burgs of Brengues, Sauliac, and Cabrerets. He
also compelled the consuls of Cajarc to treat with
him.

After a hasty meal in a little inn where I had to
be satisfied mainly with good intentions, I called
upon the schoolmaster. The poor man was spending most of his dinner-hour on the threshold of his
small school-house amidst the rocks because some
unruly or idle urchins were 'kept in.' How much
pleasanter, I thought, it would have been for him to
have produced in their case a wholesome cutaneous
irritation, and set himself, as well as the young
reprobates, free! But the French law does not
tolerate the corporal punishment of children nowadays, although the exasperated pedagogue cannot
always resist the temptation of applying his ruler
upon a bunch of grimy little knuckles. This schoolmaster, although he was past the age of fifty and
had grown corpulent, was still tied fast to the village
schoolroom that was much too small to hold thirty
children comfortably. By the aid of reading, writing,

and arithmetic, he had got into a little creek where he was safe from the stormy seas of life, and he had never allowed his ambition to draw him out into the ocean. Nevertheless, he nursed and rocked his little vanity like the rest of mortals. He had written what he termed a 'Monograph of Corn.' He brought out from his desk a copybook wherein he had set it all down with the utmost attention to upstrokes and downstrokes and punctuation. It was a pleasure to him to find somebody to whom he could read what he had written, and he had in me an attentive listener.

Wandering on by the winding Célé, the charm of the little river made me sit down upon a bank to look at the pictures that were painted on the water by the sunshine, the clouds, and the poplars. Then, continuing my journey, I saw on the opposite side of the stream a cluster of houses with an ancient church in their midst, and almost detached from this church, and yet a part of it, a tower like a campanile capped by a wooden belfry with pointed roof and far-reaching eaves. A bridge led across the water. I found the village to be Sainte Eulalie d'Espagnac. Here there existed from the early Middle Ages a celebrated convent for women of the order of St. Augustine. The founder, Aymeric d'Hébrard, was the Bishop of a see in Spain, and he brought thence Moorish slaves to cultivate the land with which he had endowed his community of a hundred nuns. Down to the Revolution most of the daughters of the nobility in the Quercy were educated here. Little is now left of the conventual building; but the church contains architectural details of much interest, and the tombs of those irreconcilable enemies of the English, Bertrand de Cardaillac, Bishop of Cahors, and the Marquis de Cardaillac—the most famous warrior of this bellicose and illustrious family.

Having reached the village of Brengues, I went immediately in search of the English rock-fortress of which I had already heard. A path led me up the steep hillside to the foot of a long line of high rocks of yellowish limestone, so escarped and so forbidding to vegetable life that I did not see even a wild fig-tree hanging from a crevice. A path ran along at the base of this prodigious wall, from the top of which stretched the arid *causse*. I had only gone a little way when I saw before me a fortified Gothic gateway jutting out from the rock to which it was attached, and extending across the path to where the hill became so steep as to sufficiently protect from assault on that side those who had a motive for defending the ledge under the high cliff. I examined this old piece of masonry with much curiosity.

The pointed form of the arch disposes of the hypothesis which has been put forward without much reflection, that this legacy of the old wars in Guyenne is part of the defences raised in the country by the unfortunate Waifré, Duke of Aquitaine, when

he was being chased from rock to rock by his
relentless enemy. Here we have work that is
evidently not anterior to the English occupation,
and which in all probability belongs to the fourteenth
or the early part of the fifteenth century. Now, as
Brengues was undoubtedly one of those places where
the English companies firmly established themselves,
and to which they clung with great tenacity, there
is very small risk of error is coming to the conclusion that it was they who built this fortified gateway. The masonry, composed of carefully-shaped
stones, and laid together with an excellent mortar
that has become as durable as the rock itself, has
been wonderfully preserved. Had it been placed
in the valley it would have been pulled down long
ago, and the materials would have been used for
building houses or pigsties. The upper part of
the wall is dilapidated, so that it is impossible to
say whether it was originally embattled or not.
There is no staircase, but the defenders had doubtless a suspended plank or beam on which they stood
when they wished to shoot arrows or bolts over the
top of the wall. On the side nearest the rock is
a splayed opening ending outwardly in a crosslet
large enough for three or four men to use at the
same time.

This gateway was only an outwork to defend the
ledge of rock. About two hundred yards farther
is a cavern some twenty or thirty feet above the
path, and only accessible by means of a ladder. It

has been walled up, openings being left here and
there for loopholes. Near the top is a row of three
windows without arches, and at the base an opening
that served for a door, and which could easily be
closed up. Although the stones were shaped for
building, they were laid together without mortar;
but the wall is so thick, and so protected by its
position, that this rough fortification has remained
almost unchanged from the date of its construction.
It is a much less finished piece of work than the
gateway, but there are other rock-fortresses in the
district, attributed by general consent to the English,
so similar to it in character that there is no reason
for doubting that the companies built this one also.
It is probable, however, that the gateway already
mentioned, and the one that corresponded to it
on the other side of the cavern, but of which
few vestiges can now be seen, were constructed
subsequently, when the science of fortification was
better understood by the *routiers*. Such a fortress
could never have been used in a military sense by
a large number of men, but to a band of brigands
and cut-throats it was a stronghold of the first order.
As they doubtless laid up in their cavern a large
store of the provisions which they obtained by
their continual forays in the surrounding region, they
were capable of withstanding a long siege even
against an enemy many times as numerous as themselves, for the reason that only a few men could
attack them at the same time, and the defenders

had an enormous advantage in the struggle. It is a very general belief in the district that there was formerly a passage by which this cavern communicated with the *causse*; no trace of it, however, has been discovered.

M. Delpen, author of a work published in 1831, and entitled 'Statistique du Département du Lot,' mentions these fortified caverns of the Quercy in the following passage, which gives a vivid picture of the kind of life that the English companies led and made others lead in the fourteenth century:

'They (the English) possessed in the Quercy the forts of Roc-Amadour, Castelnau, Verdale, Vayrac, Lagarennie, Sabadel, Anglars, Frayssinet, Boussac and Assier, and some other castles on escarped hills from which it was difficult to expel them. They also seized upon caverns formed by nature in the flanks of precipitous rocks, and fortified them with walls in which all the character of English structures can still be recognised. The garrisons that occupied these places represented six thousand lances distributed over the Quercy, the Rouergue, and High Auvergne. When they sallied forth, the earth, to use an expression of one of their chiefs, Émérigot, surnamed Black Head, trembled under their feet.* They robbed travellers, made citizens

---

* The entire passage from which these words are taken is to be found in Froissart's chronicles, and it runs as follows, the spelling being modernized: 'Que nous étions rejouis quand nous chevaussions à l'aventure et que nous pouvions trouver sur le champ un riche prieur ou marchand ou des mulets de Montpellier, de Narbonne, de Carcas-

prisoners—especially ecclesiastics—in order to extort exorbitant ransoms, they took from the peasants their beasts and their crops, and forced them to work in strengthening the dens of their spoliators with new fortifications. In fine, the Quercy was continually devastated, and the inhabitants only tilled the earth to satisfy the avidity of the English companies. The population could shield themselves from their violence only by concealing themselves in subterranean retreats, where traces of their sojourn are still observable. The English were continually recruited by all the depraved men of the provinces which they laid under contribution.'

This last remark is only too well justified by the evidence which those centuries have handed down. Indeed, to such an extent were these companies composed of Aquitanians, that one may well ask if some of them contained a single genuine Englishman. I have found no record in the Quercy of the captain of a company of *routiers* having borne an Anglo-Saxon name. Two English captains who took Figeac by surprise (a document relating to this event, written in Latin of the fourteenth

---

sone, de Limoux, de Béziers, de Toulouse, chargés de draps, de brunelles, de pelleterie, venant de la foire de Landit, d'épiceries venant de Bruges, de draps de soie, de Damas ou d'Alexandrie. Les vilains nous pourvoyaient et apportaient dans nos châteaux le blé, la farine, le pain tout cuit, l'avoine pour les chevaux, le bon vin, les bœufs, les brébis, les moutons tous gras, la poulaille et la volataille. Nous étions servis, gouvernés et étoffés comme rois et princes, et quand nous chevaussions le pays tremblait devant nous.'

century, is to be found in the municipal archives) were named Bertrand de Lebret and Bertrand de Lasale. Those who captured Martel had names equally French. There is, of course, the hypothesis that these leaders were Anglicised Normans, but the stronger probability is that they were native adventurers of Aquitaine who found it to their interest to place themselves under the protection of the King of England.

Towards the close of the fourteenth century, all those who wished to drive the English out of Guyenne rallied round the chiefs of the house of Armagnac. This great family of the Rouergue, which was ultimately absorbed by the Royal House of France and became extinct, at one time espoused the British cause; but it contributed more than any other to the final dispersion of the English companies in Guyenne. In 1381 the people of the Gévaudan, the Quercy, and High Auvergne, solicited the help of the Count of Armagnac against the companies, and he accepted the leadership of the coalition. He convened a meeting of delegates at Rodez, to which the English chiefs were invited, and the decision that was then come to did not say much for the sagacity or the valour of those who represented the majority. It was agreed that the sum of 250,000 francs—equivalent to about £200,000 to-day—should be paid to the English on condition of their surrendering the fortresses which they occupied. This fact goes far to prove that the companies were virtually independent, and that although all their outrages were ostensibly committed in the British name, they were freebooters in the fullest sense of the word. Of the sum that was to be paid to them, the clergy were to contribute 25,000 francs, the nobles 16,660. The inhabitants of the Quercy agreed to pay 50,833 francs. The captains of the companies took oath that on receiving the money they would quit Guyenne for ever. They may have kept their oath, but their followers were not to be induced to change their habits so easily. The *routiers*, still going by the name of the English companies, continued to hold the least accessible places in Guyenne, fortified in the main by nature, until long after the British sovereigns had abandoned their ambitious designs in France.

In the fifteenth century so many of the inhabitants of the Quercy had been killed or ruined by the companies that some districts were almost depopulated. In the town of Gramat there were only seven inhabitants left at the close of the Hundred Years' War. In order that the lands should not remain uncultivated, the nobles enfeoffed them to strangers from the Rouergue and other neighbouring provinces. This circumstance is supposed to account in a large measure for the differences in dialect which are to be observed in adjoining communes. There is no evidence to-day, so far as I have been able to ascertain, of English words having been introduced into the Languedocian of

Guyenne. The striking resemblance of many *patois* words to those of the English language bearing the same meaning—a resemblance that is helped by the Southern pronunciation of vowels and diphthongs—must be referred to linguistic influences far more remote and obscure than the political fact that Guyenne was intimately connected with English history for three hundred years. For example, that familiar animal the cat is called in Guyenne *lou catou* and even *lou cat;* but the word belongs to the Romance language, and is the same all through Languedoc and Provence. The fact that the English left no mark upon the language in Guyenne is almost a conclusive proof that such of the Anglo-Saxon stock as followed the Norman leaders into Aquitaine, and who remained in the country any length of time, were not sufficiently numerous to impose their idiom upon others. They probably did not preserve it long themselves; but, like the English grooms who find occupation in France to-day, they quickly adopted the language that was generally spoken around them. Patient investigation might, nevertheless, show that the English did leave some of their words, as well as their blood, in the country. It would, indeed, be astonishing if this were not so. Even the Greek colony at Marseilles and Arles, although far removed, must have influenced the dialect of Guyenne; for the peasants of the Quercy use the word *hermal* to describe a piece of waste land bordering a cultivated field, the origin of which expression was, doubtless, Hermes, the god of boundaries. This is not the only Greek word that has been corrupted, but nevertheless preserved, in the Quercynois *patois*.

Wherever the English were long established in their fastnesses amidst the rocks which form the rugged sides of the deep-cut gorges of the Quercy, many of the inhabitants have clung, century after century, to the belief that the terrible freebooters buried a prodigious amount of treasure with the intention of returning and fetching it on the first opportunity. So persistently was this tradition handed down at Brengues that many years ago a cavern, the entrance of which had been covered over with stones and earth, having been accidentally discovered on the plateau just above the Château des Anglais, it was eagerly explored, as well as a similar cavern close by. The excitement was increased by the circumstance that the discovery of these openings appeared to coincide with the indications of a local witch. It was evident that the caverns had at one time been used by men, for they contained masonry put together with mortar. By dint of excavating, hidden galleries were revealed; but although a human skeleton was discovered, no treasure was found. The explorers, however, came upon a vast collection of bones of extinct animals, and of others which, although they are now to be found both in the Arctic and in the tropical regions, have not existed in a state of nature in France during the historic period. The bones of the reindeer, for instance, were found lying with those of the hyena and the rhinoceros, many of them embedded in the calcareous breccia so frequently seen in the valley of the Célé. Here was evidence of a glacial and a torrid period, separated by an æonic gulf; but how the remains came to be piled one upon another in this way is a secret of the ancient earth. There are prodigious layers of these bones lying at a great depth in the rock, where there is no cavern to suggest that the animals entered by it, or that they were taken there by man. The beds of phosphate which English enterprise has turned to so good an account in this part of France, and which are followed in the earth just like a seam of coal or a vein of metal, are merely layers of bones. While I was at Brengues, the skeleton of a young rhinoceros was discovered in the phosphate mine at Cajarc.

On the hill above the Célé, on the side opposite to that where the Château des Anglais is to be seen, are the remains of an entrenched camp, upon the origin of which it is almost idle to speculate. In the same neighbourhood is a cavern situated high up in the face of a perpendicular rock. It is inaccessible by ordinary means; but a beam fixed at the entrance, and worn into a deep groove by a rope, shows that it was used as a refuge. A tradition says that Waifré hid himself there.

I passed the night at Brengues, and was awakened

in the early morning by the jingle of bells just beneath my window, and a man's voice repeating, 'Tè, Tè, Tè!' A couple of bullocks were being yoked, and presently they followed the man towards the fields of tobacco and maize by the little river, already shining in the sun. Very soon afterwards I, too, had begun my day's work.

In a little more than an hour I was at the next village — St. Sulpice. Here above the houses, huddled together like sheep on the lower steep of the right-hand hill, were the ruins of a castle, hanging to the rock that dwarfed it even in the days of its pride. I climbed to it, and found that it was built on terraces one above the other, formed by the rocky shelves. A considerable portion of the strong wall at the base of the structure remains, and on each terrace there is something left of the feudal fortress. Ivy, with gnarled and fantastic stocks, has so overspread the masonry in places that hardly a gray stone shows through the dense matting of sombre leaves and hoary, wrinkled stems. Multitudes of bats cling to the ruinous vaulting where the light is very dim, and lurk in the hollows of the rock. A stone thrown up will bring them fluttering down and whirling about the head of the intruder, noiselessly as if they were the ghosts that haunt the spot, but dare not reveal to the eye of man the human shape that they once wore. This castle belonged, and still belongs, to the D'Hébrard family, which was connected by marriage with the

Cardaillacs and most of the ancient aristocracy of the Quercy.

Leaving St. Sulpice, another hour's walk down the valley brought me to Marcillac, which, after Figeac, was the most important place on the Célé in the Middle Ages. It is now, however, a mere village. According to local historians, it was here that Palladius, Bishop of Bourges, retired in the fifth century to escape from the persecution of the Arians. Nothing, however, that has been written of its history, prior to the ninth or tenth century, can be accepted with any confidence. What can be safely affirmed is, that here, between the rocky cliffs that border the Célé, arose one of the earliest of the Benedictine abbeys in France. The ruined cloisters of the monastery have all the severe charm of the simple Romanesque style of the early period, but there is no means of knowing whether they date from the tenth, eleventh, or twelfth century. There are several beautiful capitals elaborately embellished with intersecting line ornament still preserved, although no value whatever is placed upon them by the inhabitants. The cloisters are used for stables, and other common farm purposes.

The abbey church must have fallen into complete ruin, when a portion of it was restored and rebuilt in the fifteenth century. Then about half the nave —the western end—was cut off, and left open to the weather. It is roofless, and the visitor walking, now in deep shadow, now in brilliant light, as the fragments of masonry may hide or reveal the sun, sees the blue sky through the arches and over the tops of the ivy-covered walls. This part of the old church shows the transition between the Romanesque and the Gothic styles.

It would have been a slight upon Marcillac had I left the place without seeing the most famous of its caverns, which goes by the name of the Grotte de Robinet. I might have looked for it in vain all day had I not taken a guide.

First, the *causse* had to be reached by ascending the cliffs on the right bank of the Célé. Then I saw before me the stony undulating land, with the sad sentiment of which I had already grown so familiar. An old woman, nearly doubled up with age and field labour, but who plied her distaff as she led her black goats to browse upon the waste, made me understand that the solitude was not altogether bereft of human life. After walking a mile or so, we descended into a deep hollow wooded with those dwarf oaks which, together with the juniper, hid at one time most of the nakedness of these calcareous tracts that stretch from gorge to gorge. One might have supposed that such a dale would have had a spring at the bottom; but no: everywhere it was parched, arid, and rocky. The rain that falls all around goes to swell some deep subterranean stream that issues no one knows where. This peculiarity of the formation explains why nearly all the *caussenards* have no water, either for themselves or their animals, except that which they collect from the skies in tanks sunk in the earth. Since the failure of the vines—which formerly flourished upon the *causses* wherever there was a favourable slope—the peasants have learnt to make a mildly alcoholic liquor by gathering and fermenting the juniper berries, which previously they had never put to any use.

We had nearly ascended the opposite side of this wooded hollow, when the guide, pointing through the sunlit trees to a very dark but narrow opening in the rocks, said, ' There it is!' We had reached the cavern. He went first, carrying aloft a wisp of burning straw, which he renewed from time to time from the bundle that he carried under his arm.

The practice of burning straw, so that people may have a good flare-up for their money, has, together with the selfish custom of throwing stones at the stalactites, gone far to spoil all the caverns of this region, which have been much visited. The Grotte de Robinet must have been dazzlingly beautiful at one time, but now most of the stalagmite and stalactite has been completely blackened by smoke. Even the rocks, over which one has to climb, and sometimes crawl, are covered with a sooty slime, which gives one the appearance, when daylight returns, of having been smeared with lampblack. I put on a blouse before entering, and had great reason to be glad that I did so. In spite of all the mischief that has been done to it, the Grotte de Robinet is a very remarkable cavern, and the time spent on the somewhat arduous and slippery task of exploring its depths is not wasted. Its length is about half a mile, and the descent, which is almost continuous, is at times very rapid. The passage connects a succession of vast and lofty spaces, which are not inappropriately termed *salles*. In some of these, the dropping water has raised from the floor of the cavern statuesque and awful forms of colossal grandeur. Some of these have been little changed by the smoke, but stand like white figures of fantastic giants. While looking at them, I thought how little I should like to be in the position of a certain *curé* of Marcillac, who spent three days and three nights in this weird company. He frequently entered the cavern alone, with a scientific object, and his familiarity with it led him to despise ordinary precautions. One day he was far underground, with only a single candle in his possession, and no matches. A drop of water from the roof put the candle out, and all his efforts to return by the way he came were futile. Meanwhile, his parishioners, hunting high and low for their *curé*, chanced to see his *soutane*, where he had left it, hanging to a bush at the entrance of the Grotte de Robinet, and when they rescued him, there was very little left of his passion for studying nature underground.

The most wonderful and the most beautiful object in the cavern is to be seen in the vast hall, which is the last of the series. This hall has a dome-shaped roof that rises to the height of about sixty feet, and it is supported in the centre, with every appearance of an architectural motive, by a single slender column that seems to have been carved with consummate skill out of alabaster. No image that I can think of conveys the picture of this exquisite stalagmite so justly as that of a column formed of the blossoms of lilies, each cup resting within another.

Having left Marcillac, I passed under the mediæval village of Sauliac, built high up on a shelf of naked rock, and then reached Cabrerets, which lies two or three miles above the junction of the Célé and the Lot. The village is at the foot of towering limestone cliffs, and many of the houses are built against the gray and yellow stone. The most interesting structure, however, is the castellated one that clings to the face of the rock far above all inhabited dwellings. It goes by the name of the Château du Diable, and it is the most considerable of all the rock-fortresses in the valleys of the Célé and the Lot which are attributed to the English companies. It possesses towers and embattlements, and it was evidently intended to defend the defile from any force advancing from the wider valley. Here, doubtless, many a desperate struggle occurred before the companies were dispersed and English influence was finally overcome in these wilds of the Quercy. At a little distance from it, the long iron of a mediæval arrow, having fastened its head in a cleft of the rock, remained sticking there for centuries, and was only recently removed. The Prefect of the Department took a fancy to it, and had not the good judgment to leave it where it had so long been an object of curiosity. There, resting in the place where the arm of the archer had cast it, it told a story of the old wars, and set the imagination working; but in a collection of local antiquities it is as dumb and almost as worthless as any other piece of old iron.

IN THE ALBIGEOIS.

A LONG dull road or street, a statue of the navigator La Perouse, a bandstand with a few trees about it, and plain, modern buildings without character, some larger and more pretentious than others, but all uninteresting. Is this Albi? No, but it is what appears to be so to the stranger who enters the place from the railway-station. The ugly sameness is what the improving spirit of our own times has done to make the ancient town decent and fit to be inhabited by folk who have seen something of the world north of Languedoc and who have learnt to talk of *le comfortable*. The improvement is undoubted, but so is the absolute lack of interest and charm; at least, to those who are outside of the *persiennes* so uniformly closed against the summer sun.

Albi, the veritable historic Albi, lies almost hidden upon a slope that leads down to the Tarn. Here is the marvellous cathedral built in the thirteenth century, after the long wars with the Albigenses; here is the Archbishop's fortified palace, still capable of withstanding a siege if there were no artillery;

here are the old houses, one of pre-Gothic construction with very broad Romanesque window, slender columns and storied capitals, billet and arabesque mouldings; another of the sixteenth century quite encrusted with carved wood; and here are the dirty little streets like crooked lanes, where old women, who all through the summer months, Sundays excepted, give their feet an air-bath, may be seen sitting on the doorsteps clutching with one bony hand the distaff and drowsily turning the spindle with the other.

To live in one of these streets might disgust the unseasoned stranger for ever with Southern life; but to roam through them in the early twilight is the way to find the spirit of the past without searching. Effort spoils the spell. Strange indeed must have been the procession of races, parties and factions that passed along here between these very houses, or others which stood before them. Romans, Romanised Gauls, Visigoths, Saracens and English; the Raymonds with their Albigenses, the Montforts with their Crusaders from the north, the wild and sanguinary *pastoureux* and the lawless *routiers*, the religious fanatics, Huguenots and Catholics of the sixteenth century, and the revolutionists of the eighteenth. All passed on their way, and the Tarn is no redder now for the torrents of blood that flowed into it.

Notwithstanding that the name Albigenses was given after the council of Lombers to the new

Manichæans, Albi was less identified with the great religious and political struggle of Southern Gaul in the twelfth and thirteenth centuries than were Castres and other neighbouring towns. If, however, it was comparatively fortunate as regards the horrors of that ferocious war, it was severely scourged by the most appalling epidemics of the Middle Ages. Leprosy and the pest had terrors greater even than those of battle. The cruelty of those feudal ages finds one of its innumerable records in the treatment of the miserable lepers at Albi. Having taken the disease which the Crusaders brought back from the East, they were favoured with a religious ceremony distressingly similar to the office for the dead. A black pall was thrown over them while they knelt at the altar steps. At the close of the service a priest sprinkled some earth on the condemned wretches, and then they were led to the leper-house, where each was shut up in a cell from which he never came out alive. The black pall and the sprinkled earth were symbols which every patient understood but too well.

In nothing is the stern spirit of those ages expressed more forcibly than in the religious buildings of Languedoc. The cathedral of St. Cecilia at Albi is the grandest of all the fortified churches of Southern France, although in many others the defensive purpose has made less concession to beauty. Looking at it for the first time, the eye is wonder-struck by its originality, the nobleness of its design, and the grandeur of its mass. The plan being that of a vast vaulted basilica without aisles, the walls of the nave rise sheer from the ground to above the roof, and are pierced at intervals with lofty but very narrow windows, the arches slightly pointed and containing simple tracery. The buttresses which help the walls to support the vaulting of the nave and choir are the most remarkable feature of the design, and, together with the tower, which rises in diminishing stages to the height of 260 feet and there ends in an embattled platform, account for the singularly feudal and fortress-like character of the building. The outline of the buttresses being that of a semi-ellipse, they look like turrets carried up the entire face of the wall. The floor of the church is many feet above the ground, and the entrance was originally protected by a drawbridge and portcullis; but these military works were removed in the sixteenth century, and in their place was raised, upon a *perron* reached by a double flight of steps, a baldachino-like porch as airily graceful and delicately florid as the body to which it is so lightly attached is majestically stern and scornful of ornament. The meeting here of those two great forces, the Renaissance and feudalism, is like that of Psyche and Mars. But in expression the porch is Gothic, for although the arches are round-headed, they are surmounted by an embroidery of foliated gables and soaring pinnacles. It can scarcely be said that the style has been broken, but the contrast in feeling is strong.

Enter the church and observe the same contrast there. Gothic art within the protecting walls and under the strong tower puts forth its most delicate leaves and blossoms. Across the broad nave, nearly in the centre, is drawn a rood-screen—a piece of stonework that has often been compared to lace, but which gains nothing by the comparison. The screen, together with the enclosure of the choir, with which it is connected, is quite bewildering by the multiplicity of arches, gables, tabernacles, pinnacles, statues, leaves, and flowers. The tracery is flamboyant, and the work dates from the beginning of the sixteenth century. The artificers are said to have been a company of wandering masons from Strasburg.

Two vast drum-shaped piers, serving to support the tower, are exposed to view at the west end of the nave; but, for the bad effect thus produced, compensation is offered by the very curious paintings, supposed to be of the fifteenth century, with which the surfaces of these piers are covered. They represent the Last Judgment and the torments of the damned. Each of the seven capital sins has its compartment, wherein the kind of punishment reserved for sinners under this head is set forth in a manner as quaint as are the inscriptions in old French beneath. The compartment illustrating the eternal trouble of the envious has this inscription:

'*La peine des envieux et envieuses.* Les envieus et envieuses sont en ung fleuve congelé plongés jusques au nombril et par dessus les frappe un vent moult froid et quant veulent icelluy vent éviter se plongent dedans ladite glace.'

All the wall-surfaces, the vaulting included, are covered with paintings. The effect clashes with Northern taste, but the absence of a columnar system affords a plausible reason for relieving the sameness of these large surfaces with colour. The Gothic style of the North, holding in itself such decorative resources, gains nothing from mural paintings, but always loses something of its true character when they are added. Apart from such considerations, the wall-paintings in the cathedral of Albi have accumulated such interest from time that no reason would excuse their removal.

This unique church was mainly built at the close of the thirteenth century, together with the Archbishop's palace, with which it was connected in a military sense by outworks. These have disappeared, but the fortress called a palace remains, and is still occupied by the Archbishop. It is a gloomy rectangular mass of brick, absolutely devoid of elegance, but one of the most precious legacies of the Middle Ages in France. It is not so vast as the papal palace at Avignon, but its feudal and defensive character has been better preserved, for, unlike the fortress by the Rhône, it has not been adapted to the requirements of soldiers' barracks. At each of the angles is a round tower, pierced with loopholes, and upon the intervening walls are fardescending machicolations. The building is still defended on the side of the Tarn by a wall of great height and strength, the base of which is washed by the river in time of flood. This rampart, with its row of semi-elliptical buttresses corresponding to those of the church and its pepper-box tower at one end, the fortress a little above, and the cathedral on still higher ground, but in immediate neighbourhood, make up an assemblage of mediæval structures that seems as strange in this nineteenth century as some old dream rising in the midst of day-thoughts. And the rapid Tarn, an image of perpetual youth, rushes on as it ever did since the face of Europe took its present form.

As I write, other impressions come to mind of this ancient town on the edge of the great plain of Languedoc. A little garden in the outskirts became familiar to me by daily use, and I see it still with its almond and pear trees, its trellised vines, the blue stars of its borage, and the pure whiteness of its lilies. A bird seizes a noisy cicada from a sunny leaf, and as it flies away the captive draws out one long scream of despair. Then comes the golden evening, and its light stays long upon the trailing vines, while the great lilies gleam whiter and their breath floods the air with unearthly fragrance. A murmur from across the plain is growing louder and louder as the trees lose their edges in the dusk, for those noisy revellers of the midsummer night, the jocund frogs, have roused themselves, and they welcome the darkness with no less joy than the swallows some hours later will greet the breaking dawn.

I left Albi to ascend the valley of the Tarn in the last week of June. I started when the sun was only a little above the plain; but the line of white rocks towards the north, from which Albi is supposed to take its name, had caught the rays and were already burning. The straight road, bordered with plane-trees, on which I was walking would have had no charm but for certain wayside flowers. There was a strange-looking plant with large heart-shaped leaves and curved yellow blossoms ending in a long upper lip that puzzled me much, and it was afterwards that I found its name to be *aristolochia clematitis*. It grows abundantly on the banks of the Tarn. Another plant that I now noticed for the first time was a galium with crimson flowers. I soon came to the cornfields for which the Albigeois plain is noted. Here the poppy showed its scarlet in the midst of the stalks of wheat still green, and along the borders were purple patches of that sun-loving campanula, Venus's looking-glass.

Countrywomen passed me with baskets on their heads, all going into Albi to sell their vegetables. Those who were young wore white caps with frills, which, when there is nothing on the head to keep them down, rise and fall like the crest of a cockatoo; but the old women were steadfast in their attachment to the bag-like, close-fitting cap, crossed with bands of black velvet, and having a lace front that covers most of the forehead. When upon this coif is placed a great straw hat with drooping brim, we have all that remains now of an Albigeois costume. As these women passed me, I looked into their baskets. Some carried strawberries, some cherries, others mushrooms (*boleti*), or broad beans. The last-named vegetable is much cultivated throughout this region, where it is largely used for making soup. When very young, the beans are frequently eaten raw with salt. Almost every taste is a matter of education.

The heat of the day had commenced when I reached the village of Lescure. This place is of very ancient origin. Looking at it now, and its agricultural population numbering little more than a thousand, it is difficult to realize its importance in the Middle Ages. The castle and the adjacent land were given in the year 1003 by King Robert to his old preceptor, the learned Gerbert, who became known to posterity as Pope Sylvester II. In the eleventh century, Lescure was, therefore, a fief of the Holy See; and in the time of Simon de Montfort the inhabitants were still vassals of the Pope. In the fourteenth century they were frequently at war with the people of Albi, who eventually got the upper hand. Then Sicard, the Baron of Lescure, was so completely humiliated that he not only consented to pay eighty gold *livres* to the consuls of Albi, but went before them bareheaded to ask pardon for himself and his vassals. Already the feudal system was receiving hard blows in the South of France from the growth of the communes and the authority vested in their consuls. What is left of the feudal grandeur of Lescure? The castle was sold in the second year of the Republic, and entirely demolished, with the exception of the chapel, which is now the parish church. Of the outer fortifications there remains a brick gateway, with Gothic arch carrying a high machicolated tower, connected to which is a fragment of the wall. To this old houses, half brick, half wood, still cling, like those little wasps' nests that one sees sometimes upon the sides of the rocks.

On entering the small fourteenth-century church, I found that it had been decorated for a funeral. A broad band of black drapery, upon which had been sewn at intervals Death's heads and tears, cut out of white calico, was hung against the wall of the apse, and carried far down each side of the nave. To me all those grinning white masks were needless torture to the mourners; but here again we are brought to recognise that taste is a matter of education.

More interesting than anything else in this church is the Romanesque holy-water stoup, with heads and crosses carved upon it, and possibly belonging to the original chapel of the castle. The chief archæological treasure, however, of Lescure is a church on a little hill above the village, and overlooking the Tarn. It is dedicated to St. Michael, in accordance with the mediæval custom of considering the highest ground most appropriate to the veneration of the archangel. It is Romanesque of the eleventh century, and belonged to a priory of which no other trace is left. The building stands in the midst of an abandoned cemetery; and at the time of my visit the tall June grasses, the poppies and white campions hid every mound and almost every wooden cross. Over the gateway, carved in the stone, is the following quaint inscription, the spelling being similar to that frequently used in the sixteenth century:

> 'Sur la terre autrefois nous fûmes comme vous.
> Mortels pensés y bien et priés Dieu pour nous.'

Beneath these lines are a skull and cross-bones, with a tear on each side.

Facing the forgotten graves, upon this spot removed from all habitations, is the most beautiful Romanesque doorway of the Albigeois. The round-headed arch widening outwards, its numerous archivolts and mouldings, the slender columns of the deeply-recessed jambs, the storied capitals with their rudely-proportioned but expressive little figures, and the row of uncouth bracket-heads over the crowning archivolt, represent the best art of the eleventh century. They show that Romanesque architecture and sculpture had already reached their perfect expression in Languedoc. The figures in the capitals tell the story of Adam and Eve, Abraham and Isaac, and of fiends busily engaged in tormenting mortals who must have been in their clutches now eight hundred years. The nave has two aisles, and massive piers with engaged columns support the transverse and lateral arches. The columns have very large capitals, displaying human figures, some of which are extraordinarily fantastic, and instinct with a wild imagination still running riot in stone. How far are we now from the minds that bred these thoughts when Southern Gaul was struggling to develop a new Roman art by the aid of such traditions and models as the Visigoth, the Frank, and the Arab had not destroyed in the country, and such ideas as were brought along the Mediterranean from Byzantium!

Lastly, I came to the apse, that part of a Romanesque church in which the artist seizes the purely religious ideal, or allows it to escape him. Here was the serenity, here the quietude of the early Christian purpose and hope. Perfect simplicity and perfect eloquence! Nothing more is to be said, except that there were stone benches against the wall and a piscina—details interesting to the archæologist. Then I walked round the little church, knee-deep in the long grave-grass, and noted the broad pilaster-strips of the apse, the stone eaves ornamented with billets, the bracket or corbel heads just beneath, fantastic, enigmatic, and not two alike.

Leaving this spot, where there was so much temptation to linger, I began to cross a highly-cultivated plain towards the village of Arthez, where the Tarn issues from the deep gorges which for many a league give it all the character of a mountain-river. I thought from the appearance of the land that everybody who lived upon it must be prosperous and happy, but a peasant whom I met was of another way of thinking. He said:

'By working from three o'clock in the morning until dark, one can just manage to earn one's bread.'

They certainly do work exceedingly hard, these peasant-proprietors and *métayers*, never counting their hours like the town workmen, but wishing that the day were longer, and if they can contrive to save anything in these days it is only by constant self-denial. A man's labour upon his land to-day will only support him, taking the bad years with the good, on the condition that he lives a life of primitive simplicity. Even then the problem of existence is often a terribly hard one to solve. In the South of France the blame is almost everywhere laid to the destruction of the vines by the phylloxera, but here in the plain of Albi the land is quite as suitable for corn as it is for grape-growing, which is far from being the case elsewhere; nevertheless, the peasants cry out with one voice against the bad times. They have to contend with two great scourges: hail that is so often brought by the thunder-storms in summer, and which the proximity of the Pyrenees may account for; and the south-east wind—*le vent d'autan* —that comes across from Africa, and scorches up the crops in a most mysterious manner. But for this plague the yield of fruit would be enormous. On the other hand, the region is blessed with lavish sunshine from early spring until November, and a half-maritime climate, explained by the neighbourhood of the ocean—not the Mediterranean—renders long periods of drought such as occur in Provence and Lower Languedoc rare. In the valleys the soil is extremely fertile, and, favoured by moisture and warmth, its productive power is extraordinary. Four crops of lucern are taken from the same land in the course of a season. Unfortunately, these valleys being mere gorges—cracks in the plain, with precipitous rocky sides—the strip of land bordering the stream at the bottom is usually very narrow.

On reaching Arthez, the character of the country changed suddenly and completely. Here the plain with its tertiary deposits ended, and in its stead commenced the long series of schistous rocks wildly heaped up and twisted out of their stratification, by which the Tarn is hemmed in for seventy miles as the crow flies, and nearly twice that distance if the windings of the gorge be reckoned. When the calcareous region of the Gévaudan is reached, the schist, slate, and gneiss disappear. On descending to the level of the river at Arthez, I saw before me one of the grandest cascades in France—the Saut de Sabo.

It is not so much the distance that the river falls in its rapid succession of wild leaps towards the plain as the singularly chaotic and savage scene of dark rocks and raging waters, together with the length to which it is stretched out, that is so impressive. The mass of water, the multitude of cascades, and the wild forms of the rocks, compose a scene that would be truly sublime if one could behold it in the midst of an unconquered solitude; but the hideous sooty buildings of a vast iron foundry on one bank of the river are there to spoil the charm.

I stayed in the village of Arthez for food and rest, but not long enough for the mid-day heat to pass. When I set forth again on my journey, the air was like the breath of a furnace; but as the slopes were well wooded with chestnuts, there was some shelter from the rays of the sun. There were a few patches of vineyard, the leaves showing the ugly stains of sulphate of copper with which they had been splashed as a precaution against mildew, which in so many districts has followed in the wake of the phylloxera, and hastened the destruction of the old vines. The Albigeois has ceased to be a wine-producing region, and, judging from present signs, it will be long in becoming one again.

The valley, deepening and narrowing, became a gorge, the beginning of that long series of fissures in the metamorphic and secondary rocks which, crossing an extensive tract of Languedoc and Guyenne, leads the traveller up to the Cevennes Mountains, through scenery as wild and beautiful as any that can be found in France, and perhaps in Europe. But the difficulties of travelling by the Tarn from Arthez upwards are great, and, indeed, quite forbidding to those who are not prepared to endure petty hardships in their search for the picturesque. Between Albi and St. Affrique, a distance that cannot be easily traversed on foot in less than four days, railways are not to be thought of, and the line of route taken by the *diligence* leaves the Tarn far to the north. In the valley the roads often dwindle away to mere paths or mule-tracks, or they are so rocky that riding either upon or behind a horse over such an uneven surface, with the prospect of being thrown into the Tarn in the event of a slip, is unpleasant work. Those who are unwilling to walk or unable to bear much fatigue should not attempt to follow this river through its gorges. All the difficulties have not yet been stated. Along the banks of the stream, and for several miles on either side of it, there are very few villages, and the accommodation in the auberges is about as rough as it can be. The people generally are exceedingly uncouth, and between Arthez and Millau, where a tourist is probably the rarest of all birds of passage, the stranger must not expect to meet with a reception invariably cordial. Even a Frenchman who appears for the first time in one of their isolated villages, and who cannot speak the Languedocian dialect, is looked upon almost as a foreigner, and is treated with suspicion by the inhabitants. This matter of language is in itself no slight difficulty. French is so little known that in many villages the clergy are compelled to preach in *patois* to make themselves understood.

This region I had now fairly entered. The road had gone somewhere up the hills, and I was walking beside the river upon sand glittering with particles of mica. This sand the Tarn leaves all along its banks. It is one of the most uncertain and treacherous of streams. In a few hours its water will rise with amazing rapidity and spread consternation in a district where not a drop of rain has fallen. Warm winds from the south and south-west, striking against the cold mountains in the Lozère, have been condensed, and the water has flowed down in torrents towards the plain. The river is as clear as crystal now, and the many-coloured pebbles of its bed reflect the light, but a thunderstorm in the higher country may change it suddenly to the colour of red earth.

The path led me into a steep forest, where I lost sight of the Tarn. The soil was too rocky for the trees—oaks and chestnuts chiefly—to grow very tall; consequently the underwood, although dense, was chequered all through with sunshine. Heather and bracken, holly and box, made a wilderness that spread over all the visible world, for the opposite side of the gorge was exactly similar. Shining in the sun amidst the flowering heather or glowing in majestic purple grandeur in the shade of shrubs stood many a foxglove, and almost as frequently seen was its relative *digitalis lutea*, whose flowers are much smaller and of a pale yellow. Now and again a little rill went whispering downward through the woods under plumes of forget-me-nots in a deep channel that it had cut by working age after age. Reaching at length a spot where I could look down into the bottom of the fissure, I perceived a small stream that was certainly not the Tarn. I had been ascending one of the lateral gorges of the valley, and had left the river somewhere to the north. My aim was now to strike it again in the higher country, and so I kept on my way. But the path vanished, and the forest became so dense that I was bound to realize that I was in difficulties. I resolved to try the bank of the stream, and reached it after some unpleasant experience of rocks, brambles and holly. Here, however, was a path which I followed nearly to the head of the gorge and then climbed to the plateau. There the land was cultivated, and the musical note of a cock turkey that hailed my coming from afar, as he swaggered in front of his harem on the march, led me to a spot where a man was mowing, and he told me where I should find the Tarn, which he, like all other people in the country, pronounced Tar.

Evening was coming on when I had crossed this plateau, and I saw far below me the village of Marsal on the banks of the shining Tarn. The river here made one of those bold curves which add so much to its beauty. The little village looked so peaceful and charming that I decided to seek its hospitality for that night.

There was but one inn at Marsal that undertook to lodge the stranger, and very seldom was any claim of the sort made upon it. The peasant family who lived in it looked to their bit of land and their two or three cows to keep them, not to the auberge. The bottles of liquor on the shelf were rarely taken down, except on Sundays, when villagers might saunter in, to gossip and smoke over coffee and *eau de vie*, or the glass of absinthe, which, since the failure of the vines in the South of France, has become there the most convivial of all drinks, although it makes men more quarrelsome than any other. In these poor riverside villages, however, where a mere ribbon of land is capable of cultivation—which, although exceedingly fertile, is constantly liable to be flooded by the uncertain Tarn—men have so little money in their pockets that water is their habitual drink, and when they depart from this rule they make a little dissipation go a very long way.

I found this single auberge closed, and all the family in an adjoining field around a waggon already piled with hay, to which a couple of cows were harnessed. My appearance there brought the pitchforks suddenly to a rest. If I had been shot up from below like a stage-devil, these people could not have stared at me with greater amazement and a

PORCH OF THE CATHEDRAL OF ALBI.

more frank expression of distrust. First in *patois*, and then, seeing that I was at a loss, in scarcely intelligible French, they asked me what my trade was, and what object I had in coming to Marsal. I tried to explain that I was not a mischievous person, that I was travelling merely to look at their beautiful rocks and gorges, but I failed completely to bring a hospitable expression into their faces. An old man of the party was the worst to deal with. He put the greatest number of questions and understood the least French, and all the while there was a most provokingly keen, suspicious glitter in his little gray eyes. Presently he beckoned me, and led the way, as I thought, to the inn; but such was not his intention. He stopped at the door of the communal school, where the schoolmaster was already waiting for me, for he had evidently been warned of the presence of a doubtful-looking stranger, who had come to the village on foot with a pack on his back, and who, being dressed a trifle better than the ordinary tramp, was probably the more dangerous for this reason. Like most of the village schoolmasters in France, this gentleman was also secretary at the *mairie*, a function highly stimulating to the sense of self-importance, and no wonder, considering that the person who fills it frequently supplies the mayor, who may scarcely be able to sign his name to official documents, with such intelligence as he may need for his public duties.

This schoolmaster was affable and pleasant, but

as a crowd quickly collected to see what would happen, he was not going to let a good opportunity slip of showing how indispensable he was to the safety of the village. He said that personally he was quite satisfied with my explanations, but that in his official capacity he was compelled to ask me for my papers. These were forthcoming, and the serious official air with which he pretended to read the English passport from beginning to end was very pretty comedy, considering that he did not understand a word of the language.

Having asserted his importance, and made the desired impression, he invited me into his house, introduced me to his young wife, who was charmingly gracious, and who would have been pleased to see any fresh face at Marsal—English or Hottentot. I was really indebted to the schoolmaster, for he harangued in *patois* the people of the inn drawn up in line, and by seizing a word here and there, I made out that I was a respectable Englishman travelling to improve my mind, and that they might receive me into their house without any distrust. And they did receive me, almost with open arms, when their doubts were removed.

The old man slunk off, and I never saw him again; but the young couple to whom the inn had been given up now proved to me that their only wish was to please. They were rough people, but sound at heart and honest, as the French peasants, when judged in the mass, undoubtedly are. The hostess, who, by-the-bye, gave me a soup-plate in which to wash my hands, was greatly perplexed to know how to get up a dinner for me, and, as she told me afterwards, she went to the schoolmaster and held a consultation with him on the subject. An astonishing dish of minced asparagus fried in oil was concocted in accordance with his prescription. It was ingenious, but I preferred her dish of barbel from the Tarn, notwithstanding the multitudinous bones which this fish perversely carries in its body, to choke the enemy, although nothing could be more absurd than such petty vengeance.

The schoolmaster's wife said to me, with a suggestion of malice at the corners of her mouth, that she was afraid I should be troubled by a few fleas at the auberge.

'Oh, bast!' observed her husband; 'monsieur in his travels has doubtless already encountered a flea or two.'

'Yes, and other *bestioles*,' said I.

Madame's local knowledge did not deceive her, but her expression 'a few fleas' did not at all represent the true state of affairs. And I had forgotten the precious powder and the little pair of bellows, without which no one should travel in Southern France.

The morning air was fresh, and the fronds of the bracken were wet with dew, when I left Marsal, and took my course along the margin of the river through meadows that dwindled away into woodlands, where the rocky sides of the gorge rose abruptly from the stream. Haymakers were abroad, and I heard the sound of their scythes cutting through the heavy swathes with all their flowers; but the sunshine had not yet flashed down into the deep valley, and the grasshoppers were waiting to hail it from their watch-towers in the green herbage and on the purple heather. As the breeze stirred the leaves of the wood, it brought with it the perfume of hidden honeysuckle. Golden oriels were busy in the tops of the wild cherry trees, feeding upon the ripe fruit, and calling out their French name, *loriot;* and when they flew across the river, a gleam of brilliant yellow moved swiftly over the rippled surface. For an hour or so I remained in the shade of trees, and then the sandy path met a road where the gorge widened and cultivation returned. Here I left the stream for awhile.

Now came sunny banks bright with the common flowers that deck most of the waysides of Europe. Bedstraw galium and field scabious, ox-eyes and knapweed, bladder-campions and ragged robins, mallows and crane's-bill — all the flowers of the English banks seemed to be there. Where the bare rock showed itself, yellow sedum spread its gold, and in the little clefts stood stalks of cotyledon, now turning brown. At the base of the rocks, where there was still some moisture, were the blue flowers of the brooklime veronica, and the brighter blue of the forget-me-not. Having passed a village,

I met the Tarn again. Here the beauty of the rushing water, and all that was pictured upon it, tempted me to sit down upon a bank; but I had no sooner chosen the spot than I changed my intention. A red viper was curled up there, and sleeping so comfortably that it really seemed unkind to wake it with a blow across all its rings. When I thought, however, of the little consideration it would have shown me had I sat upon it, I added it without compunction to the number of *aspics* I had already slain.

My mind was taken off the contemplation of this good or evil deed by a scene that seemed to contain as much of the picturesque as the eye could seize and the mind dwell upon, without being bewildered and fatigued. I had turned the bend of the wooded gorge, and, looking up the river, saw what resembled a dyke of basalt stretching sheer across the stream, with a ruined castle on a bare and apparently inaccessible pinnacle, another ruin on the opposite end of the ridge, and, between the two, a little church on the brink of a precipice. Houses were clustered at the foot of the rocks by the blue water.

This was Ambialet, so called from the extraordinary loop which the Tarn forms here in consequence of the mass of schistous rock which obstructs its direct channel. After flowing about two miles round a high promontory, where dark crags jut above the dark woods, the stream returns almost to the spot from which it was compelled to deviate, and the lower water is only separated from the upper by a few yards of rock. There are several similar phenomena in France, but there is none so remarkable as that at Ambialet.

Although nothing is now to be seen of its defensive works, except the ruined castle upon the high rock, Ambialet was one of the strongest places in the Albigeois. Now a small and poor village, it was in the Middle Ages an important burg, with its consuls, its council of *prud'hommes*, and its court of justice. It became a fief of the viscounts of Beziers, and was thus drawn into the great religious conflict of the twelfth and thirteenth centuries, the Viscount of Beziers having espoused the cause of Count Raymond of Toulouse. An army of Crusaders, which had been raised to crush the Albigenses, having Simon de Montfort at its head, appeared before Ambialet in 1209, and, although the burghers were quite capable of withstanding a long siege, they were so much impressed by the magnitude of the force brought against them, and also by Simon's sinister reputation, that they surrendered the place almost immediately. But when the army was campaigning elsewhere, these burghers, growing bold again, attacked the garrison that had been left in the town and castle, and distinguished themselves by one of those treacherous massacres which were among the small incidents of that ruthless war. When Simon reappeared in the Albigeois, the people of Ambialet, cowards

AMBIALET.

again, laid down their arms. The castle was soon afterwards the meeting-place of De Montfort and Raymond VI.; but the interview, which it was hoped would lead to peace, had no such result, and the war was carried on in Languedoc and Guyenne with renewed fury.

Ambialet was enjoying comparative freedom and self-government in an age when many a town was still in the midnight darkness of feudal servitude. It had its communal liberties and organization before the eleventh century. There is a very interesting charter in existence, dated 1136, by which Roger, Viscount of Beziers and Albi, recognises and confirms these liberties. Although it opens in Latin, the body of the charter is in the Romance language. It shows that the idiom of Southern Gaul in the twelfth century was a little nearer the Latin than that which is spoken now. The document is full of curious information. It tells us that the inhabitants of Ambialet were liable to be fined if they did not keep the street in front of their houses clean. Perhaps the towns in the South of France were less foul in the twelfth century than most of them are now. We learn, too, that the profits in connection with the most necessary trades were fixed in the interest of the greater number. Thus, the butchers were required to take oath that they would reserve for their own profit no more than the head of the animal that they killed. What sort of face would a butcher of to-day make if he were asked to work on such terms? The tavern-keepers had to take oath that they would buy no wine outside of the boundaries of the viscounty of Ambialet, which shows what was thought in the twelfth century of the practice of purchasing in the cheapest market to the neglect of communal interests. The price of wine, like that of bread, was fixed, and five worthies (*prohomes*) were appointed to examine weights and measures, and to confiscate those which were not just. The concluding part of the charter confirms the right of the youth of Ambialet to their traditional festivals and merry-making: 'E volem e auctreiam que lo Rei del Joven d'Ambilet puesco far sas festas, tener sos senescals e sos jutges, e sos sirvens e sos officials,' etc. The whole passage is worth giving in English, because historians tell us very little about the festive manners of the twelfth century:

'We wish and order that the King of Youth of Ambialet shall keep his festivals, have his seneschals, judges, servants, and officials, and that on the day appointed for the merry-making, the King of Youth shall demand from the most recently married man in the viscounty, and woman who shall have taken a husband, a pail of wine and a quarter of walnuts; and if they refuse, the king can order his officers to break the doors of their house, and neither we nor our bailiffs shall have the right to interfere. And any person who shall have cut ever so little from the leaves of the elm, planted upon the place, shall be sentenced by the King of Youth to pay a pail of wine, and the king can enforce it as above. Moreover, we declare that on the first day of May the youth shall have the right to set up a maypole, and any person who shall cut a portion of it shall owe a pail of wine, and the king can compel him to pay it, for such is our wish. We have granted this favour to the youth because, having been a witness of their merry-making, we have taken great pleasure and satisfaction therefrom.'

This custom has been continued to the present day. The youth of Ambialet have their annual festival, and the most recently married couple of the commune are called upon to 'pay' their pail of wine, although the exact measure is not strictly enforced.

The rocks at Ambialet at one time supported a multitude of dwellings, of which there would be no trace now had they been entirely of masonry. In addition to partial chambers made with the pickaxe, one sees here and there a series of stairs cut out of the mica-schist. The strength of the burg made it a place of refuge for numerous families in the Albigeois, who had retreats upon these rocks to which they repaired in time of danger. All that made up the grandeur and importance of the place has passed away. Among those who now guide the plough and scatter the grain for bread are descendants of the old nobility of the Albigeois.

Fascinated by the quietude and picturesque decay

of this beautiful spot by the farm, instead of leaving it in a few hours, as I had intended, I remained there for days. Let no wayfarer, if he can help it, be the slave of a programme.

On the side of the promontory already mentioned, a rough bit of ancient forest, steep and craggy, stretches down to the strip of cultivated land beside the river. Here chance led me to take up my abode in an old farm-house—a long building of one story, with dovecot raised above the roof, and massive walls that kept the rooms cool even in the sultry afternoons. It was half surrounded by an orchard of plum, peach, apple, and cherry trees, and at the border of this were three majestic stone-pines, whose vast heads were lifted so high and seemed so full of radiance that they appeared to belong more to the sky than to the earth. The gleam of the oriel's golden breast could be seen amidst the branches, but the little birds that flew up there were lost to sight in the sunny wilderness of tufted leaves.

On the stony slope above the orchard, the stock of an old and leafless vine, showing here and there over the purple flush of flowering marjoram and the more scattered gold of St. John's-wort, told the story of the perished vineyard. For centuries a rich wine had flowed from these slopes, but at length the phylloxera spread over them like flame, and now where the vine is dead the wild-flower blooms. A little higher a fringe of broom, the blossom gone, the pods blackening and shooting their seeds in the sun, marked the line of the virgin wilderness. Then came tall heather and bracken, dwarf oak and chestnut, box and juniper, all luxuriating about the blocks of mica-schist, a rock that holds water and is therefore conducive to a varied and splendid vegetation, wherever a soil can rest upon it. Towards the summit the trees and shrubs dwindled away, and then came the dry thyme-covered turf scenting the air. The tall thyme, the garden species in the North, had already flowered, but the common wild thyme of England, the *serpolet* of the French, was beginning to spread its purple over the stony ground. A great wooden cross stood upon the ridge, and hard by, buffeted by the wintry winds and blazed upon by the summer sun, was the ancient priory of Nôtre Dame de l'Oder.

I ring the bell. Presently a little wicket is pulled back, and a dark eye glitters at me from the other side of the door. It belongs to a serving brother, who, perceiving that I am not in petticoats, allows me to enter.

While I am waiting for the Père Etienne, a Franciscan of wide learning, whose acquaintance had already brought me both pleasure and profit, I sit in the cloisters watching another Father counting the week's washing, which has just been brought in, and neatly folding up handkerchiefs and undergarments. He has placed a board across a wheelbarrow, and the heap of linen is upon this. Seated upon a stool, he leisurely takes each great coarse handkerchief with blue border, which, like the rest of the linen, has not been ironed, folds it into four, lays it upon another board, smooths it with his large, thin yellow hand, and so goes on with his task without saying a word or raising his eyes. He is a gaunt, angular, sallow man of about fifty, with hollow cheeks and long black beard. He has a melancholy air, and does his work as though he were thinking all the while that it is a part of the sum of labour he has to get through before reaching that perfect state of felicity in which there is no more washing to be done or counted. If there were only monks in the priory, this one would have very little to do in looking after the linen; but there are many boys who, although they are being educated with a view to the religious life, have not yet put off such worldly things as shirts.

Very different from the sombre-looking Franciscan, bent over the wheelbarrow, is the Père Etienne. He is as cheerful and sprightly as if he were now convinced that a convent is the pleasantest place on earth to live in, and that outside of it all is vanity and vexation. He teaches the boys Latin, Greek, English, and the physical sciences. Although he has never been out of France and Italy, he can speak English, and actually make himself understood. He is a botanist, and he and I have already spent some hours together in his cell before a table strewn with floras and plants, both dry and fresh.

This time we are joined by a young monk who has been gathering flowers on the banks of the Tarn, and has placed them between the leaves of a great Latin Bible.

These meetings, and the library of the priory, with its valuable works by local historians, strengthened the spell by which Ambialet held me. The monks whom one occasionally meets in Languedoc are generally men of better culture than the ordinary rural clergy, most of whom show plainly enough by their ideas and the vigorous expressions which they rarely hesitate to use in any company that they are sons of the soil. As priests, situated as they are, this coarseness of manners and circumscribed range of ideas, so far from being a disadvantage, forms a bond of union between them and the people. A man to be deeply pitied is he who, having a really superior and cultivated mind, is charged with the cure of souls in some forlorn parish where nobody has the time or the taste to read. Such a priest must either bring his ideas down to those of the people around him, or be content to live in absolute intellectual isolation. He may turn to the companionship of books, it is true, but his library is very small; and if, as is probable, his income is not more than £40 a year, he is too poor to add to it. Such a revenue, when the bare needs of the body have been met, does not leave much for satisfying a literary appetite.

The priory of Nôtre Dame de l'Oder was founded

in the twelfth or thirteenth century by the Benedictines, but a church already existed on the spot as early, it is supposed, as the eighth century. The one now standing, and which became incorporated with the priory, probably dates from the eleventh. If the interior is cold by the severity of the lines scarcely broken by ornament, the artistic sense is warmed by the beauty of the proportions and general disposition. The apse, with its three little windows, has the perfect charm of grace and simplicity. A structural peculiarity, to be especially noted as one of the tentative efforts of Romanesque art, is the use of half-arches for the vaulting of the two narrow aisles. Unfortunately, the plastering mania, which has robbed the interior of so many French churches of their venerable air, has not spared this one. A singularly broad flight of steps, partly cut in the rock and covered with tiles, leads up to the portal; but as the building has been closed to the public since the application of the law dispersing religious communities, these steps look as if they belonged to the Castle of Indolence, so overgrown with grass are they and abandoned to the wandering wild-flowers. Great muleins have been allowed to spring up from the gaps between the lichen-spotted tiles.

When there was a regular community of monks here, the ancient pilgrimage to Nôtre Dame de l'Oder was kept up, and near the top of the *via crucis*, which forms a long succession of zigzags upon the bare rock, a dark shrub or small tree allied to box may be seen railed off with an image of the Virgin against it. According to the legend, a Crusader returning from the Holy Land made a pilgrimage to the sanctuary upon these rocks at Ambialet, and planted on the hill the staff he had brought with him. This grew to a tree, to which the people of the country gave the name of *oder*. In course of time it came to be so venerated that Notre Dame d'Ambialet was changed to Notre Dame de l'Oder. The existing tree is said to be a descendant of the original one.

The monks at the priory told me that nearly all the old historical documents relating to Ambialet had been taken away by the English and placed in the Tower of London. In various parts of the Quercy, I had also been told exactly the same with regard to the documents connected with the early history of the locality. There are people who still speak of this as a proof of the intention of the English to return. How the belief became so widespread that the English placed the documents which they carried away in the Tower of London, I am unable to explain.

Memory takes me back again to the farmhouse by the Tarn. It is well that there is plenty of space, for the household is numerous. There are the farmer, his wife and children, an aged mother whose voice has become a mere thread of sound, and who thinks over the past in the chimney-corner, sometimes with a distaff in her hand ; two old uncles, a youth of all work, who has been brought up as one of the family, and a little bright-eyed, barelegged servant girl, whose brown feet I still hear pattering upon the floors. One of the old men is a white-bearded priest of eighty-five, who has spent most of his life in Algeria, and has himself come to look like the patriarchal Arab in all but the costume. He has no longer any sacerdotal work, but he has other occupation. His special duty is to look after a great flesh-coloured pig, and many a time have I seen him under the orchard trees following close at the heels of the grunting beast while reading his office. His old breviary, like his *soutane*, is very much the worse for wear, the leaves having been thumbed nearly to the colour of chocolate ; but if he had a new one now, he would find it hard to believe that it had the same virtue as the other. Notwithstanding his years, he can do harder work than watching a pig. I have seen him haymaking and reaping, and always the merriest of the party. Before taking the fork or the sickle in hand, he would hitch up his *soutane*, and reveal a pair of still active sacerdotal legs in white linen drawers. The sight of the old man bending his back while reaping, his white beard brushing the golden corn, was pathetic or comic as the humour might seize the beholder. As gay as any of the cicadas that keep the summer's jubilee in the sunny tree-tops, he sings songs that have nothing in common with psalms, and he needs little provocation to dance. French has become an awkward language to him, but his tongue is nimble enough both in Languedocian and Latin. When he hears that the evening soup is ready, he hurries the pig home, flourishes his stick above his head in imitation of the Arabs, and shouts in his cheeriest voice, 'Oportet manducare!'

The other uncle's chief business is to look after a couple of cows, and as the farm has no pasturage but the orchard, he is away with them the greater part of the day along the banks of the Tarn. One evening I met him by the river, and he stopped me to quote a passage from the Georgics which he had recalled to mind. His face beamed with satisfaction. I knew that he had not been brought up to cow-tending, but was, nevertheless, taken aback when the unfortunate old bachelor wished me to share the pleasure he felt in having brought to mind a long-forgotten passage of Virgil. The surprises of real life never cease to be startling. Speaking to me afterwards of the growing extravagance of all classes, he said:

'When I was young there were only two *cafés* in Albi, and none but the rich ever entered them. Now every man goes to his *café*. I remember when, in middle-class families in easy circumstances, coffee was only drunk two or three times a year, on festive occasions.' Very different is the state of things now in France.

The figure of the old man bending upon his stick glides away by the dark willow-fringe of the Tarn, and I am standing alone in the solemn splendour of the luminous dusk—the clear-obscure of the quickly passing twilight, beside the bearded corn, whose gold is blended with the faint rosiness that spreads through the air of the valley, and lets free the fragrance of those flowers which keep all their sweetness for the evening. There is still a gleam of the lost sun upon the priory walls, and over the dark rocks and wooded hollows floats a purple haze. The dusk gathers apace, and the poplars that rise far above the willows along the river, their outlines shaded away into the black forest behind them, stand motionless like phantom trees, for not a leaf stirs; but the corn seems to grow more luminous, as if it had drunk something of the fire as well as the colour of the sun, while the horns of the sinking moon gleam silver-bright just over the topmost trees, painted in sepia upon a cobalt sky. How weird, phantasmal, enigmatic the forms of those trees now appear! Some like hell-hags, with wild hair flying, are rushing through the air; others, majestic, solitary, wrapped about with dark horror, are the trees of Fate; some have their arms raised in the frenzy of a torturing passion; others look like emblems of Care when hope and passion are alike dead; each touches the spring of a sombre thought or a fantastic fancy.

On the road to Villefranche, about half a mile

from Ambialet, is a mine which has been abandoned from time immemorial, and which the inhabitants say was worked by the English for gold. I have noticed, however, throughout this part of France, that nearly everything that was done in a remote age, whether good or evil, is attributed by the people to the English, and that they not infrequently make a curious confusion between Britons and Romans. As for the Visigoths, Ostrogoths, and Arabs, all traditions respecting them appear to have passed out of the popular mind. In the side of a stony hill on which scarcely a plant grows, a narrow passage, a few feet wide, has been quarried, and air shafts have been cut down into it through the solid rock with prodigious labour. I followed this passage until a falling in of the roof prevented me from going any farther. I could perceive no trace of a metallic vein, so thoroughly had it been worked out, but scattered over the hillside with schist, talcose slate, and fragments of quartz, was a great deal of scoriæ, showing that metal of some kind had been excavated, and that the smelting had been done on the spot. That the mine was worked for gold seems quite probable, inasmuch as a lump of mineral containing a considerable quantity of the precious metal was picked up near the entrance some years ago. Besides the scoriæ, I found upon the hillside much broken pottery, and from the shape of several fragments it was easy to restore the form of earthenware pots which were probably used for smelting purposes. There is no record to show who the people were who were so busy upon these rocks glittering with mica and talc. They may have belonged to any one of the races who passed over the land from the time of the Romans.

One morning, still in the month of July, I broke away from the charms of Ambialet, and shouldering again my old knapsack — which, by travelling hundreds of miles in all weathers, had become disgracefully shabby, but which was a friend too well stitched together to be thrown aside on account of ill-looks—I continued my journey up the valley of the Tarn. I had agreed to walk with the parish priest as far as the village of Villeneuve, and having found him at the presbytery, we passed through the churchyard on the edge of the rock. Here there is a remarkable cross, with the figure of Christ on one side and that of the Virgin on the other, not carved in relief, but in that early mediaeval style which consisted of hollowing out the stone around the image. The *curé* frankly declared that, if anyone offered him a large new cross in the place of this little one, he would be glad to make the exchange. It is unfortunate that so many rural priests place but little value upon religious antiquities other than images and relics which have a legend. Their appreciation of ecclesiastical art is too often regulated by the practical and utilitarian order of ideas. To dazzle the eye of the peasant may, and does, become the single aim of church ornamentation. Hence the brassy, vulgar altars, and those coloured plaster images of modern manufacture that one sees with regret in so many of the country churches of France.

I soon took my last look at Ambialet, its rocks and ruins on which the wild pinks nodded, and its stone-covered roofs overgrown with white sedum. I was struck by the number of prickly plants on the sandy banks of the Tarn. Those which now made the best show of bloom were the star-thistle centaurea and *ononis repens*. The appearance of this last was very curious, for in addition to its pink pea-blossoms it seemed to be sprinkled over with little flowers the colour of forget-me-nots. These, however, were not flowers at all, but small flying beetles painted the brilliant blue of myosotis. Another plant that showed a strong liking for these banks was the horned poppy (*glaucium luteum*), which I had only found elsewhere near the sea-coast. Brown stalks of broomrape were still standing, and I lighted upon a lingering bee-ophrys, a plant which by its amazing mimicry makes one look at it with awe as if it were something supernatural.

It was an invitation to lunch at a presbytery that was the reason for my companion taking a walk of about eight miles. Passing through a small village on the way he called for the *curé* there, who was also an expected guest. This priest had obtained a reputation throughout the district for his humour, his eccentricity, and contempt for appearances. He had passed most of his life alone, cooking his food, making his bed, and probably mending his clothes, without the help of any woman. Being now over eighty years of age, he had realized the necessity of changing his ways, and a woman not much younger than himself had succeeded in obtaining a firm footing in his paved kitchen, which was also the dining-room and *salon*. His presbytery in the steep and rocky village street was no better built or more luxuriously furnished than the dwellings of his peasant parishioners. Here we found the old white-haired man, gay and hospitable, anxious to offer everything he had in the house to the visitor, but only able to think of two things which might be acceptable—snuff and sausage. '*Un peu de saucisson?*' he said to me, with a winning smile after handing me his snuff-box. I assured him I could eat nothing then. '*Tè!* and so you are really English, monsieur?—*Un peu de saucisson?*'

The *curé* had been shut up in this village so many years, speaking nothing but Languedocian to his parishioners, even when preaching to them, that his French had become rather difficult to understand. I was keenly alive to the exceptional study of human nature presented by this fine specimen of an old rustic priest, who was not the less to be respected because he took a great deal of snuff, hated shaving, wore hob-nailed shoes of the roughest make, and a threadbare, soup-spotted *soutane* with frayed edges. He was not a bit ascetic, and although he had lived so many years by himself, his good-humour and gaiety continually overflowed. It may be that a housekeeper tends to sour a priest's temper more than anything else, and this one knew it. The sacerdotal domestic help must be fifty years old when she enters the presbytery. Spinster or widow, she has that inherent purpose of every woman to be, if she can, the mistress of the house in which she lives. If she encounters no other woman in the field, against whom if she tried conclusions she would be broken like the earthen pot in the fable, she generally succeeds in achieving her ambition, although she may be in name a servant. There are such phenomena as hen-pecked priests, and those who peck them have no right whatever to do it. It is a state of things brought about by too much submission, for the sake of peace, to a mind determined to be uppermost while pretending to be humble.

When we left again for Villeneuve, we were three in number, and the old *curé* trudged along over the rocky or sandy paths as nimbly as either of his companions. He pointed out to me a spot in the Tarn where he said was a gulf the bottom of which had never been sounded. There are many such holes in the bed of this river, which receives much of its water from underground tributaries.

I was looking at the mournful vine-terraces, now mostly abandoned and grass-grown. 'Ah!' said the octogenarian, shaking his head, and for once wearing a melancholy expression, 'the best wine of the South used to be grown there.' Near a village a very tall pole, probably a young poplar that had been barked, had been raised in a garden, and painted with stripes of red, white, and blue. It was described to me as a 'tree of liberty,' and I was told that the garden in which it was placed belonged to the mayor for the current year. Every fresh mayor had a fresh tree.

At the village of Villeneuve I parted from my companions, who went to lunch with the *curé*, together with several other ecclesiastics. These occasional meetings and junketings at one another's houses are the chief mundane consolation of the rural priests, who are as weak as other mortals in the presence of a savoury dish, and, when they can afford to do so, they enter into the pleasures of hospitality with Horatian zest. Poor as they often are, they generally know the faggot that conceals a drop of old wine to place before the guest. The people in the South believe that the bounty of the Creator was intended to be made the most of, and the type of priest that one meets most frequently there in the richer parishes thinks that the next good thing to a clear conscience is a good table.

I lunched at the auberge, and I had for my companion a ruby-faced cattle-dealer of about fifty. He spent his life chiefly in a trap, followed by an old cattle-dog of formidable build and determined expression of mouth. This animal was now lying down near the table, so tired and footsore from almost perpetual running that he thought it too much trouble to get up and eat. I read in his eye that he was in the habit of breathing every day of his life a canine curse on the business of cattle-dealing. His master seemed a good-natured man, but he had a fixed idea that was unfortunate for the dog. He considered that the beast ought to be able to run from thirty-five to forty miles a day, and that if he got sore paws it was his own fault.

'And do you never give him a lift?'

'Never!' roared the cattle-dealer, laughing like an ogre.

The dog being now ten years old, I was not surprised to hear that he sometimes tried to lose himself just before his master was starting upon a long round. Considering his age, and all the running he had done in return for board and lodging, I thought his diplomacy excusable; but the cattle-dealer used strong language to express his loathing of such depravity and ingratitude in a dog old enough to be serious, and on which so much kindness had been lavished.

This man had a very bad opinion of the inhabitants of that part of the Rouergue which I was about to cross, and he strove to convince me that it was very imprudent of me to think of travelling on foot and alone through such a wild country. Had I told him that I carried no other arm but my oak stick with iron spike, he would have been still more vehement. Frenchmen like the companionship of a revolver. I do not. In the first place, it makes me imagine there is an assassin lurking in every thicket; secondly, I do not know where to carry it conveniently so that it would be of use in time of need. I place confidence in my stick, and take my chance. To tell the plain truth, I did not believe what my table companion said about the dangerous character of the inhabitants. The reason he gave for their exceptional wickedness was that they were very poor, but this view was contrary to my experience of humanity.

While we were talking over our coffee, there was a rising uproar in the village street. Looking out of the window, we saw two men fighting in the midst of a crowd.

'Ah!' exclaimed the cattle-dealer, with a sonorous chuckle, 'that ought to give you an idea of the capacities of the inhabitants.' Then, entering into the spirit of the battle, he shouted: 'Leave them alone—leave them alone! It is not men who are fighting; it is the juice of the grape!'

Both combatants soon had enough of it, and very little damage was done on either side. The scene was more ludicrous than tragic. After all, it was well, perhaps, that these men had not learnt how to use their fists, and that with them pushing, slapping, and rolling upon one another satisfied honour.

The hostess of this inn, while cooking the inevitable fowl for lunch, basted it after the Languedocian fashion, of which I had taken note elsewhere. Very different is it from what is commonly understood by basting. A curious implement is used for the purpose. This is an iron rod, with a piece of metal at one end twisted into the form of an extinguisher, but with a small opening left at the pointed extremity. The extinguisher, if it may be so termed, is made red-hot, or nearly so, and then a piece of fat bacon is put into it, which bursts into flame. A little stream of blazing fat passes through the small opening, and this is made to trickle over the fowl, which is turned upon the spit by clockwork in front of the wood fire. The fowl or joint thus treated tastes of burnt bacon: but the Southerners like strong flavours, and revel in grease as well as garlic.

Fat bacon is the basis of all cookery in Guyenne and Upper Languedoc, where the winters are too cold for the olive to flourish, and where butter is rarely seen. The *cuisine* is substantial, but not refined.

A little beyond Villeneuve I found Trébas, a pleasant river-side village, with a ferruginous spring that has obtained for the place a local reputation for healing. Here I left the Tarn again, and followed its tributary, the Rance, for the sake of change. This stream ran at the bottom of a deep gorge, the sides of which were chiefly clothed with woods, but here and there was a patch of yellow corn-field and green vineyard. Reapers, men and women, were busy with their sickles, singing, as they worked, their Languedocian songs that troubadours may have been the first to sing; but nature was quiet with that repose which so quickly follows the great festival of flowers. Already the falling corn was whispering of the final feast of colour. All the earlier flowers of the summer were now casting or ripening their seed. I passed a little village on the opposite side of the gorge. The houses, built of dark stone, even to the roofs, looked scarcely different from their background of bare rock. Weedy vine-terraces without vines told the oft-repeated story of privation and long-lasting bitterness of heart in many a little home that once was happy. I found the grandeur of solitude, without any suggestion of human life, where huge rocks of gneiss and schist, having broken away from the sides of the gorge, lay along the margins and in the channel of the stream. Here I lingered, listening to the drowsy music of the flowing water, and the murmuring of the bees amongst the purple marjoram and the yellow agrimony, until the sunshine moving up the rocks reminded me of the fleet-winged hours.

Continuing my way up the gorge, I presently saw a village clinging to a hill, with a massive and singular-looking church on the highest point. It was Plaisance, and I knew now that I had left the

Albigeois, and had entered the Rouergue. Having decided to pass the night here, and the auberge being chosen, I climbed to the top of the bluff to have a near view of the church. It is a remarkable structure representing two architectural periods. The apse and transept are Romanesque, but the nave is Gothic. Over the intersection of the transept is a cupola supported by massive piers. Engaged with these are columns bearing elaborately carved capitals embellished with little figures of the quaintest workmanship. In the apse are two rows of columns with cubiform capitals carved in accordance with the florid Romanesque taste, as it was developed in Southern France.

Although the little cemetery on the bluff was like scores of others I had seen in France—a bit of rough neglected field with small wooden crosses rising above the long herbage, tangled with flowers that love the waste places, I yielded to the charm of that old simplicity which is ever young and beautiful. I strolled amongst the grave mounds, and passing the sunny spot where the dead children of the village lay side by side, under the golden flowers of St. John's-wort, reached the edge of the rock, whose dark nakedness was hidden by reddening sedum, and looked at the wave-like hills, their yellow cornfields, vine terraces and woods, the gray-green roofs of the houses below, and lower still the stream flashing along through a desert of pebbles.

Descending to the valley, I noticed the number and beauty of the vine trellises in the village. One, commencing at a Gothic archway, extended from wall to wall far up a narrow lane, and here the twilight fell an hour too soon. I wandered down to the pebbly shore of the Rance, where bare-footed children, sent out to look after pigs and geese, were building castles with the many-coloured stones, while others on the rocky banks above were singing in chorus, like a somewhat louder twittering of sedge warblers from the fringe of willows. I wandered on until all was quiet save the water, and returned to the inn when the fire on the hearth was sending forth a cheerful red glow through the dusk. The soup was bubbling in the chain pot, and a well-browned fowl was taking its final turns upon the spit.

I dined with a commercial traveller, one who went about the country in a queer sort of vehicle containing samples of church ornaments and sacerdotal vestments. His business lay chiefly with the rural clergy, and, like most people, he seemed convinced that circumstances had pushed him into the wrong groove, and that he had remained in it too long for him to be able to get out of it. For twenty years he had been driving over the same roads, reappearing in the same villages and little towns, watching the same people growing old, and spending only three months of the year with his family in Toulouse. He declared the life of a commercial traveller, when the novelty of it had worn down, to be the most abominable of all lives. He was one of the most pleasant, and certainly the most melancholy, of commercial travellers whom I had met in my rambles. He left the impression on me that there was more money to be made nowadays in France by travelling with samples of *eau de vie* and groceries than with church candlesticks and chasubles. Nevertheless, although he had his private quarrel with destiny, he was not at all a gloomy companion at dinner.

A person who had not had previous experience of French country inns would have been astonished at the order in which the dishes were laid on the table. The first course after the soup was potatoes (*sautées*); then came barbel from the stream, and afterwards veal and fowl. The order is considered a matter of no importance; the main thing aimed at in the South of France is to give the guest plenty of dishes. If there is any fish, more often than not it makes its appearance after the roast, and I have even seen a custard figure as the first course. By living with the people one soon falls into their ways, accepting things as they come, without giving a thought to the conventional sequence.

Among other things that one has to grow accustomed to in rural France, especially in the South, is the presence of beds in dining-rooms and kitchens. At first it rasps the sense of what is correct, but the very frequency of it soon brings indifference. In the large kitchen of this rather substantial auberge there was an alcove, a few feet from the chimney-place, containing a neatly tucked-up bed with a crucifix and little holy-water shell by the side. It was certainly a snug corner in winter, and I felt sure that the stout hostess reserved it for herself.

ACROSS THE ROUERGUE.

At an early hour in the morning I was wayfaring again. I had made up my mind to reach St. Affrique in a day's walk. There were some thirty miles of country to cross, and I had, moreover, to reckon with the July sun, which shines very earnestly in Southern France, as though it were bent on ripening all the fruits of the earth in a single day. By getting up earlier than usual I was able to watch the morning opening like a wild rose. When we feel all the charm that graces the beginning of a summer day, we resolve in future to rise with the birds, but the next morning's sun finds most of us sluggards again.

I returned towards the Tarn, which I had left the day before, but with the intention of keeping somewhat to the south of it for awhile. However beautiful the scenery of a gorge may be, the sensation of being at the bottom of a crevice at length becomes depressing, and the mind, which is never satisfied with anything long, begins to wonder what the world is like beyond the enclosing cliffs, and the desire to climb them and to look forth under a

wider range of sky grows stronger. Such change is
needed, for when there is languor within, the impressions from without are dull. The country
through which I now passed was very beautiful
with its multitude of chestnut-trees, the pale yellow
plumes of the male blossom still clinging to them
and hiding half their leaves; but here again was the
sad spectacle of abandoned, weedy, and almost leafless vineyards upon stony slopes which had been
changed into fruit-bearing terraces by the long
labour of dead generations.

The first village I came to was Coupiac, lying in
a deep hollow, from the bottom of which rose a
rugged mass of schistous rock, with houses all about
it, under the protecting shadow of a strong castle
with high round towers in good preservation. It
was a mediæval fortress, but its mullioned windows
cut in the walls of the towers and other details
showed that it had been considerably modified and
adapted to changed conditions of life at the time of
the Renaissance. A troop of little girls were going
up to it, and teaching Sisters, who had changed it
into a stronghold of education, were waiting for
them in the court. Hard by upon the edge of the
castle rock was a calvary. The naked schist, ribbed
and seamed, served for pavement in the steep little
streets of this picturesque old village, where most of
the people went barefoot. This is the custom of
the region, and does not necessarily imply poverty.
Here the *sabotier's* trade is a poor one, and the

cobbler's is still worse. In the Albigeois I was the neighbour of a well-to-do farmer who up to the age of sixty had never known the sensation of sock or stocking, nor had he ever worn a shoe of wood or leather.

No female beauty did I see here, nor elsewhere in the Rouergue. Plainness of feature in men and women is the rule throughout this extensive tract of country. But there is this to be said in favour of the girls and younger women, that they generally have well-shaped figures and a very erect carriage, which last is undoubtedly due to the habit of carrying weights upon the head, especially water, which needs to be carefully balanced.

How the peasants stared at me as I passed along! The expression of their faces showed that they were completely puzzled as to what manner of person I was, and what I was doing there. Had I been taking along a dancing-bear they would have understood my motives far better, and my social success with them would have been undoubtedly greater. As it was, most of them eyed me with extreme suspicion. Not having been rendered familiar, like the peasants of many other districts, with that harmless form of insanity which leads people to endure the hardship of tramping for the sake of observing the ruder aspects of human life, the lingering manners of old times, and of reading the book of nature in solitude, they thought I must perforce be engaged upon some sinister and wicked work. And now this reminds me of an old man at Ambialet, whom I used to send on errands to the nearest small town. He liked my money, but he could never satisfy his conscience that it was not something like treason to carry letters for me, for he had the feeling to the last that he was in the pay of the enemy. 'Ah!' he growled one day (not to me), 'I have always heard it said that the English regretted our beautiful rocks and rich valleys. They are coming back! I am sure they are coming back!' I used to see him looking at me askance with a peculiarly keen expression in his eyes, and as his words had been repeated to me I knew of what he was thinking. He was the first man of his condition who to my knowledge called rocks beautiful. The peasant class abhor rocks on account of their sterility, and because the rustic idea of a beautiful landscape is the fertile and level plain. In searching for the picturesque and the grandeur of nature, it is perfectly safe to go to those places which the peasant declares to be frightful by their ugliness.

Leaving Coupiac behind me, I turned towards the east. The road, having been cut in the side of the cliff, exposed layers of brown argillaceous schist, like rotten wood, and so friable that it crumbled between the fingers; but what was more remarkable was that the layers, scarcely thicker than slate, instead of being on their natural plane, were turned up quite vertically. I was now ascending to the barren uplands. Near the brow of a hill I passed a very ancient crucifix of granite, the head, which must originally have been of the rudest sculpture, having the features quite obliterated by time.

A rural postman in a blouse with red collar had been trudging up the hill behind me, and I let him overtake me so that I might fall into conversation with him, for these men are generally more intelligent or better informed than the peasants. I have often walked with them, and never without obtaining either instruction or amusement. When we had reached the highest ground, from which a splendid view was revealed of the Rouergue country—a crumpled map of bare hills and deep dark gorges—the postman pointed out to me the village of Roquecésaire (Cæsar's Rock), on a hill to the south, and told me a queer story of a battle between its inhabitants and those of an adjacent village. The quarrel, strange to say, arose over a statue of the Virgin, which was erected not long since upon a commanding position between the two villages. 'Now, the Holy Virgin,' said the postman, in no tone of mockery, 'was obliged to turn her back either to one village or the other, and this was the cause of the fight!' When first set up, the statue looked towards Roquecésaire, to the great satisfaction of the inhabitants; but the people of the other village, who thought themselves equally pious, held that they had been slighted; and the more they looked at the back of the Virgin turned towards them the angrier they became, and the more determined not to submit to the indignity. At length, unable to keep down their fury any longer, they sallied forth one day, men, women and children, with the intention of turning the statue round. But the people of Roquecésaire were vigilant, and, seeing the hostile crowd coming, went forth to give them battle. The combat raged furiously for hours, and it was watched —so said the postman—with much excitement and interest by the *curé* of Montclar—the village we were now approaching— who, happening to have a telescope, was able to note the varying fortune of war. At length the Roquecésaire people got the worst of it, and they were driven away from the statue, which was promptly turned round. Although many persons were badly knocked about, nobody died for the cause. The energetic intervention of the spiritual and temporal authorities prevented a renewal of the scandal, and it was thought best, in the interest of peace, to allow the statue to be turned half-way to one village and half to the other.

The postman was a little reserved at first, not knowing to what country I belonged, but when he was satisfied that I was not a German, he let his tongue rattle on with the freedom which is one of the peculiarities of his class. He confided to me that the best help to a man who walked much was absinthe. It pulled him up the hills and sent him whisking across the plains.

'I eat very little,' said my black-bearded, bright-

eyed fellow-tramp; 'but,' he added, 'I drink three
or four glasses of absinthe a day.'

'You will eat still less,' I said, 'if you don't soon
begin to turn off the tap.'

Considering the hard monotony of their lives and
the strain imposed upon physical endurance by walking from twenty to twenty-five miles a day in all
weathers, the rural postmen in France are a sober
body of men. This one told me that he walked
sometimes eight miles out of his way to carry a
single letter.

Thus gossiping, we reached Montclar, on the
plateau, a little to the south of the deep gorge of
the Tarn. Here we entered an auberge, where the
postman was glad to moisten his dry throat with the
green-eyed enemy. This inn was formerly one of
those small châteaux—more correctly termed *maisons
fortes*, or manors—which sprang up all over France
in the sixteenth and seventeenth centuries. The
inhabited part of the building was reached by a
spiral staircase enclosed by a tower. A balcony
connected with the principal room enabled me to
read an inscription cut in a stone of the tower:
'Tristano Disclaris, 1615.' But for this record left
by the founder, his name would probably have
passed, long ago, out of the memory of men.

I found that the chief occupation of the people in
this house was that of making Roquefort cheeses;
indeed, it was impossible not to guess what was
going on from the all-pervading odour. And yet

I was still many miles from Roquefort! However, I knew all about this matter before. I was not twenty miles from Albi when I found that Roquefort cheese-making was a local industry. In fact, this is the case over a very wide region. The cheeses, having been made, are sent to Roquefort to ripen in the cellars, which have been excavated in the rock, and also to acquire the necessary reputation. While my lunch was being prepared I looked into the dairy, which was very clean and creditable. On the ground were large tubs of milk, and on tables were spread many earthenware moulds pierced with little holes and containing the pressed curds.

The hostess was a buxom, good-tempered woman with rosy cheeks. She told me that she could not give me anything better than ham and eggs. She could not have offered me anything more acceptable after all the greasy cooking, the steadfast veal and invariable fowl which I had so long been compelled to accept daily with resignation. By a mysterious revelation of art she produced the ham and eggs in a way that made me think that she must surely be descended from one of the English adventurers who did all manner of mischief in the Rouergue some five or six centuries ago. Such ham and eggs in her case could only be explained by the theory of hereditary ideas. Nevertheless, she had become French enough to look at me with a dubious, albeit a good-natured eye. My motive in coming there and going farther without having

any commercial object in view was more than she
could fathom. After my visit to the dairy I fancy
her private notion was that I was commissioned by
the English Government to find out how Roquefort
cheese was made, with a view to competition. At
length, as we talked freely, she let the state of her
mind with regard to me escape her unawares by
putting this question plump :

'How is it the gendarmes have not stopped you?'

'That I cannot tell you,' said I, much amused by
her candour; 'but you may be sure of this, I am
not afraid of them.'

Her husband was listening behind the door, and
I observed an expression of relief in his face when I
took up my pack and departed. If I was to be
pounced upon, he preferred, for his own peace of
mind and the reputation of his house, that it should
be done elsewhere. All the village had heard of
my coming, and when I reappeared outside there
was a small crowd of people waiting to have a good
look at me. I thought from these signs that I was
likely to be asked to show my papers again by some
petty functionary; but no, I was allowed to pass on
without interference. Perhaps the postman had
given a good account of me, the absinthe having
touched his heart. There is much diplomacy in
getting somebody on your side while travelling alone
through these unopened districts far from railways.
Wandering among the peasants of the Tarn and the
Aveyron teaches one what ignorance really means,

what blindness of intellect goes with it. And yet
their enlightenment by the usual methods would be
a doubtful blessing to themselves and others.

I was now descending to the valley, and not long
after leaving the village an attempt to escape from
the winding hot road led me into one of those
wildernesses which are to me infinitely more pleas-
ing than the most artistic gardens, with their
geometric flower-beds and their counterfeit lakes
and grottoes. The surface of the land was thrown
or washed up into dark-brown hillocks of broken
argillaceous schist, which repelled vegetation, but
the hollows were wooded with mountain oak and
many shrubs. Farther down there were other
hillocks, equally bare, but formed of the blue-look-
ing lias marl which the husbandman detests with
good reason, for its sterility is incorrigible. This
terre bleue, as the peasants call it, was not the only
sign of a change in the formation; fragments of
calcareous stone were mixed with the brown soil. I
was leaving the dark schist and was approaching
those immense accumulations of jurassic rock, whose
singular forms and brilliant colours lend such extraordinary grandeur to the scenery of the Upper Tarn.
There was also a change in the vegetation. A large
species of broom, four or five feet high, covered with
golden blossom the size of pea-flowers, although the
common broom had long passed its blooming, now
showed itself as well as roseroot sedum, neither of
which had I seen while coming over the schist.

The cicadas returned and screamed from every tree.
I captured one and examined the musical instrument—a truly marvellous bit of mechanism—that it carried in each of its sides. It is not legs which make the noise, as is the case with crickets and grasshoppers, but little hard membranes under the wings are scraped together at the creature's will. The sound is not musical, for when it is not a continuous scissor-grinding noise, it is like the cry of a corncrake with a weak throat; but what delight there is in it! and how it expresses that joy in the present and recklessness of the morrow, which the fabulist has in vain contrasted with the virtuous industry of the ant in order to point a moral for mankind!—vainly, because the *cigale's* short life in the sunlit trees will ever seem to men a more ideal one than that of the earth-burrowing ant, with its possible longevity, its peevish parsimony, and restless anxiety for the future. I could have lain down under a tree like a gipsy in this wild spot, and let the summer dreams come to me from their airy castles amongst the leaves, if I had not made up my mind to reach St. Affrique before night. There was another reason which, although it clashes with poetry, had better be told for the sake of truth. Insects would soon have taken all pleasure from the siesta. Great black ants and great red ones, little ants too, that could have walked with comfort through the eye of a fine needle, notwithstanding their wickedness, and intermediate species of the same much-praised family,

would have scampered over me and stung me, and flies of bad propensities would have settled upon me. An enthusiastic entomologist has only to lie down in the open air in this part of France at the end of July or in August, and he will soon be able to observe, perhaps feel, sufficient insects travelling on their legs or on the wing to satisfy a great deal of curiosity. Often the air is all aflutter with butterflies, many of them remarkable for their size or the beauty of their colouring. One I have particularly noticed; not large, but coloured with exquisite gradations of bright-yellow, orange, and pale-green.

I believe I added to my day's journey by my excursion across country, but the time would have passed less pleasantly on the road. The winding yellow line, however, appeared again, and I had to tramp upon it. And a hot, toilsome trudge it was, through that long narrow valley with scrubby woods reaching down to the road, but with no habitations and no water. It was the desert. The afternoon was far advanced when the country opened and I saw a village of coquettish appearance, for most of the houses had been washed with red, and many of the window-shutters were painted green.

I was parched with thirst, for the sun had been broiling me for hours; therefore, when I saw this village on the hillside, I hurried towards it with the impatience of a traveller who sees the palm-trees over a well in the sands of Africa. In a place that could give so much attention to colour there must surely be an auberge, I thought. And I judged rightly, for there were two little inns. I found the door of the first one closed, and learnt that the people were out harvesting. I walked on to the next, and found that likewise closed, and was again informed that all the family were out in the fields. The whole village was nearly deserted; almost everyone was busy reaping and putting up the sheaves. I stopped beside the village pump and reflected upon my misery. I had resigned myself to water, when a woman carrying a sickle opened the door of one of the inns. Some friendly bird must have told her of my thirst and weariness—perhaps the merry little quail that I heard as I came up from the plain crying 'To-whit! To-whit!' That blessed auberge actually contained bottled beer. And the room was so cool that butter would not have melted in it. These southern houses have such thick stone walls that they have the double advantage of being warm in winter and delightfully cool in summer. I had some difficulty in resisting the temptation to stop the night at this inn; but I did resist it, and was again on the road to St. Affrique before the heat of the day had passed.

Another toilsome trudge, during which I met an English threshing-machine being dragged along by bullocks, and the familiar words upon it made me feel for awhile quite at home. The apparition, however, gave me a shock, for the antique flail is still the instrument commonly used for threshing in the southern provinces of France.

At a village called Moulin, lying in a rich and beautiful valley, I met the Sorgues, one of the larger tributaries of the Tarn, and for the rest of my journey I had the companionship of a charming stream. Evening came on, and the fiery blue above me grew soft and rosy. Rosy, too, were the cornfields, where bands of men and women, fifteen or twenty together, were reaping gaily, for the heat of the day was gone, the freshness of the twilight had come, and the fragrance of the valley was loosened. I had left the last group of reapers behind, and the silence of the dusk was broken only by the tree crickets and the rapids of the little river, when a woman passed me on the road and murmured '*Adicias!*' (God be with you!). '*Adicias!*' I replied, and then I was again alone. Presently there was a jangling of bells behind, and I was soon overtaken by three horses and a crowded *diligence*. The sound of the bells grew fainter and fainter, and once more I was alone with the summer night. The stars began to shine, and the river was lost in the mystery of shadow, save where a sunken rock made the water gleam white, and broke the peace with a cry of trouble.

It was late when I reached St. Affrique, and I believe no tramp arrived at his bourne that night more weary than I, for I had been walking most of the day in the burning sun. But although I lay down like a jaded horse, I was too feverish to sleep. To make matters worse, there was a cock in the yard just underneath my window, and the fiendish creature considered it his duty to crow every two or three minutes after the stroke of midnight. How well did I then enter into the feelings of a man I knew who, under similar provocation, got up from his bed, and, taking a carving-knife from the kitchen, quietly and deftly cut off the cock's head before the astonished bird had time to protest. Having stopped the crowing and assured himself that it would not begin again, he went back to bed and slept the sleep of the innocent.

I was out early the next morning, looking at the extraordinary astronomical dials of the parish church, covering much of the surface of the outer walls. All the straight lines, curves, and figures, and the inscriptions in Latin, must have the effect of convincing the majority of the inhabitants that their ignorance is hopeless. Such a display of science must be like wizard symbolism to the common people. The dials are exceedingly curious, and there are some really astonishing calculations, as, for instance, a table showing the 'number of souls that have appeared before the Tribunal of God.' Near a great sundial are these solemn words : 'Sol et luna faciunt quae precepta sunt eis ; nos autem pergrimamur a Domino.' The church itself is one of the most fantastically ugly structures imaginable. All possible tricks of style and taste appear to have been played upon it. It is a jumble of heavy Gothic and Italian, and the apse is twisted out of line with the nave, in which respect, however, it is like the cathedral of Quimper. As I left the church a funeral procession approached, women carrying palls by the four corners a little in front of the coffin, according to the custom of the country when the dead person is of their own sex.

St. Affrique is a small town of about 7,000 inhabitants, lying in a warm valley and surrounded by high hills, the sides of which were once covered with luxuriant vineyards. These slopes, arid, barren, and sun-scorched, are perfectly suited to the cultivation of the vine, the fig, and the almond; but the elevation is still too great for the olive. According to the authors of 'Gallia Christiana,' a saint named Fricus, or Africus, came at the beginning of the sixth century into the valley of the Sorgues, and was the founder of the burg. St. Affrique was a strong place in the Middle Ages, and for this reason it was disturbed less by the English than some other towns in the Rouergue. After the treaty of Brétigny the consuls went to Millau and swore fealty to the King of England, represented there by John Chandos.

As I toiled up the side of the valley in the direction of Millau, I noticed the Rocher de Caylus, a large reddish and somewhat fantastically shaped block of oolitic rock, perched on the hill above the vineyards. Here the lower formation was schistous, the upper calcareous. The sun was intensely hot, but there was the shade of walnut-trees, of which I took advantage, although it is said to be poisonous, like that of the oleander.

When I reached the plateau there was no shade whatever, baneful or beneficent. If there was ever any forest here all vestige of it has disappeared. I was on the border of the Causse de Larzac, one of the highest, most extensive, and hopelessly barren of the calcareous deserts which separate the rivers in this part of France. Not a drop of water, save what may have been collected in tanks for the use of sheep, and the few human beings who eke out an existence there, is to be found upon them. Swept by freezing winds in winter and burnt by a torrid sun in summer, their climate is as harsh as the soil is ungenerous.

But although I was sun-broiled upon this *causse*, I was interested at every step by the flowers that I found there. Dry, chaffy, or prickly plants, corresponding in their nature to the aridity and asperity of the land, were peculiarly at home upon the undulating stoniness. The most beautiful flower then blooming was the catananche, which has won its poetic French name, *Cupidon bleu*, by the brilliant colour of its blossom. Multitudes of yellow everlastings also decked the solitude.

On reaching the highest ground the crests of the bare Cevennes were seen against the cloudless sky to the south. A little to the east, beyond the valley of the Cernon, which I intended to cross, were high hills or cliffs, treeless and sterile, with hard-cut angular sides, terminating upwards in vertical walls of naked stone. These were the buttresses of the Causse de Larzac. The lower sides of some of the hills were blue with lias marl, and wherever they were steep not a blade of grass grew.

Having descended to the valley, I was soon climbing towards Roquefort by the flanks of those melancholy hills which seemed to express the hopelessness of nature after ages of effort to overcome some evil power. And yet the tinkling of innumerable sheep-bells told that even here men had found a way of earning their bread. I saw the flocks moving high above me where all was wastefulness and rockiness, and heard the voices of the shepherds. There were the Roquefort sheep whose milk, converted into cheese of the first quality, is sent into distant countries whose people little imagine that its constituents are drawn from a desert where there is little else but stones.

I came in view of the village, clinging as it seemed to the steep at the base of a huge bastion of stark jurassic rock. Facing it was another barren hill, and in the valley beneath were mamelons of dark clay and stones partly conquered by the great broom and burning with its flame of gold. When I reached the village I felt that I had earned a rest.

Cheese, which has been the fortune of Roquefort, has destroyed its picturesqueness. It has brought speculators there who have raised great ugly square buildings of dazzling whiteness, in harsh contrast with the character and sombre tone of the old houses. Although the place is so small that it consists of only one street and a few alleys, the more ancient dwellings are remarkable for their height. It is surprising to see in a village lost among the sterile hills houses three stories high. The fact that there is only a ledge on which to build must be the explanation. What is most curious in the place is the cellars. Before the cheese became an important article of commerce these were natural caverns, such as are everywhere to be found in this calcareous formation, but now they are really cellars which have been excavated to such a depth in the rock that they are to be seen in as many as five stages, where long rows of cheeses are stacked one over the other. The virtue of these cellars from the cheese-making point of view is their dryness and their scarcely varying temperature of about 8° Centigrade summer and winter. But the demand for Roquefort cheese has become so great that trickery now plays a part in the ripening process. The peasants have learnt that 'time is money,' and they have found that bread-crumbs mixed with the curd cause those green streaks of mouldiness, which denote that the cheese is fit for the market, to appear much more readily than was formerly the case when it was left to do the best it could for itself with the aid of a subterranean atmosphere. This is not exactly cheating; it is commercial enterprise, the result of competition and other circumstances too strong for poor human nature. In cheese-making, breadcrumbs are found to be a cheap substitute for time, and it is said that those who have taken to beer-brewing in this region have found that box, which here is the commonest of shrubs, is a cheap substitute for hops. The notion that brass pins are stuck into Roquefort cheese to make it turn green is founded on fiction.

Having remained at Roquefort long enough to see all that was needful, to lunch and to be overcharged—commercial enterprise is very infectious—I turned my back upon it and scrambled down a stony path to the bottom of the valley where the Cernon—now a mere thread of a stream—curled and sparkled in the middle of its wide channel, the yellow flowers and pale-green leaves of the horned poppy basking upon the rocky banks. Following it down to the Tarn, I came to the village of St. Rome de Cernon, where the houses of dark-gray stone, built on a hillside, are overtopped by the round tower of a small mediæval fortress which has been patched up and put to some modern use. I thought the people very ill-favoured by nature here, but perhaps they are not more so than others in the district. The harshness of nature is strongly reflected in all faces. Having passed a man on the bank of the stream washing his linen—presumably his own—with bare arms, sinewy and hairy like a gorilla's, I was again in the open country; but instead of following donkey-paths and sheep-tracks

I was upon the dusty highroad. Well, even a *route nationale*, however hot and dusty, so that it be not too straight, has its advantages, which are felt after you have been walking an uncertain number of miles over a very rough country, trusting to luck to lead you where you wished to go. The feeling that you may at length step out freely and not worry yourself with a map and compass is a kind of pleasure which, like all others, is only so by the force of contrast and the charm of variety. I knew that I could now tramp along this road without troubling myself about anything, and that I should reach Millau sooner or later. It was really very hot—ideal sunstroke weather, verging on 90° in the shade: but I had become hardened to it, and was as dry as a smoked herring. For miles I saw no human being and heard no sound of life except the shrilling of grasshoppers and the more strident song of the cicadas in the trees. By-and-by houses showed themselves, and I came to the village of St. Georges beside the bright little Cernon, but surrounded by wasteful, desolate hills, one of which, shaped like a cone, reared its yellow rocky summit far towards the blue solitude of the dazzling sky. I passed by little gardens where great hollyhocks flamed in the afternoon sunshine, then I met the Tarn again and reached Millau, a weary and dusty wayfarer.

I stopped in Millau (sometimes spelt Milhau) more than a day, in order to rest and to ramble—moderately. Although the town, with its 16,000 inhabitants, is the most populous in the department of the Aveyron, it is so remote from all large centres and currents of human movement that very little French is spoken there. And this French is about on a par with the English of the Sheffield grinders. In the better-class families an effort now is made to keep *patois* out-of-doors for the sake of the children; but there is scarcely a middle-aged native to whom it is not the mother-tongue. The common dialect is not quite the same throughout Guyenne and Languedoc; but the local variations are much less marked than one would expect, considering that the *langue d'oc* has been virtually abandoned as a literary vehicle for centuries. The word *oc* (yes), which was once the most convenient sound to distinguish the dialect from that of the northern half of France, is not easy to recognise nowadays in the conversation of the people. The *c* in the word is not pronounced—perhaps it never was—and the *o* is usually joined to *bè*, which has the same meaning as *bien* in the French language. Thus we have the forms *obè*, *opè*, and *apè* according to the district, and all equivalent to 'yes.' All these people can understand Spanish when spoken slowly. Many can catch your meaning when you speak to them in French, but reply in *patois*. I had grown accustomed, although not reconciled, to this manner of conversing with peasants; but I was surprised to find on entering a shop at Millau that neither the man nor his wife there could reply to me in French.

This town lies in the bottom of a basin; some of the high hills, especially those on the east, showing savage escarpments with towering masses of yellow or reddish rock at the summits. The climate of the valley is delightful in winter, but sultry and enervating in summer. It is so protected from the winds that the mulberry flourishes there, and countless almond-trees rise above the vines on the burning hillsides.

Millau presents a good deal of interest to the archæologist. Very noteworthy is the ancient market-place, where the first and upper stories project far over the paving and are supported by a colonnade. Some of the columns, with elaborately carved Romanesque capitals, date from the twelfth century, and look ready to fall into fragments. At one end of the square is an immense modern crucifix — a sure sign that the civic authorities do not yet share the views of the municipal councillors of Paris in regard to religious emblems. Protestants, however, are numerous at Millau as well as at St. Affrique, both towns having been important centres of Calvinism at the time of the Revocation of the Edict of Nantes; and after the forced emigration many of the inhabitants must have strongly sympathized with their persecuted neighbours, the Camisards. Nevertheless, the department of the Aveyron, taken in its entirety, is now one of the most fervently Catholic in France.

The church is Romanesque, with a marked Byzantine tendency. It has an elegant apse, decorated in good taste ; but the edifice having received various patchings and decorations at the time of the Renaissance, the uniformity of style has been spoilt. The most striking architectural feature of the town is a high Gothic belfry of octagonal form, with a massive square tower for its base.

In the Middle Ages the government of this town was vested in six consuls, who received twenty gold florins a year as salary, and also a new robe of red and black cloth with a hood. In 1341 they furnished forty men-at-arms for the war against the English, but the place was given up to Chandos in 1362. The rising of 1369 delivered the burghers again from the British power, but for twenty-two years they were continually fighting with the English companies.

The evening before I left Millau I strolled into the little square where the great crucifix stands. I found it densely crowded. Three or four hundred men were there, each wearing a blouse and carrying a sickle with a bit of osier laid upon the sharp edge of the blade along its whole length, and firmly tied. All these harvesters were waiting to be hired for the following week. They belonged to a class much less numerous in France than in England—the agricultural labourers who have no direct interest in the soil that they help to cultivate and the crops that they help to gather in. I have often met them on the dusty roads, frequently walking with bare feet, carrying the implements of their husbandry and a little bundle of clothes. It must be very hard to ask for work from farm to farm. I can enter fully into the attachment of the French peasant to his bit of land, which, although it may yield him little more than his black bread, cannot be taken from him so long as he can manage to live by the sweat of his brow. Many of these peasant proprietors can barely keep body and soul together; but when they lie down upon their wretched beds at night, they feel thankful that the roof that covers them and the soil that supports them are their own. The wind may howl about the eaves, and the snow may drift against the wall, but they know that the one will calm down, and that the other will melt, and that life will go on as before—hard, back-breaking, grudging even the dark bread, but secure and independent. Waiting to be hired by another man, almost like a beast of burden—what a trial is here for pride! Happily for the human race, pride, although it springs naturally in the breast of man, only becomes luxuriant with cultivation. The poor labourer does not feel it unless his instinctive sense of justice has been outraged.

THE BLACK CAUSSE.

ONE cannot be sure of the weather even in the South of France, where the skies are supposed, by those who do not know them, to be perpetually blue. The 'South of France' itself is a very deceptive term. The climate on one side of a range of mountains or high hills may be altogether different from that on the other. In Upper Languedoc and Guyenne the climate is regulated by three principal factors: the elevation of the soil, the influence of the Mediterranean, and the influence of the Atlantic. On the northern side of the Cevennes, the currents from the ocean, together with the altitude, do much to keep the air moist and comparatively cool in summer; whereas on the other side of the chain, where the Mediterranean influence—in a large measure African—is paramount, the climate is dry and torrid during the hot months. A liability to sudden changes goes with the advantages of the more favoured region. This was enforced upon me at Millau.

At seven o'clock the sky, lately of such a fiery blue, was of a most mournful smokiness, and the rain fell in a drenching spray. It was mountain weather, and I blamed the Cevennes for it. But I was in the South, and at a season when bad weather is seldom in earnest, so I did not despair of a change when the sun rose higher. It came, in fact, at about eight o'clock, when, a breeze springing up, the clouds, after a short struggle, were swept away. The market-women spread out upon the pavement their tomatoes, their purple *aubergines*, their peaches, and green almonds; the harvesters, long hesitating, went out into the fields to reap; and I, leaving the Tarn, took my way up the valley of the gleaming Dourbie. Millau was soon nearly hidden in its basin, but above it, on the sides of the surrounding hills, scattered amongst the sickly vines, or the vigorous young plants which promised in a few years to make the stony soil flow once more with purple juice, were the small white houses of the wine-growers. Where I could, I walked in the shade of walnut and mulberry trees, for the heat was great, and the rain that had fallen rose like steam in the sun-blaze from the herbage and the golden stubble. In this low valley all corn except maize had been gathered in, and Nature was resting, after her labour, with the smile of maternity on her face. Nevertheless, this stillness of the summer's fulfilment, this pause in the energy of production, is saddening to the wayfarer, to whom the vernal splendour of the year and the time of blossoming seem like the gifts of yesterday. The

serenity of the burnished plains now prompts him
upward, where he hopes to overtake the tarrying
spring upon the cool and grassy mountains. Although the mountains towards which I was now
bearing were the melancholy and arid Cevennes,
I wished the distance less that lay between me and
their barren flanks, where the breeze would be
scented with the bloom of lavender. There were
flowers along the wayside here, but they were the
same that I had been seeing for many a league,
and they reminded me too forcibly of the rapid
flight of the summer days by their haste—their
unnecessary haste, as I thought—in passing from the
flower to the seed. A sprig of lithosperm stood
like a little tree laden with Dead Sea fruit, for the
naked seeds clung hard and flinty where the flowers
had been. The glaucium, although still blooming,
had put forth horns nine inches long, and the wild
barley, so lately green, was now a brown fringe
along the dusty road. And thus all these familiar
forms of vegetable life, which we notice in our
wanderings, but never understand, come and go,
perish and rise again—so quickly, too, that we have
no time to listen to what they say; we only feel
that the song which they sing along the waysides of
the world is ever joyous and ever sad.

In the lower part of this valley were scattered
farmhouses, which looked like small rural churches,
for their high rectangular dovecots at one end had
much the air of towers with broach spires. Through-

out Guyenne one is amazed at the apparently extravagant scale on which accommodation has been provided for pigeon-rearing. There are plenty of pigeons in the country, but the size of their houses is usually out of all proportion to the number of lodgers, and dovecots without tenants are almost as frequently seen as those that are tenanted. They are seldom of modern construction; many are centuries old. All this points to the conclusion that people of former times laid much greater store by pigeon-flesh than their descendants do. It may have been that other animal food was relatively more expensive than at the present day.

But as I ascended the valley the breadth of cultivated land grew narrower, and the habitations fewer. On either side the cliffs rose higher, and the walls of jurassic rock, above the brashy steeps, more towering, precipitous, and fantastic. Where vegetable life could draw sustenance from crumbling stones stretched a veritable forest of box. Now, in a narrow gorge, the Dourbie frolicked about the heaps of pebbles it had thrown up in its winter fury. Strong wires, attached to high rocks, crossed the gorge and the stream, and were made fast to the side of the road. Bundles of newly-cut box at the lower end showed the use to which these wires were put. Far aloft upon the heated rocks women were cutting down the tough shrub for firewood or manure, for it is put to both uses. It serves a very useful purpose when buried in dense layers between the vine rows. When I looked aloft, and saw those petticoated beings toiling in the terrible heat, I thought it a pity that there was no society to protect women as well as horses from being cruelly overworked. Let social reformers ponder this truth: The more the man is encouraged to shirk work, the more the woman will have to toil to make up for wasted time. As it is, women everywhere, except perhaps in England, work harder than men, as far as I can speak from observation.

I was on my way to Vieux Montpellier—the 'Devil's City'—and already the scenery began to take the character to be expected of it in such a neighbourhood. It seemed as though the demon builder of the fantastic town, sporting with man's architectural ideals before his appearance on the earth, had hewn the red and yellow rocks above the Dourbie into the ironic semblance of feudal towers and heaven-pointing spires.

The highest limestone rocks in this region, those which rise from the plateau or *causse* and strike the imagination by the strangeness of their forms, are dolomite: in the gorges they approach the character of lias towards the base, and not unfrequently contain lumps of pure silex embedded in their mass. The redness which they so often show, and which, alternating with yellow, white, or gray, adds to the grandeur of their rugged outlines, is due to the iron which the rock contains.

A young gipsy-woman, carrying a child upon her shoulders, and holding on to a dusky little leg on each side of her neck, followed in the wake of an old caravan drawn by a mule of resigned countenance—a beast that seemed to have made a vow never to hurry again, and to let the flies do their worst. She vanished upon the winding road, and presently I saw another wayfarer seated on the bank beside the stream, binding up a bleeding foot under the trailing traveller's joy. Before reaching the village of La Roque-Sainte-Marguerite, I passed a genuine rock dwelling. A natural cavern, some twenty or thirty feet above the level of the road, had been walled up to make a house. It had its door and windows like any other dwelling, and some convenient crevice in the rock had probably been used for a chimney.

Having taken an hour's rest and a light meal in the village, I commenced the ascent towards the 'Devil's City.' A mule-path wound up the steep side of the gorge, which had been partly reclaimed from the desert by means of terraces where many almond-trees flourished, safe from the north wind. Very scanty, however, was the vegetation that grew upon this dry stony soil, burning in summer, and washed in winter of its organic matter by the mountain rains. Tall woody spurges two feet high or more, with tufts of dusty green leaves, managed to draw, however, abundant moisture from the waste, as the milk that gushed from the smallest wound

attested. An everlasting pea, with very large
flowers of a deep rose-colour, also loved this arid
steep. I was wondering why I found no lavender,
when I saw a gray-blue tuft above me, and welcomed
it like an old friend. The air was soon scented with
the plant, and for five days I was in the land of
lavender. On nearing the buttresses of the plateau
the ground was less steep, and here I came to pines,
junipers, oaks, and the bird-cherry prunus. But the
tree which I was most pleased to find was a plum,
with ripe fruit about the size of a small greengage,
but of a beautiful pale rose-colour.

I am now upon the *causse* and already see the
castellated outworks of the 'Devil's City.' The city
itself lies in a hollow, and I have not yet reached it.
The mule-path fortunately leads in the right direction. On my way multitudes of very dark, almost
black, butterflies flutter up from the short turf, which
is flecked with the gold of yellow everlastings.
Here and there a solitary round-headed allium nods
from the top of its long leafless stem. I walk over
the shining dark leaves and the scarlet beads of the
bearberry, and am presently roaming in the fantastic
streets of the dolomitic city. To say streets is
scarcely an exaggeration, for these jutting rocks
have in places almost the regularity of the menhirs
of Carnac. But the megalithic monuments of
Brittany are like arrow-heads compared to the
stones of Montpellier-le-Vieux. In placing these
and in giving them that mimicry of familiar forms at

times so startling to human eyes, Nature has been
the sole engineer and artist. There is but one
theory by which the working cause of the existing
phenomena can be brought to our understanding.
It is that these honeycombed and fantastically-
shaped masses of dolomite or magnesian limestone
represent the skeletons of vaster rocks whose less
resisting parts were washed away by the wearing
action of the sea. Some are formed of blocks of
varying size, lying one upon another, with a pinnacle
or dome at the summit; others show no trace of
stratification, but are integral rocks which in many
cases appear to have been cut away and fashioned
to the mocking likeness of some animal form by a
demon statuary. Now it is a colossal owl, now a
frightful head that may be human or devilish, now
some inanimate shape such as a prodigious wine-
glass which fixes the eye and excites the fancy. A
mass of rock on which can be seen half sitting,
half reclining, a monstrous stony shape with head
hideously jovial, has been named the 'Devil's Chair.'

I saw this spot under circumstances very favourable to the full reception of its fantastic, mysterious,
and gloomy influence. It was late enough in the
afternoon for the feeling of evening and of the coming
night to be in the air, especially here, where dark
pines stood in the mimic streets and squares like
cypresses in a cemetery. The awful mournfulness
of the shadowy groves was deepened by my own
solitariness, for although surrounded by frightful

shapes that caricatured humanity, mine was the only human form that moved amongst the dumb but fiend-like rocks and the pines, which moaned and whispered like unhappy ghosts. I was alone in the 'Devil's City,' and perchance with the devil himself. When a hawk flew over and screamed it was welcome, although there was nothing cheerful in its cry. There could be no severer trial perhaps to the nerves of a superstitious person than to take a solitary walk by moonlight through Montpellier-le-Vieux. The sense of the weird and the horrible would give him too many cold shudders for him to enjoy the grandeur and the strangeness of the scene.

The superstitious horror in which this spot has always been held by the peasants—chiefly shepherds —of the district, together with the fact that the rustic, uninfluenced from without, never speaks of rocks except in terms of contempt, however extraordinary their forms may be, must be the reason why Montpellier-le-Vieux has only been known of late years to persons interested in such curiosities of nature. To the geologist it is fascinating ground, as, indeed, is the whole expanse of these *causses* of Guyenne and Upper Languedoc, so fissured and honeycombed—a region of gorges and caverns, of subterranean lakes and rivers, of bottomless pits and mysterious streams.

It is said that the dolomitic city owes its name, Montpellier-le-Vieux, to the shepherds of Lower

Languedoc, who from time immemorial have brought their flocks in summer to pasture upon these highlands. In their dialect they call Montpellier, which is to them what Paris is to the peasants of the Brie, 'Lou Clapas'—literally, a heap of stones. On seeing rocks covering several acres, and looking like the ruins of a great city of the past, they could think of no better name for it than 'Lou Clapas Biel,' or 'old heap of stones.' This turned into French becomes Montpellier-le-Vieux.

The 'Devil's City' can be recommended to the botanist, who need not fear that the flowers he will find there will wither at his touch like those gathered for Marguerite by her guileless lover. The ever-crumbling dolomite has formed a soil very favourable to a varied flora. As I had, however, to reach the gorge of the Tarn before nightfall, and it was still far off, I only took away two souvenirs of the diabolic garden—a white scabious and a bit of rock-potentil.

The name given to the tract of country I was now crossing—the Causse Noir, fitly describes it. It is singularly dark and mournful, and almost uninhabited. It is not, strictly speaking, a plateau, but a succession of valleys and low hills like the bed of the ocean. The barren land is thickly overgrown with box and juniper, and these shrubs, which often attain a height of six or eight feet, sufficiently account for the sombre tone of the landscape. Here and there savage little gorges run up between the dismal hills, with trees of larger growth, such as oaks and pines, in the hollows. There is good reason to believe that all these *causses* were at one time more or less covered by forests; but the reason commonly given for their disappearance—namely, that they were burnt down during the religious wars—is less likely to be the true one than that they gradually perished because it was nobody's business to protect the seedlings from sheep and goats— animals capable of changing the world into a treeless desert, but which, fortunately, cease to be profitable when they come down from the sterile highlands, where they thrive best, into the rich plains and valleys. The disastrous floods which occur with such appalling suddenness in the valleys of the Tarn and the Lot are due in a large measure to the nudity of the *causses* and the Cevennes, where these mountains turn northward and cross the Lozère to meet the Auvergne range. The French Government nurses the hope that it will be able some day to cover much of the baldness of this extensive region with magnificent pine-forests, and planting actually goes on in places; but what with the nibbling flocks, and the increasing severity of the winters, the measure of success already obtained by such laudable efforts is not encouraging.

I wished to reach Peyreleau that night, but how to get there I knew not otherwise than by persistently keeping in a north-easterly course, and despising all natural obstacles. I was attracted by what looked like a road running up between two hills in the right direction; but when I came to it I found that it was the dry channel of a stream. I nevertheless took advantage of it, as I have of many another such in the South, although there are few watercourses whose beds can be walked upon with comfort. I was lucky now beyond my expectations, for it was not long before I struck a road which I was sure could lead nowhere but to Peyreleau. It first took me through a darkly-wooded gorge, where evening stood like a nun in a chapel. The brilliant sky had changed to a sad gray. There was to be no gorgeous sunset, with rosy after-glow, softening with transparent colour the harshness of the dark box and darker juniper. No: the day that commenced sadly was ending sadly—going to its grave in a gray habit with drawn cowl. A great falcon passed slowly on its way under the dull sky, but no bird nor beast uttered a sound. The Causse Noir was as silent as a crypt.

I became very uncertain where this road over the dismal solitude was going to lead me, for it turned about in such a way as to put me out of my reckoning. At length I saw a deep gorge yawning below, and this told me that I had reached the edge of the *causse*. Oh, the sublime desolation of these heights and depths in the solemn evening! How mournful then is the silence of the innumerable gray stones and monstrous rocks which try to speak to us like creatures once eloquent and possessing the knowledge of wondrous changes, and the key to problems that everlastingly distress the human mind, but on which the curse of dumbness has lain for ages!

I thought that I must have wandered beyond the peopled world, when suddenly I saw, far down in the bottom of the widening valley, a village or small town at the foot of a cone-shaped hill. The little river running near satisfied me that I was in view of Peyreleau. The descent was tedious and long, notwithstanding the loops that I cut off of the curling road by scrambling down the steep sides of the gorge over the loose stones and lavender. It was still daylight when I reached a small hotel, outside of which some tourists were smoking cigarettes and drinking beer while waiting for dinner. Until then I had not seen a tourist after leaving Albi. All through the Albigeois and the Rouergue, I was looked upon as an animal of unknown species, and possibly noxious; but here I was recognised at once as one of a familiar tribe, of small brain development, but harmless. I had entered a region which for several years past had drawn to it many persons—mostly French—who had heard of the grand gorge, or cañon, of the Tarn.

I had been told that the right way—the one followed by all sensible people—of seeing the gorge from Sainte-Énimie to Le Rozier was to come down the stream in a boat; but circumstances, or my own perversity, had led me once more to do the thing that was considered wrong. Instead of coming down the swift stream like a fly on a leaf, my intention was to crawl up the gorge by such goat or mule paths as were available on the margin of the river or on the ledges of the cliffs. Thus I should not be obliged to treat every fresh view as if it were a bird on the wing, but could dawdle as long as I pleased over this or that object without being a trouble to anybody.

It was far from unpleasant, however, to spend an evening at this water-side inn with people fresh from Paris, bringing with them the spray of the sea that beats against the shores of high-strung life. Nor was it unpleasant to find a little refinement in the kitchen again, and to eat trout not saturated with the essence of garlic.

THE CAÑON OF THE TARN.

At an early hour next morning I was making my way up the gorge beside the Tarn; but before leaving Peyreleau, I wandered about its steep streets—in some places a series of steps cut in the rock—noted Gothic doorways, and houses with interior vaulting, and climbed to the top of a machicolated tower built over the ivy-draped wall of a ruined castle. The place is very charming to the eye; but in this region one soon becomes a spoilt child of the picturesque, and the mind, fatigued by admiration, loses something of its sensibility to the impressions of beauty and grandeur, and is capable of passing by almost unmoved what, where Nature deals out her surprises with a calmer hand, might engrave upon the memory images of lasting delight. This is the chief reason, perhaps, why I hate the hurry of the sightseer who, even in his pleasure, makes himself the bondman of time and the creature of convention.

It was pleasant and easy walking on the bank of the river, for as yet the cliffs were far apart, and in the valley there were strips of meadow and flowering buckwheat. The water, where it was not broken into white anger by the rocky channel, was intensely green with the reflection of poplar and alder, although of crystal clearness. I watched the large trout swimming in the pools, and wished I had a rod, but consoled myself with the thought that if I had brought one I should probably have not seen a fish. Opportunities are never so ready to show themselves as when we have not the means of seizing them. While I was looking at the river, a boat shot into view round a bend of the gorge and came down like an arrow over the rapids. It contained a small party of tourists and two boatmen, who stood in the flat-bottomed craft with poles in their hands, with which they kept it clear of the rocks. I understood at once the delicious excitement of coming down the Tarn in this fashion. Bucketfuls of water are often shipped where the stream rushes furiously between walls of rock; but the men have become so expert with practice that the risk of being capsized is very slight. In a few minutes the boat had vanished, and then the gorge became wilder and sterner; but just as I thought the sentiment of desolation perfect, a little goatherd, who had climbed high up the rocks somewhere with his equally sure-footed companions, began to sing, not a pastoral ditty in the Southern dialect, but the 'Marseillaise,' thus recalling with shocking incongruity impressions of screaming barrel-organs at the fête of St. Cloud.

The gorge narrowed and the rocks rose higher,

the topmost crags being 1,000 or 1,200 feet above the water. Although everything here was on a grander scale, all the strong peculiarities of formation which I had remarked elsewhere in Guyenne and Languedoc, wherever the layers of jurassic rock have split asunder and produced gorges more or less profound, were repeated in this cañon of the Tarn.

Competent geologists, however, have noted a distinctive difference, namely: that, of all the rivers running in the fissures of the *causses*, the Tarn is the only one whose water does not penetrate to the beds of marl beneath the lias; and this is said to partly explain the great height and verticality of the cliffs, for when the water reaches the marl it saps the foundations of the rocks, and these, subsiding, send their dislocated masses rolling to the bottom of the gorge.

I overtook a man and two boys who were hauling and pushing a boat up-stream. The man was wading in the water with a towing-rope over his shoulder, and the boys were in the punt plying their boat-hooks against the rocks and the bed of the river. They made very slow headway on account of the strength and frequency of the rapids. In coming down the Tarn, all that the boatman has to do is to use his *gaffe* so as to keep clear of the rocks; but the return-journey is by no means so pleasant and exciting.

I passed a little cluster of hovels built against the

rock, and here a kind woman offered me some sheep's milk, which I declined for no better reason than because it was sheep's.

Towards mid-day I reached the village of Les Vignes, which takes its name from the vineyards which have long been cultivated here, where the gorge widens somewhat, and offers opportunities to husbandry. The great cliffs protect vegetation and human life from the mountain climate which prevails upon the dismal Causse Méjan and the Causse de Sauveterre, separated by the deep fissure. Until tourists came to the Tarn, Les Vignes was quite cut off from the world, but now it is a halting-place for the boatmen and their passengers ; and a little auberge, while retaining all its rustic charm, provides the traveller with a good meal at a fair price. The rush of strangers during the summer has not yet been sufficient to spoil the river-side people between Sainte-Enimie and Peyreleau by fostering that spirit of speculation which, when it takes hold of an innkeeper, almost fatally classifies him with predatory animals.

On reaching the auberge I walked straight into the kitchen as usual. A fowl and a leg of mutton were turning on the spit, and the hostess was very busy with stewpans and other utensils on various parts of her broad hearth. I soon learnt that a party of several persons had arrived before me, and that all these preparations were for them. My application for a meal was not met with a refusal, but it was evident that I should have to wait until others were served, and that, they having bespoken the best of everything in the house, my position was not as satisfactory as could be desired. I suppose I must have looked rather sad, for one of the party who had so swooped down upon the little inn and all its resources suggested that I should take my meal at their table. I should have accepted this offer with more hesitation had I known that they had brought with them the *pièce de résistance*, the leg of mutton, nearly as large as an English one, that was browning upon the spit before the blazing wood. After thinking myself unlucky, it turned out that I was in luck's way.

I was presently seated at a long table with about a dozen others of both sexes, all relatives or old friends. They belonged to the small town of Severac, and had driven in two queer countrified vehicles about fifteen miles in order to spend a happy day at Les Vignes. They were terribly noisy, but boundlessly good-natured. Not only was I made to share their leg of mutton, but also the champagne which they had brought with them. The modest lunch that I had expected became a veritable feast, and having been entangled in the convivial meshes, I had to stay until the end of it all. The experience was worth something as a study of provincial life and manners. These people —husbands and wives and friends—had come out with the determination to enjoy themselves, and their enjoyment was not merely hearty; it was hurricane-like. There were moments when pieces of bread and green almonds were flying across the table, and the noise of voices was so terrific that the quiet hostess looked in at the door with a scared expression which made me think she was wondering how much longer the roof would be able to remain in its right place. Then, the jokes that were exchanged over the table were as broad as the humour of the South is broad. I felt sorry for the women, but quite unnecessarily. Although the local colour was not refined, human nature present was frank, hospitable, and irresistibly warm-hearted. The vulgarity of the party was of the unselfish sort, and therefore amusing. The enjoyment of each was the enjoyment of all; and even when the tempest of humour was at its height, not a word was said that was intended to be offensive. As a compliment to me, they all rose to their feet, glasses in hand, and the hostess was again startled by a mighty rush of sound repeating the words 'Vive l'Angleterre!' far up and down the valley.

Instead of going on to La Malène that afternoon, as I had intended, I went after crayfish with one of the members of this jovial party, who had brought with him the necessary tackle for the sport. There are various ways of catching crayfish; but in this district the favourite method is the following: Small wire hoops, about a foot in diameter, are covered with netting strained nearly tight, and to this pieces of liver or other meat are tied. A cord a few yards long, fastened to the centre of the netting, completes the tackle. The baited snare is thrown into the stream, not far from the bank, and generally where the bottom is strewn with stones. No more art is needed. The crayfish, supposing them to be in the humour to eat, soon smell the meat or divine its presence, and, coming forth from their lairs beneath the stones, make towards the lure with greedy alacrity. Their movements can be generally watched, for although they are not delicate feeders, they are as difficult as Chinamen to please in the matter of water, and are only to be found in very clear streams. As is the case with their congeners—the sea crayfish and the crab—greediness renders them stupid, and, rather than leave a piece of meat which is to their taste, they will allow themselves to be pulled with it out of the water. It sometimes happens that the netting is covered with these creatures in a few minutes, and that all the trouble the fisherman has is to haul them up. But they are capricious, and, notwithstanding their voracity, there are times when they will not leave their holes upon any consideration. Such was their humour to-day. The cause of their sullenness was said to be a wind that rippled the surface of the water; but, whatever the reason, not a crayfish did we catch.

The breeze which was supposed to have upset the temper of the crustaceous multitude in the

Tarn blew up bad weather before night. The panic-stricken leaves upon the alders and poplars announced the change with palsied movements and plaintive cries; the willows whitened, and bent towards the stream; and muttered threats of the strife-breeding spirits in nature seemed to issue from caverns half hidden by sombre foliage. As the gorge darkened, the gusts grew stronger, and the moaning rose at times to a shriek. Now the thunder groaned, the lightning flashed, and the face of the river gleamed. I returned to the inn just as the hissing rain began to fall. I was by this time alone, for the party from Severac had left at the approach of the storm.

As I took my solitary evening meal in a low building cut off from the inn, composed of a large *salle-à-manger*—the same in which the feast was held—and a bedroom, where I was to pass the rest of the night, I could not help contrasting the exuberant joviality of the morning with the absolute want of it now. The place seemed much too big for me; I had rather it had been half as large, to have got rid of half the shadow. Instead of the tempestuous laughter, there was the thunder's roar. There was also the lightning's flash to drive the shadows out of the corners from time to time. It was a wild and awful night.

I was busily building around me a vaporous rampart of tobacco-smoke, as a barrier to gloomy suggestions from without, when the door suddenly opened, and in walked two gendarmes—one a very self-important-looking brigadier, with thin sharp nose and keen, weasel-like eyes. My immediate impression was that they had come to question me respecting my intentions—inasmuch as I was not going to work in the same way as other tourists—and possibly to ask me for my papers; but I was mistaken. They had merely taken shelter from the rain, and they had not found a refuge too soon, for their appearance was that of half-drowned rats. The brigadier called for a bottle of beer, and while he and his younger companion were drinking it I learnt from their conversation what business had taken them out of doors that night. Their object was to surprise the fish-poachers at the illegal, but very exciting and picturesque, sport of spearing by torchlight. Now, as I had already seen these night-poachers at work on the Tarn, I may as well describe their method here.

I was walking one dark night on the bank of the river near Ambialet, when a glare of lurid light suddenly shot up from the water some distance in front of me, illuminating the willows, and even the black woods, on each side of the gorge. I imagined myself at once in a Canadian forest, near an Indian camp-fire. The light came gliding in my direction, and presently I distinguished the forms of men in a boat, all lit up by the glare. One was punting; another was holding aloft, not a torch, but blazing brushwood which I afterwards learnt was broom—

that he replenished from a heap in the boat; and a third was in the stern, gazing intently at the water, and holding in his hand a staff, which he plunged from time to time to the bottom of the stream. I understood that this was the *pêche au flambeau*, of which I had already heard.

The Tarn being in summer shallow, and of crystal clearness except in time of flood, it offers every facility for this kind of fishing. The flat-bottomed boat glides along with the current; the fish, dazzled by the sudden light, sink at once to the bottom, and lie there stupefied until they are either speared or the cause of their bewilderment passes on. The spear-head used is a small trident. When the moon is up, the fish are not to be fascinated by artificial light; consequently the darkest nights are chosen for this kind of poaching.

The two gendarmes, then, had been looking for poachers, and, not liking the weather, they had been unable to resist the auberge light that beckoned them indoors. While they were talking, in walked the most hardened and skilful poacher of the place, whose acquaintance I had made earlier in the day, and who made no secret to me of his business. So far from being abashed by the presence of the gendarmes, he gave them a genial salutation, and, sitting down beside them, talked to them as if he had been on the pleasantest terms with them for years. He was a man of about fifty, who boasted to me that he had been a poacher from the age of fifteen, and had never been caught. He therefore an artful old fox, and one very difficult to run down. He made the most of his opportunities in all seasons, and laughed at those who troubled their heads about the months which were open or closed. His coolness in the presence of the gendarmes was charming. He actually offered to furnish the brigadier with a dish of trout at any time on a day's notice, and argued that they had no right to seize a net wherever found, because the meshes were not of the lawful size. 'If you doubt it,' said the brigadier, 'just show me yours.' Then he added with a grin: 'I shall pinch you some day, *mon vieux.*' The other did not seem to believe it, and I am inclined to think that no one will 'pinch' him but Death.

Of the few really attractive callings left, that of the poacher must be given a prominent place, especially in France, where the law is not too severe upon a man who tries to make an honest living by breaking the law so far as it relates to fish and game. The excitement of catching wild creatures must be greatly increased by the risk that the hunter or fisher runs of being caught himself. A poacher is by no means looked down upon in France. He is considered a useful member of society, especially by hotel-keepers. I know a very respectable beadle of a singularly pious parish who is an inveterate poacher. On week-days he is slinking about the woods and rocks with his gun, and has generally a hare or a partridge in his bag; but on Sundays he wears a cocked hat, a gold-laced coat with a sword at his side, and he brings down his staff upon the church pavement with a thundering crack at those moments when the wool-gathering mind has to be hurried back and fixed upon the sacredness of the ritual. He is a well-knit, agile fellow, who knows every inch of his ground, and he has led the gendarmes who have surprised him such dances over rocks, and placed them in such unpleasant positions, that they have come to treat him with the respect and consideration due to a man of his talent and resource. The French poacher must not be judged by the same ethics as the English poacher. Generally speaking, game is not preserved in France. There are extensive tracts everywhere where anybody can shoot, provided that he has satisfied the license formality and observes the regulations with regard to the seasons. The poacher is a man who thinks it waste of money to pay for a gun-license, and a waste of opportunities to respect the breeding season. If he is a fisher, he not only scoffs at the close time, but uses illegal means to achieve his purpose, such as nets with meshes smaller than they should be, and the three-pronged spear. In the Tarn and other French rivers the fish have been destroyed in a woeful manner by poison and dynamite, but it is the rock-blaster and the navvy, not the regular poacher, who is chiefly to be blamed for this. Men who have the constant handling of dynamite, and who move from place to place, are rapidly destroying the life of the rivers and streams. Having noted a good pool, they return by night and drop into it a dynamite cartridge, the explosion of which brings every fish, big and small, to the surface. With these destructive causes, which do not belong to the natural order of things, should be mentioned another that does, namely, the frequency of floods in the season when the trout are spawning. But for this drawback, and the unfair methods of fishing, the Upper Tarn would be one of the finest trout streams in the world. As it is, an expert angler would find plenty of sport on the banks of the river above Le Rozier, and as all anglers are said to be lovers of nature, he would never be dull in the midst of such entrancing scenery as is to be found here.

The storm having spent its fury, the gendarmes and the poacher left, and I was again alone. Although it was not yet ten o'clock, there was the quietude of midnight around me. The village was asleep, and I should have thought Nature asleep had I not heard the harsh scream of an owl as I entered my bedroom and threw open the window. The clouds had broken up, and the moon was shining above the great rocks at the foot of which I knew that the owl was flying silently and searching with glowing eyes for the happy, unsuspecting mouse or young hare amidst the thyme and bracken. Can Nature never rest? Is there no peace without bloodshed under the sun and moon, no respite from ravin even when the night is hooded like a dead monk?

I turned from the moonlit clouds, the rushing dark water, the long white reach of pebbles, and made a little journey round my room. The people who owned this inn may not have been very prosperous, but they were evidently rich in faith. The walls were ornamented with rosaries yards long—probably from Lourdes—and religious pictures. There were also statuettes of sacred figures, a large crucifix, and close by the bed a holy-water stoup. The inhabitants of the Lozère, like those of the Aveyron, are not only believing, they are zealous, and in their homes they surround themselves with the emblems of their faith. These are the only works of art which the villagers possess—almost their only books.

At seven the next morning I had left Les Vignes, and was making my way up the gorge, whose rocky walls drew closer together, became more stupendous, fantastic, and savagely naked. All cultivation disappeared. A rock of immense size, pointing to the sky, but leaning towards the gorge, soon attracted my notice, as it must that of any traveller who comes within view of it. This monolith, over 200 feet in height, has its base about 500 feet above the stream, but it is only a jutting fragment of the prodigious wall. It has received the name of L'Aiguille, from its needle-like shape. Below this, and partly in the bed of the stream, is another prodigious block of dolomite called La Sourde, and here the channel is so obstructed by the number and size of the rocks which have fallen into it, that the river has forced a passage beneath them, and does not reappear until the obstacle is passed. But although the water vanishes, its muffled groan arises from mysterious depths. This, together with the monstrous masses of dolomite, wrinkled, white and honeycombed, the narrowness and gloomy depth of the gorge, the fury of the water as it descends amongst the blocks to leap into its gulf, makes the imagination ask if something supernatural has not happened here. But the geologist says that this chaos of tumbled-down rocks is simply the result of a 'fault' in the stratification, and that, the foundations having given way, the masses of dolomite fell where they now lie.

In the Middle Ages, however, geology was an undiscovered science, and the human mind was compelled—perhaps with much advantage to itself—to seek supernatural causes in order to explain the mysterious phenomena of nature, many of which, so far as subsidiary causes are concerned, have ceased to be mysterious. This spot—called the Pas de Souci—has, therefore, its poetic and miraculous legend. St. Enimie, when she established her convent near the fountain of Burlats, higher up the Tarn, interfered with the calculations of the devil, who had found the numerous orifices in this region communicating with the infernal kingdom exceedingly convenient for his terrestrial enterprises. He therefore lost no time in entering upon a tug-of-war with the saintly interloper. But she was more than a match for him. Her nuns, however, were of weaker flesh, and so he tried his wiles upon them. Their devotions and good resolutions were so much troubled by the infernal teaser of frail humanity that St. Enimie, realizing the great danger, rose to the occasion. One day or night she caught the devil unawares in the convent and tried to chain him up; but he was too strong or too crafty for the innocent virgin, and made his escape down the gorge of the Tarn, intending to reach his own fortress by the hole down which the stream plunges at the Pas de Souci, and which the peasant believes existed from the beginning of the world. St. Enimie followed at his heels as closely as she could, and he led her a wild scamper over the rocks. She hoped that St. Ilère, her confessor, who lived in a cavern of the gorge, would stop the fiend in his flight, but the saint was so busy praying that he did not notice the arch-enemy as he sped on his frantic course. St. Enimie was quite out of breath and ready to drop from exhaustion when she drew near the Pas de Souci, a little in the rear of the tormentor of souls, and he was just about to plunge into the gulf. The saint threw herself upon her knees, and exclaimed: 'Help me, O ye mountains and crags! Stop him, fall upon him!' Thereupon there was a great commotion of the ancient rocks far above under the calm sky, and they fell, one after the other, with a frightful crash. It was, however, the immense block, since named La Sourde, that stopped the devil; the others he shook off as if they had been pebbles. When La Sourde struck him it was more than he could contend with, and it flattened him out. The Needle Rock was just about to tumble, when La Sourde cried out: 'Hold on, my sister! You need not trouble yourself; I have him fast!' This explains why the Needle Rock has ever since looked so undecided. For centuries La Sourde bore the impress of a sanguinary hand, left upon it by Satan in his frantic efforts to get free, but some years ago it was washed away by an exceptionally high flood.

A little beyond this impressive and legendary spot, the gorge, widening, displays an immense concavity on the left, nearly semicircular. Here among the spur-like rocks which jut out from its steep sides —much clothed, however, with vegetation—was the hermitage of St. Ilère, and the spot where it is supposed to have been is a place of pilgrimage. Here, too, are numerous caverns, in some of which many implements of the Stone Age have been found, as well as the bones of extinct animals and others which disappeared from Europe before the historic period. To those who have the special knowledge that is requisite, the caverns of the Causses de Sauveterre and Méjan offer great enticement, for only a few of their secrets, covered by the darkness of incalculable ages, have yet been brought to light.

Again the cliffs draw closer together, and the tower-like masses on the brink of each precipice lift their inaccessible ramparts higher and higher in the blue air. Gray-white or ochre-stained layers and monoliths shine like incandescent coals in the unmitigated radiance of the sun. I pass a little group of houses in the hollow of overhanging rocks, splashed by the shadow of the wild fig-tree's leaves. One side of the gorge is all luminous with sunbeams, down to the lathy poplars leaning in every direction by the edge of the torrent, their leaves still wet with last night's rain. Another boat is being tugged laboriously up the rapids, a mule taking the first place at the end of the rope. The impetuous water looks strong enough to carry the beast off his legs; but he, like the boatman, is used to the work, and has good nerves. The path—if path it can be called, when it has lost all trace of one—now leads over large pebbles which are not pleasant to walk upon; but presently the way along the water-side is absolutely closed by vertical rocks some hundred feet high.

To enter the mad torrent in order to get beyond these terrible rocks, forming a narrow strait, was an undertaking only to be thought of if the case were desperate. I believed that there must be a path somewhere running up the cliff, and after going back a little I found one. It led me four or five hundred feet up the side of the gorge; but on looking down the distance seemed much less, because the rocks rose a thousand feet higher. I was gazing at the loftiest peak on the opposite side, when two eagles suddenly appeared in the air above it; and so long as I remained did they continue to circle over it without any apparent movement of their wings. The eyrie upon this needle-like point is well known; according to the popular belief, it has always been there.

It was in vain, however, that I searched the horizon for the vultures, whose principal stronghold —a long ledge of rock, protected from above by an overhanging cornice, and beyond the range of a fowling-piece from below—is immediately over the river in this part of the gorge. Had I left Les Vignes before daybreak, I might have seen them start off all together, the brown vultures and their black cousins, the arians, in quest of carrion; but now there was not one to be seen. As the vulture has become a rare bird in France, inhabiting only a few localities where there are very high and inaccessible rocks, and where man is crestfallen in the presence of nature, it is to be hoped that they will not be driven from the great gorge of the Tarn by being too frequently shot at in the breeding season, when they are obliged to show themselves at all hours of the day. No peasant would think of wasting a cartridge upon them; but the sharp-shooting tourist, armed with a rifle, may be tempted to do so. He would probably fire many bullets before he succeeded in striking a bird five or six hundred feet above him; and even if the shot took effect, there would be very small chance of the vulture falling where it could be picked up. The bombardment would do them little damage; but it might, if often repeated, prove too trying to their nerves, and, notwithstanding their conservative principles, they might be driven at length to quit these rocks inhabited by their ancestors for centuries. To the naturalist this district is of fascinating interest, on account of the large number of carnivorous birds of various species by which it is still haunted. Besides the common brown eagle, three kinds of vulture, several species of falcons, hawks, and owls, the raven family appears to be fully represented, with the exception of the jackdaw, which possibly finds itself too weak and too slow of flight to live in the midst of such strong and ferocious air-robbers as those which have established themselves in these grand solitudes. Among smaller birds of different habits, the red partridge and the water-ousel are frequently seen. The rock-partridge, or *bartavelle*, is also found, but is rare. The four-legged fauna is not represented by the wolf or the boar, the forests being too scanty to afford them sufficient cover, and the largest wild quadrupeds are the badger and the fox.

Descending the path by steps cut in the rock, I again reached the margin of the Tarn. Gradually the gorge opened, slopes appeared, and upon these were almond-trees and vines planted on terraces. Flowers, too, which had little courage to bloom in the dim depths where the cliffs seemed ready to join again, and the sunbeam vanished before it dried the dew, now took heart under the broader sky. Great purple snapdragons hung from clefts in the rocks, inula flashed gorgeously yellow, white melilot raised its graceful drooping blossoms, and hemp-agrimony made the bees sing a drowsy song of the brimming cup of summer.

Some vestiges of a castle appeared upon a high-jutting craggy mass, marking the site of the Château de Montesquieu, one of the strongest fortresses of the gorge in the Middle Ages.

I guessed rightly by the vines and almonds that La Malène was not far off. Soon came that sight, ever welcome to the wayfarer—the village where he intends to seek rest and refreshment. The inn here was as unpretentious as the one at Les Vignes; but with hare, *en civet*, a dish of trout, and a bottle of the wine grown upon the sunny terrace above the houses, I had as good a meal as any hungry tramp has a right to expect. As for myself, I never expect anything so sumptuous, and in this way I let luck have a chance of giving me now and then a pleasant surprise. The trout in the Upper Tarn do not often reach a large size, because by growing they become too conspicuous in such clear water; but their flesh obtains that firmness which is the gift of mountain streams. The wine grown upon the slopes of the gorge is a *petit vin* with a sparkle in it, and it comes as a delightful change to those who have been drinking the tasteless, deep-coloured wines of the Béziers and Narbonne region, with which the South of France has been flooded since the new vineyards upon the plains and slopes of the Mediterranean have been yielding torrents of juice. The fruit of no plant is so dependent upon the soil for its flavour as that of the vine. Chalk produces champagne, and some of the best wines of Southern France are grown upon calcareous soils where the eye perceives nothing but stones. The plant loves to get its roots down into the crevices of a rock. I now drank the fragrant light wine of the Gévaudan—the calcareous district of the Upper Tarn—with a pleasure not unmixed with sorrow; for the phylloxera had found its way up the gorge, and the vineyards were already sick unto death. The pest had come some years later here than in districts nearer the plains; but it had too surely come, and the fear of poverty was gnawing the hearts of the poor men—many of them old—who had been bending their backs such a number of years, and their fathers before them, upon those terraces which had been won from the desert at the price of such long labour.

Before continuing my journey up the gorge, I climbed to the little church overlooking the village, and which stands in the midst of the rough burying-ground where the dead must lie very near the solid rock. It is a plain Romanesque building, presenting the peculiarity not often seen of exterior steps leading to the belfry. Against an inner wall is a tablet, which tells of certain men of Florac who 'pro Deo et rege legitime certantes coronati sunt, die 11 mensis Junii, anni 1793.' They were guillotined by the Revolutionists at Florac.

I passed the Château de la Caze, a small but well-preserved castle, showing the transition from the feudal to the Renaissance style, and still surrounded by its moat. It has five towers, and is a picturesque building; but I thought it gloomy in the deep shade of the gorge and the surrounding trees. It must be gloomier still at night when the owls shriek and hoot. If it is not haunted, it must be because there are so many abandoned solitary great houses in this part of France that the ghosts have become rather spoilt and hard to please.

What is the pale yellow flame that I see burning by the river where a slanted beam strikes down from a crenellated bastion of ruddy rock? Reaching the spot, I find two pale-yellow flames, one hanging from the bank, the other trembling upon the stream. The evening primrose has lit its lamp from the sunbeam.

More rocks there are to climb, for the river again rushes between upright walls. The path goes along the edge of a horrid precipice, then descends abruptly by steps cut in the rock.

At a very poor hamlet, clinging to the side of the

gorge at a sufficient height to be safe from the floods, I ask a woman if anybody there sells wine. 'Yes,' she replies, 'he does,' pointing at the same time to a tall old white-haired man, who beckons me to follow him. He hobbles along with a stick, dragging one leg, and leads the way into his house under a rock. It is a mere hovel, but it has a wooden floor, and there are signs of personal dignity—what is known in England as 'respectability'—struggling with poverty. Perhaps the ancient clock, whose worm-eaten case reaches from the floor to the ceiling, and whose muffled but cheery tick-tack is like the voice of an old friend, impressed me in favour of this poor home as soon as I entered.

The crippled man, having given me his best chair, disappeared into his cellar scooped out of the rock, and presently returned with a bottle of wine. Then he brought out a great loaf of very dark bread, which he placed upon the table with the wine, and a plateful of green almonds. The French peasants observe the wholesome rule of never drinking red wine without 'breaking a crust' at the same time. I made my new acquaintance break a crust with me and share the contents of the bottle. Then he talked freely of the cares that weighed upon him. He told me that he and others who lived in the gorge had always depended upon their wine to buy bread.

'And are the vines in a very bad way?'

'The year after next will see the last of them.'

Many persons, he added, would be obliged to leave the district because it would become impossible for them to live there. While we were talking two or three little barefooted boys, whose clothes had been patched over and over again, but still showed gaping places, watched and listened in the open doorway with round-eyed attention. They were robust children with health and happiness in their faces, in spite of the hard times, for the mountain air fed them, and their troubles were yet to come. They were the old man's grandchildren, and I suppose I was looking at them more keenly than I should have had I reflected, for he made excuses for their neglected appearance with an expression of pain. Then, changing the subject suddenly, he said:

'What country do you belong to?'

'To England.'

'Ah, c'est un riche pays!'

I told him that it was rich and poor like other countries, and that the people there had no vines at all to help them. 'It is a rich country all the same,' repeated the old man, for the impression had somehow become deeply fixed in his mind. There I see him still seated at the rough table, and behind his broad bent back the wide fireplace against the bare rock blackened with smoke.

I had left this hamlet, and was on the bank of the Tarn, when I heard the patter of bare feet upon the pebbles behind me. Turning round, I saw the eldest of the boys who had been watching me in the doorway. He had an idea that I should go wrong, and followed stealthily to see. He now told me that if I continued by the water I should soon be stopped by rocks, and I accepted his offer to show me the way up the cliff. His recklessness in running over the sharp stones made me ask him if they did not hurt his feet. 'Oh no!' he replied; 'they are used to it.' It is indeed astonishing what feet are able to get used to. The boy's joy at the few sous which I gave him was almost ecstatic. He had hardly thanked me when he set off running homeward to show how he had been rewarded for his sharpness in thinking that I should lose my way, and allowing me to do so before saying a word.

I was by the river-side not far from Sainte-Énimie when a rather alarming noise broke the silence and became rapidly louder. I looked up the steep cliff, and saw to my consternation a great stone bounding down the rocks and crashing through the vines. As I seemed to be in the line of it I hastened on. I had only gone about ten yards when it bounded into the air and, passing sheer over the path and bank, plunged into the Tarn with a mighty splash. I reckoned that had I remained where I was it would have just cleared my head. It was a fragment of rock which, from its size, might well have been two hundredweight. The same thing happened earlier in the day, but that time I was not so unpleasantly near. The heavy rain of the previous night, coming after a long period of drought, was probably the cause of these already-loosened stones starting upon their downward career. All these calcareous rocks are breaking up. The process of disintegration and decomposition is slow, but it is sure. Every frost does something to split them, and every shower of rain entering the crevices does something to rot them; so that even they cannot last. The Tarn is carrying them back to the sea, to be deposited again, but somewhere else.

I was at Sainte-Enimie before sunset, and there I found the air laden with the scent of lavender. True, all the hills round about were covered with a blue-gray mantle; but I had never known the plant when undisturbed give out such an aroma before. Looking down from the little bridge to the waterside, my wonder ceased. There in a line, with wood-fires blazing under them, were several stills, and behind these, upon the bank, were heaps of lavender stalks and flowers such as I had never seen even in imagination. There were enough to fill several bullock-waggons. The fragrance in the air, however, did not come so much from these mounds as from the distilled essence. It was evident that Sainte-Enimie had a considerable trade in lavender-water.

I spent an unhappy evening, for the inn where I

stopped—it called itself a hotel—had been made uninteresting by enterprise; and a couple of tourists from the South, with whom it was my lot to dine, caused me unspeakable misery by talking of nothing else but of a bridge which they had lately seen. If I should ever be near it, I think the recollection of that evening will make me avoid it. It may be a miracle in iron, but none the less shall I owe it an everlasting grudge. These gentlemen from Carcassonne were typical sons of the South in this, that the sound of their own voices acted upon their imagination like the strongest coffee blended with the oldest cognac. They would have been amusing, nevertheless, but for the horrible intensity of their resolve to make me see that nightmare of a bridge. If one had taken breath while the other spoke, or rather shouted, I should have suffered less; but they both shouted together, and their struggle to get the better of one another by force of lung, gesticulation, and frenzied rolling of the eyes became a duel, whereby the solitary witness was the only person harmed. What a relief to me if they had gone down to the river bank and fought it out there! No such luck, however. Had there been no listener, they, too, might have wished the bridge in the depths of Tartarus.

If I passed an unhappy evening at Sainte-Enimie, I spent a worse morning. There was a change of weather in the night, and when the day came again, it was a blear-eyed, weeping day, with that uniform gray sky with steam-like clouds hiding half the hills which, when seen in a mountainous region by a person bent on movement, is enough to give him 'goose flesh.' I now felt a longing to leave the Cevennes and to return to the lower country, but there seemed no chance of escape. The rain continued hour after hour—and such rain! It was enough to turn a frog against water. As the people of the inn seemed incapable of showing sympathy, I went out to look at the town under a borrowed umbrella. It was certainly not much to look at, especially under circumstances of such acute depression. I walked or waded through a number of miry little streets where all manner of refuse was in a saturated or deliquescent state cabbage-stumps and dead rats floating in the gutters, potato-peelings and bean-pods sticking to the mediæval pitching—everything slippery, nasty, and abominable. There were old houses, as a matter of course; but who can appreciate antiquities when his legs are wet about the knees and his boots are squirting water? Nevertheless, I tried to notice a few things besides the vileness underfoot. One was a rudely-carved image of the Virgin in a niche covered by a grating. This was in such a dark little street that it seemed as if the sun had given up all hope of ever shining there again. I struggled through the slush to the church, built, with the town, on the side of a hill rising from the Tarn. I found a Romanesque edifice—old, but rough, and offering no striking feature, save the arched recesses in the exterior surface of the wall. A little higher upon the hill was the convent founded by St. Enimie; but the original building disappeared centuries ago.

On returning to the inn I passed the Fontaine de Burlats, where St. Enimie was cured of her leprosy in the Merovingian age. It was a change to see something that really seemed to enjoy the incessant downpour and to enter into the spirit of it. The fountain would be remarkable in another region by the volume of water that gushes in all seasons like a little river out of the earth; but there are so many such between the Dordogne and the Tarn, wherever the calcareous formation has lent itself to the honeycombing action of water, that this copious outflow loses thereby much of its claim to distinction.

The legend of St. Enimie is fully set forth in a Provençal poem of the thirteenth century by the troubadour Bertrand de Marseilles, who received his information from his friend the Prior of the monastery at Sainte-Enimie, which in the Middle Ages was the most important religious house in the Gévaudan. The MS. is preserved in the library of the Arsenal, Paris. It was at the express recommendation of St. Hère that Enimie sought the fountain of Burla (now Burlats), and bathed her afflicted body in its pure waters. The passage of the poem containing this injunction is as follows:

> 'Enimia verges de Dyeu,
> Messatges fizels ti suy yeu.
> Per me ti manda Dieus de pla
> Que t'en anes en Gavalda,*
> Car, lay trobaras una fon
> Que redra ton cors bel e mon
> Si te laves en l'aygua clara.
>
> *   *   *   *
>
> A nom Burla ; vay l'en lay
> Non ho mudar per negun play.'

The relics of the saint were destroyed or lost at the time of the Revolution ; but high upon the side of a neighbouring hill a chapel has been raised to her, and it is a place of pilgrimage.

* Gévaudan.

IN THE VALLEY OF THE LOT.

THE rambler in the highlands of the North knows so well what the wretchedness of being shut up by bad weather in a mountain inn means, that he may have grown reconciled to it, and have learnt how to spend a day under such circumstances pleasantly. But to me, a sun-lover, to whom the charm of the South has been irresistible, such a trial is one that taxes to the utmost all the powers of endurance. Hence it is that, when I think of Sainte-Enimie, I can recall nothing but impressions of dismal wetness. This may seem shocking to those who have seen, under a different aspect, the little town on the Upper Tarn, named after the Merovingian saint. Be it remembered, however, that I was shut up hour after hour in an inn crowded with peasants in damp blouses, shouting *patois* at each other, and clutching great cotton umbrellas, whose fragrance, under the influence of moisture, was not idyllic. In that abominable little auberge, that styled itself a hotel, I decided to go no farther up the Tarn, but, as soon as the weather would set me free, to cross the *causse* that separated me from the Lot, and to descend the valley of this river towards the warmer and dryer region of the plains.

Not until the afternoon were there any signs of improvement in the weather; and then, as soon as the clouds grew lighter, I started without waiting for the rain to stop. It was Sunday, and outside the old church was a crowd of men and boys, who had come for vespers. The women did not join them, but passed through the door as they arrived. Throughout rural France, wherever religion keeps a firm hold on the peasant, it is the custom of the men to gather for gossip in front of the church some time before the service, and, just as the bell stops, to make a rush at the doorway, and struggle through the opening like sheep into a fold when there is a dog at their heels. While looking at these men, I was again struck by the prevailing tendency of the peasants of the Lozère to develop long, sharp noses—a feature that often gives them a very weasel-like expression.

Having passed the ruins of the monastery, whose high loopholed walls and strong tower showed that it had once been a fortress as well as a religious house, I was soon rising far above the valley of the Tarn. The winding road led me up the flanks of stony hills, terraced everywhere for almond-trees; but after two or three hours of ascent the almonds dwindled away, and the country became an absolute desert of brashy hills, showing little asperity of outline, but mournful and solemn by their wastefulness and abandonment to a degree that makes the traveller ask himself if he is really in Europe, or has been transported by magic to the most arid steppes of Asia. But there is a plant that thrives in this desert, that loves it so much as to give to it a tinge of dusty blue as far as the eye can reach on every side. Needless to say that this is the lavender. It was in all its flowering beauty as I crossed the treeless waste, and it gave to the breath of the desert what seemed to be the mystical fragrance of peace.

Leaving the highway to Mende, I took a rough road on the left, which, according to the map, led directly to Chanac by the Lot. I should recommend no one else to take it unless he have more hours of daylight before him than I had. Again I ran a near risk of passing the night in the open air. The road became little better than a track; then it crossed others, and it was a very pretty puzzle to tell which was the one for me and which was not. It is true that I could have made straight towards the Lot by the compass, but the descent of the precipitous cliffs into the deep gorge, unless one knows the paths, is only a task to be undertaken at nightfall with a light heart by those who have had no experience of this savage district. When my perplexity was at its worst I saw a shepherd, whose form, wrapped in the long brown homespun cloak called a *limousine*, stood solemnly against the evening sky. I made towards him, thinking that he would help me out of my difficulty; but no: either he did not understand a word I said, or did not choose to give any information. Perhaps he thought me an escaped madman, or a dangerous tramp, with whom it was better to hold no conversation. The sun was setting when I reached a wood of scattered firs—a more melancholy spot at that hour than the bare *causse*. The weather had been fine for some hours, but now a storm that had been gathering broke. As the wind blew the rain in slanting lines, the level sun shone through the vapour and the streaming atmosphere. Looking above me, as I sheltered myself behind a wailing fir, I saw that the dreary world was spanned by two glorious rainbows. But although the scene was so wildly beautiful, the spirit of desolation was upon me, and I felt like a homeless wanderer. I was roaming among the firs in the dusk, when I met a shepherd boy, who put me on a path that joined the main road to Chanac. Then began the descent into the valley of the Lot. It was very long; the winding road passed through a black forest of firs, and the dark night fell when I was still far from the little town. The walk was gloomy, but in all gloom there is something that is grand and elevating—something that gives a sense of expansion to the soul. The cries of the unseen night-birds, the solemn mystery of the enigmatic trees wrapped in darkness, make us feel the supernatural that surrounds us, and is a part of us, more than the visible movement of life in the light of the sun.

At length the oil-lamps of Chanac flashed brightly in the hollow below, and not long afterwards I was sitting at a table in an upper room of a comfortable old inn, the lower part of which was filled with roisterers, for it was Sunday night. I dined with a Government functionary—an inland revenue *contrôleur*, who happened to be a Frenchman of the reserved and solemn sort that cultivates dignity. By dint of being looked up to by others he had acquired the fixed habit of looking up to himself. All the time that I was in his company I felt that, had he been an angel dining with a modern Tobias, he could scarcely have shown greater anxiety not to sit upon his wings. Moved by the genial spirit of the grape, or not wishing, perhaps, to crush me altogether with the weight of his official importance, his ice began to melt a little at about the second or third course. Forgetting discretion, he actually smiled. The meal, which had been prepared in anticipation of his coming, was a much more splendid entertainment than would have been got up for me had I been alone. The cook's masterpiece was a very cunningly contrived pasty—a work of local genius that I was quite unprepared for. Even M. le contrôleur, had he not checked himself in time, would have beamed at this achievement; but he would never have forgiven himself such an admission of weakness common to mortals not in the service of the Government. Just before the dessert a superb trout that had been drawn out of the sparkling Lot was brought in, and it had been mercifully spared the disgrace of being sprinkled with chopped garlic.

While we were dining the wassailers in the great kitchen and general room downstairs became more and more uproarious. Dancing had commenced, and it was the *bourrée*, the delightful *bourrée* of Auvergne (the Upper Lot here runs not very far from the Cantal) that was being danced. It is a measure that has no local colour unless it is accompanied by violent stamping. The *contrôleur* looked very scandalized, and said it was abominable that the house should be given up to such tumult and disorder. I observed, however, that as the joyousness of the party downstairs increased my companion's face became animated by an expression that was not one of genuine anger, and as soon as he had drunk his coffee he remarked in a tone of indifference that, as the evening had to be spent somehow, it might be less disagreeable to see what was going on below than simply to hear it. I soon followed him, and found that he was enjoying himself thoroughly, although discreetly, in a quiet corner. The kitchen was filled with young fellows in blouses, some sitting at tables drinking and smoking, others standing; all were shouting, whistling or raising peals of laughter that might have brought the house about their ears had it been built by a modern contractor. In the centre of the room the bare-armed kitchenmaid, who had left the platters, and a young peasant in a blouse were dancing, their backs turned to each other, moving their arms up and down like puppets in a barrel-organ, and banging the floor with their sabots, with the full conviction that the greater the noise the greater the fun. And this was the opinion of all except the stout hostess, who looked on at the scene with a distressed countenance from behind a mighty pile of dirty plates. The musicians were spectators who whistled in a band the air of the *bourrée*, which is enough to make the most sedate Canon who ever sat in a stall dance, or at least to remember with charity the promptings of his adolescence.

When the kitchenmaid went back to her plates—to the great relief of her mistress, who would have sternly condemned her tripping if thoughts of business had not beset her practical mind—two young men stood up and danced another *bourrée*. With the exception of the scullion and household drudge there was no chance of getting a female partner. In these villages and small towns the girls are kept out of harm's way. They go to bed at eight or nine, and are hard at work either in the fields or in the house, or washing by the stream, all through the hours of daylight. The priests, wherever they have influence—and in the South they have a great deal—set their faces strongly against dancing by the two sexes, except under very exceptional circumstances. They are right; they have peculiar facilities for knowing the variety of human nature with which they have to deal. Humanity is fundamentally the same everywhere, but what is fundamental is modified by race and climate. Temperament, fashioned by causes innate and local, exercises an immense influence upon practical morality.

And so the revel went on. As the glasses were refilled the noise grew louder and the smoke denser. I soon had enough of it, and taking a candle I climbed to my bedroom, leaving the *contrôleur* in his corner. Before going to bed I did a little sewing, having borrowed a threaded needle from the landlady with this object in view. The wayfarer should be ready to help himself as far as he can, and although sewing is not, perhaps, the most manly of accomplishments, no tourist should be incapable of sewing on a button or closing up a rent that makes the village children laugh.

My walk across the *causse* separating two rivers had tired me, but I might as well have remained downstairs for all the sleep that I enticed. As the hours wore on the uproar, instead of subsiding, became more terrific. These Southerners have voices of such rock-splitting power that, when twenty or thirty of them, inspired by Bacchus, or excited by discussion, shout together, one asks if it would be possible for devils on the rampage to raise a more hideous tumult. The house trembled as from a succession of thunderclaps. Midnight struck, and the uproar was unabated. At one it had entered upon the quarrelsome phase, and at two there was a fight. Chairs or tables were overthrown, there was a smashing of glass, a rapid scuffling of feet, and the screaming and howling as of a menagerie on fire. Above the fiendish din rang out the shrill voice of the hostess, who was evidently trying to separate the combatants, and who seemed to be successful, for the hurricane suddenly lulled.

This hostess was a woman of words, but the landlady of an inn near Rodez, which I entered one summer evening, showed herself under similar circumstances to be a woman of action. Two young men who were sitting at a table, after a very brief difference of opinion, stared fixedly and fiercely into each other's face, and then sprang at one another like a couple of tom-cats. Presently the stronger took the other up in his arms, carried him out through the door, and, having pitched him considerately upon the manure-heap in the yard, returned to his place with the expression of the victorious cat. But he reckoned without his hostess. She was not tall, but her cubic capacity took up more place in the world than that of two or three ordinary mortals. With her great bare arms folded across her ample person she waddled towards the triumphant young man, and there was a look in her eye that made him wriggle uneasily upon his chair. I think he was tempted to run away, but shame

nailed him to his seat. As soon as the pair were at
close quarters, one of the folded bolster-like arms
made a sudden movement, and the back of the
strong rough hand, hardened by forty years or more
of toil, covered for an instant the youth's nose and
mouth. That single movement of a female arm,
the muscular development of which a pugilist might
have envied, shed more blood than all the clawing,
tugging, and butting of the male combatants had
caused to flow. 'That is to teach you,' said the
strong woman, 'not to fight in my house again!'

But I am forgetting that I am now at Chanac.
When I went down into the kitchen at about seven
o'clock, after two or three hours' sleep, the landlady
and the other women of the inn looked very tired
and sheepish. They were prepared to hear some
strong criticism of the night's proceedings, such as
they would be sure to get when the *contrôleur* came
down.

'You seem to have had some good amusement
last night, and to have kept it up well,' said I.

'Oh, monsieur,' exclaimed the hostess, shaking
her head dolefully, 'what a night it was!'

And she went on shaking her head, while the
kitchen-maid—the one who danced the *bourrée*, and
was now listlessly rinsing glasses innumerable—
giggled behind her mistress's back. She evidently
thought that it was a good sort of night. In making
up the bill I think that the regretful aubergiste, who
felt that the reputation of her house had received a

CIGALA, THE SHOEBLACK.

cruel blow, and that all the mothers in the place were reviling her for encouraging their sons in dissipation, must have left the bed out of the reckoning, considering that she could not honestly charge me for a night's rest which I did not get. At any rate, the bill was ridiculously small.

Now, with the help of daylight, I can see what the little town is like. The houses—many of which have late Gothic doorways—are clustered about the sides of an isolated hill or mamelon in the valley of the Lot, beyond which rise the high cliffs covered with dark woods. The town is still dominated by the tall rectangular tower that helped to protect it in the Middle Ages, and near to this is the church, which is both Romanesque and Gothic, and is rich in curious details. The sanctuary is separated from the rest of the choir by the graceful arcade of numerous little arches supported by tall and slender columns, which is one of the most charming and characteristic features of the Auvergnat style. The carving of the capitals exhibits in a delightful manner the hardihood and florid fancy of this singularly interesting development of Byzantine-Romanesque taste. Upon one of the piers of the sanctuary are a pair of symbolical doves dipping their beaks into the chalice that separates them, and upon another are two grotesque and fantastic beasts facing one another with frightful jaws wide open.

The walk from Chanac down the valley through the rest of the department of the Lozère I did not

do fairly. The sun was so hot and the way so
tedious that I at length yielded to the temptation of
the railway that I met here, and rode some fifteen
or twenty miles. It was not until the next morning
at St. Laurent d'Olt that I braced myself up to the
task of faring on foot by the river through the
department of the Aveyron. Here in the upper
country the stream retains its ancient name, the Olt,
which is merely an abbreviation of Oltis, unless it
be the Celtic origin of the Latin word. It is easy
to see how in rapid speech L'Olt became changed
to Lot. The *t* is still pronounced.

The valley down which I now took my way from
St. Laurent was broad and green, but the high
rocky cliffs which shut it off from the outer world
drew nearer as I went on. An old tramp who had
a bag slung over his back stopped me and said that
he was 'dans la misère.' Doubtless he guessed that
I was not quite so deep in it as himself, and that I
might be able to spare him something. As I always
look upon the tramp with a fraternal interest, however disreputable he may appear, because my own
wayfaring has helped to teach me contempt for
appearances, I stopped to talk with the aged
wanderer while hunting for some stray sous. His
matted gray beard and sunken cheeks gave him the
air of a Job of the studios; but no such luck had
probably ever befallen him as to be asked to pose
for thirty sous the hour. Such a sum would be
more than he could gather in a day, even after

selling the surplus of his begged crusts. He talked to me of 'the picturesque,' which proved that he had not grown gray and half doubled up without learning something of the world's wisdom. I learnt from him that between the spot where we met and St. Geniez there was only a hamlet, but that I should be able to find a house there where I could get a meal.

The old man went hobbling away, wondering, perhaps, when he would meet another foreign imbecile on the tramp, and I was soon alone upon the margin of the river's broad bed of sand, strewn with pebbles like the seashore. The stream was still fresh from the mountains, and it had the joyousness and bounding movements of young life. It was very narrow now, and many plants had grown up since the spring upon its far-shelving banks of mica-glittering sand and many-coloured pebbles; but often its swollen waters had rolled through this smiling valley, a raging and uncontrollable force, spreading terror and destruction.

The cliffs drew nearer and rose higher, and then the river ran through a gorge nearly impassable, and abandoned to all the wildness of nature. The partial loop here formed by the Lot is hidden and defended by a forbidding wilderness of rocks and forest, as if it were one of the last retreats of the fluvial deities, where they can defy the curiosity of man. The adventurous spirit prompted me to explore it, but the lazy one said, 'Leave it.' I took the advice of the latter, and went on by the road, which now left the river, and ascended towards the plateau under cliffs of red sandstone. The thirsty sun had by this time drained almost every flower-cup of its dew; but the freshness of the morning still lingered in the hollows of the rocks, and in the shade of the chestnut, the walnut, and elm. As the earth warmed, it became quieter. All creatures seemed to grow drowsy, except the sociable little quails that kept calling to one another, 'How are you?' and the flies of wicked purpose, which become more and more enterprising as the temperature rises.

It was long since I had seen a human being, when I heard the click-clack of loose *sabots* coming nearer. Presently a couple of young bulls showed their grim visages round a corner, and after them came a very small girl with a very long stick. She looked about six years old, and she had great trouble to keep her little brown feet inside the wooden shoes, which were many sizes too large for her. How was it that those big, and perhaps bad-tempered, animals allowed themselves to be driven and beaten by that child, whereas they would have turned upon a dog double her size, and done their best to toss him over the chestnut trees? What is it that the brutes see below the surface of the human being to inspire them with such respect and fear of this biped, even when he or she has just crawled out of the cradle? These bulls, by-the-bye, stopped and looked at me in a way that was anything but respectful, and I delayed the study of the metaphysical question until I could watch them from the rear.

I found on the top of the hill the village or hamlet that the old tramp had mentioned; but there was no sign of an inn—indeed, there was no sign of anybody being alive in the place. I threaded the steep little lanes between the houses and hovels, up to the ankles in dirty straw that had been turned out of the animals' sheds, but saw nothing moving except fowls. I knocked at various doors, and obtained no response. It was clear that all the people, including the children, were away in the fields, and had left the village to take care of itself. Hungry and thirsty, I was resigning myself with a heavy heart to trudge on, when I observed a column of blue smoke rise suddenly from a chimney, and I was not long in finding the house to which it belonged. It was a dilapidated building, very wretched now, but with an air of bygone superiority. This was chiefly shown in the Renaissance doorway, a rather elaborate piece of work, over which was the date 1602. I ascended the steps with a little misgiving, for I thought that perhaps some cantankerous person whose family had seen better times might be living there, and that my questions as to food and drink might meet with surly answers. I knocked, nevertheless, with my stick upon the old door studded with nail-heads. It was opened, and before me stood a woman who looked old, but who

was probably middle-aged; she was very poorly
clad, very imperfectly washed, but on her tired and
toil-worn face there was no forbidding expression.
I told her that I was looking for an auberge, and
she said that hers was one *au besoin*. It was the
only one that answered at all to the name there-
abouts. So the smoke had led me to the right
place. I followed the heiress of the dilapidated
house—she was a descendant of the original owner
—through the dingy kitchen, where upon the hearth
the fire of sticks that she had just lighted was
blazing cheerfully, into a back room, where there
were two beds without linen, and with nothing but
patchwork quilts over big bundles of dry maize
leaves. It is thus that many of the peasants of the
Aveyron sleep. This is not a part of France where
the study of cleanliness and comfort is carried to
excess. If the floor of the room that I now entered
had ever been washed, the boards must have forgotten the scrubbing sensation a century or more
ago. The appearance of everything indicated that
I was in a fleas' paradise; but as it was by no means
the first of the kind of which I had had experience,
I merely took the precaution of keeping my feet off
the ground, so as to offer as few travelling facilities
as possible to the enemy. The room, although it
was dirty, was cheerful; for the sunshine streamed
in through the open window, and the view of the
green valley beneath and the woods beyond soon
drove the fleas out of mind. Upon the sill were

plums laid out on wooden trays to dry in the sun and become what English people call prunes.

The excellent woman, who installed me before a little table on which she laid a cloth, said that she had little to offer me; but that all she had was, at my service. She first fished out of the wood-ashes in which it was preserved one of those dry, stringy sausages with which everyone who knows this part of France must be familiar. Then she brought in some white bread which a presentiment of my coming had perhaps caused her to buy a month before, for it was green with mildew. She thought that I should prefer this to the very dark bread of her own making. The choice was perplexing. My meal was chiefly made upon a dish of firm cream like that of Devonshire, with plums and fresh cob-nuts for dessert. Then my hostess made me some coffee, a luxury rarely used in the house; and when she had set it on the table, I induced her to stay and talk awhile. The conversation was made easier because, notwithstanding her poverty, she spoke French with much more facility than most of the people in these rural districts. She told me that her husband and children had not yet returned from the fields, and that she was at home because she was so tired after threshing buckwheat all yesterday in the sun.

'In winter,' I said, 'you have an easier time?'

'Oh no! In winter we are always working at something or another. We then make our linen from the hemp, patch up the clothes, prepare the walnuts for pressing, and blanch the chestnuts.* We have always something on hand.'

But while there was any work to be done out-of-doors, there they were busy from sunrise until dusk. Supper over, the beasts were looked after. 'Then,' she added, 'we say our prayers and go to bed.' She volunteered no statements respecting her ancestry, but when I questioned her concerning the house, she said that her family had been living in it for nearly 300 years. At one time they were the principal people in the district. It was true that they had come down in the world, but she felt thankful for the blessings that had been given her, and was satisfied. The family were all in good health, and that was the main thing. Her mother was still living with her - eighty-seven years of age, and had never been ill in her life.

Here was a simple but eloquent story of human vicissitude and uncertainty that was told without a word of regret or repining, and as though it were a tale of no interest to anybody. This poor, humble woman before me, whose back was still aching from the movement of bending and lifting

---

* *Blanchir les châtaignes.* In Guyenne, after the first sale of chestnuts in their natural state, the peasants prepare a large quantity of those that remain in a special manner, which consists of removing the first and second skins, and artificially drying the nuts until they become quite hard. They will then keep an indefinite period, and can be boiled for food when required. In the winter evenings, while the women work at their distaffs, the men frequently skin chestnuts either for drying or for food the next day.

the flail hour after hour, was, by right of birth, what we call in England a 'gentlewoman.' But she was poor, and ignorant of all books except the one that contained her prayers. She was not less a peasant than any of the women around her, nor did she wish to be thought anything better. That her ancestors were gentlemen, that they may have borne a forgotten title (many that were borne in France have been forgotten by the descendants), was as nothing to her. She clung only to what, in her simple but grand philosophy, was really to be valued—the blessings of life and health, opportunities of labour, independence, and faith in God.

This woman would only take the equivalent of a shilling for her wine, her coffee, and her food; then she made me drink some of her *eau de noix* (spirit prepared with the juice of green walnuts), and as I left she pressed more nuts and plums upon me.

The old woman who had never been ill was waiting for me under a tree. She could not speak a word of French, but she said a great deal in *patois*, of which all that I could make out was that she was afraid the *calour* (heat) would hurt me if I left so early in the afternoon. A little beyond the village I passed a party of threshers, men and women—two rows of them facing each other like dancers; the figures bending and straightening in unison, and all the flails whirling together in the air. They had spread a large cloth upon the ground, and were thrashing out the grain upon it.

A block of granite cropping out of the sandstone indicated a change in the formation, and this came, for the rocks gradually passed into gneiss and schist, frequently covered with moss and ferns, golden-rod in bloom, and purple heather. St. Geniez by the Lot was reached long before sundown; but although I had the time, I was not tempted to walk any farther that day.

The little town is picturesquely situated on the river-bank, and it has some old houses with turrets, and other interesting details. There is a late Gothic church that was formerly attached to an Augustinian monastery, of which part of the cloisters remains. Inside the edifice every flagstone covers a tomb, and in several instances masons' hammers and other tools are carved upon them.

It fell out that several commercial travellers and superior pedlars came into St. Geniez on the same day as myself, but in more genteel fashion, for they had their traps, and would not for all the world have risked their reputation for respectability, and rendered themselves despicable in the eyes of customers, by entering on foot. Nevertheless, their first impression (as I afterwards learnt), when I sat down with them to dinner at the comfortable inn, which, thanks to their patronage, had found the courage to style itself a hotel, was that I might be a new rival in the field. But the difficulty was to guess the particular field that I had marked out for my own distinction and the confusion of competitors. Was I in the grocery line, or the oil and colour line? Was I *dans les spiritueux* or *dans les articles d'église*? Then they had a suspicion that I was, perhaps, a German traveller trying to open up a fresh market for potato spirit, or those scientific syrups which are said to change any alcohol into 'old cognac' or the most venerable Jamaica rum. This may have accounted for the somewhat chilly reserve that fell upon my table companions as I took my seat among them. But, as this was unpleasant for everybody, I soon found an opportunity of dispelling the mystery that hung over me. Then they threw off all restraint, and showed themselves to be the jolly, rollicking, good-natured beings that these men almost invariably are. They were much more polite to me than Englishmen generally are to strangers, who are felt to be something like intruders—recognising me as a guest, and insisting upon my helping myself first to every dish that was brought on the table. It is customary for tourists to speak of the French commercial traveller as a very ridiculous or vulgarly offensive person. I have found these so-called 'bagmen' to be among the most pleasant-mannered, agreeable, and intelligent people whom I have met while roaming in provincial France. I have been disturbed at night by their uproariousness, for they are convivial to a fault; but in my immediate relations with them I have always found them frank, kindly, and courteous.

Before eight o'clock the next morning I had left St. Geniez behind me in the light mist, and was again on the banks of the Lot. At a waterside village called Sainte-Eulalie — a saint so much venerated by the French in the Middle Ages that a multitude of places have been named after her — was a church with a broad tower and low broach spire. I was struck by the noble simplicity and elegance of the Romanesque apse, which was much in the Auvergnat style. The village was very picturesque, partly on account of its position by the sunny, babbling water, and partly because of its numerous old houses, some with projecting stories, and others with exterior staircases communicating with an open gallery covered by the prolonged eaves of the roof. Outside of the doors mushrooms (*boleti*), after being cut in slices, were spread in the sun to dry. As I continued my way down the valley I met several women and girls returning from the chestnut woods on the hillsides carrying baskets of these *cèpes* on their heads. Although I hoped to sleep that night at Espalion, I soon left the direct road and struck off across country to the south-west in order to take in the village of Bozouls, a place that some soldier whom I had met told me was like Constantine in Algeria. I therefore left the valley of the Lot, and proceeded to cross the hills and tablelands which separated me from the gorge of its tributary, the Dourdou.

In taking by-paths to reach the *causse*, I passed over hillocks of chocolate-coloured marl mixed with broken schist and flints: here the broom and juniper, the heather and bracken, flourished. At length I felt the fresh breeze and drank the invigorating air of the limestone plateau. Descending the hill beyond, on the road to Rodez, I passed a very strange-looking spot where huge flat blocks of bare gneiss, laid together as though giants of the Titanic age had here been trying to pave the world, sloped with extraordinary regularity towards the highway. And these prodigious slabs of gneiss now lay amidst schistous marl and calcareous rock.

Farther down in the valley was a small village of which the houses were dwarfed by a gloomy stronghold, apparently of the fifteenth century, whose four high and massive towers, occupying the angles of a small quadrilateral, gave it the appearance of a vast *donjon*. At a small inn kept by a blacksmith I was able to get a meal and the rest that was now needed. The blacksmith's wife, a pleasant young woman, who seemed much amused at the sight of a being from the outer and, to her, half-fabulous world, drew part of a duck out of the grease in which it had been preserved, and gave me this with rice for my lunch. During the repast I was not a little worried by the questions of the blacksmith and some other village worthies who were drinking coffee in the small room that had to do for everybody, and who had so placed themselves that they could watch me at their ease. Such a strange bird as myself did not drop into their midst every day. They were not unfriendly, but their curiosity was troublesome, and I perceived that nothing that I might have said would have removed the impression from their minds that I was a mysterious character.

The country beyond this village was not unpleasant to the eye, with its vineyards on the slopes and its green pasturage in the valleys, but the hours went by drearily as I tramped upon the long road. I felt solitary, and was not in the mood to be interested easily; nevertheless, I lingered on the wayside awhile before a remarkable relic of the past: a rectangular machicolated tower of great height and strength rising out of a dark grove of trees. The afternoon was drawing towards evening, when I descended suddenly into a deep and narrow ravine where the sunshine was lost, and the twilight dwelt with greenness and dampness. At the bottom the Dourdou ran swiftly over its pebbly bed. After following it a little distance I found myself between towering walls of jurassic rock, vertical towards the summit, capped on each side by a long row of houses. There was also a church, likewise on the edge of the precipice. This was Bozouls—a place scarcely known beyond a small district of the Aveyron, but one of the most curious in France. The traveller, when he reaches the gorge, after

crossing a somewhat monotonous country, is quite
unprepared for such a startling revelation of the
sentiment of human fellowship in the midst of the
savagery of nature. Why did men build houses in
rows on the brink of these frightful precipices? It
appears to have been all done for the sake of the
artist and the lover of the picturesque. And yet
Bozouls grew to be a village in an age when men of
work and action only knew two kinds of enthusiasm
—war and religion. Either a castle or a religious
foundation must have been the beginning of this
community. There are no remains of a fortress,
but the church is very old, and its elaborate architecture suggests that it was at one time attached to
a monastic establishment. After crossing the stream
I climbed to this church by a path that wound about
the rocks, and found it an exceedingly interesting
example of the Southern Romanesque. The portal
opens into a narthex, where there is a very primitive
font like a low square trough. The nave entrance
has two columns on each side supporting archivolts,
and upon the capitals of these columns are carved
figures of the quaintest Romanesque character,
illustrating Biblical subjects. The nave has an
aisle on each side scarcely four feet wide, and most
of the separating columns are out of the perpendicular. The capitals here are wrought with
acanthus-leaves or little figures. The sanctuary
and apse are in the style of Auvergne, with this
peculiarity, that the capitals of the slender columns

are singularly massive, and bear only the mere outline of the acanthus-leaf for ornament.

The long street of the village, white and sun-baked, running within a few yards of the precipice, was almost as deserted as the church. But for a Sister who stood by the convent gate like a statue of Eternal Silence, and a man who was killing a wretched calf in the middle of the road, I might have asked myself if this fantastic Bozouls was not some spectral village, reproducing the past in all except the living beings who had gone down into their graves. When I recrossed the Dourdou, the light was several tones lower than it was when I first descended to the bottom of the ravine, and the vegetation was of a deeper and sadder green. And the stream rushed onward with a low wail, and a distressful cry, as of a soul passing down the Dark Valley and not yet free from the panic of death.

When I had reached the plateau that I had left an hour or more ago, the sun was about to set. As I knew that the *diligence* to Espalion would soon pass, I preferred to wait for it rather than to walk any farther. The south wind was blowing with such force that I lay down on the leeside of a bush to be sheltered from it. Here I watched the sun burning dimly in a yellow haze on the edge of the world. The wind wailed amongst the leaves of the hawthorn-bushes, but over the brown land, flushed with the sad yellow gleam, came the sound of cattle-bells, softening the harshness of the solitude, and bringing almost a smile upon the careworn face of Nature. I watched the dingy golden light rising up the stubble of the hills. Now the sun began to dip behind a knoll; a far-off tree stood in the line of vision, and I could see the leaves shaking as if in frenzy against the disc of sullen fire. Then from the edge of the western sky shot up into the yellow haze fair colours of pink and purple that seemed to say: 'The south wind may blow and burn the beauty of the earth, but the west wind will come again, its light wings laden with refreshment and joy.' The sun was gone, the shadows of night were being laid upon the dreary land, when the wavy clouds about the brightening moon became like a shower of rose-petals; the breeze grew softer and softer, for it was, in the language of the peasant, the 'sun-wind,' and the nocturnal peace began to reign over the sadness of the day's death.

The sound of jingling bells coming rapidly nearer roused me from my contemplative mood. The *diligence*, so called, was in sight, and a few minutes later I took my place in the very stuffy box on wheels, nearly filled with women and bundles. As it was only a drive of some seven or eight miles to Espalion, the town was reached in good time for dinner. I sat at a side-table in the large room of the inn, at the door of which the coach stopped. The central table was already occupied by half a dozen persons—all fat, vulgar, and noisy. They were examples of the *petit bourgeois* class whom one meets rather too frequently wherever there are towns in this part of France, and with whom the disposition to grossness is equally apparent in mind and body. There were women in the party, but had they been absent, the language of the men would have been no coarser. These fat and middle-aged women, married, doubtless, and highly respectable after their fashion, when struck by each gust of humour, such as might issue from the mouth of a foul-minded buffoon at a fair, rolled like ships at sea.

I passed a troubled night at Espalion, for there were a couple of feathered fiends just underneath the window crowing against each other with maddening rivalry. One, an old cock, had a very hoarse crow, and seemed to be suffering from chronic laryngitis brought on by an abuse of his vocal powers; and the other was a young cock with a very squeaky crow, for he was still taking lessons, and, as is the case with many beginners, he had too much enthusiasm.

I had had more than enough of this duo before the night was through, and was out very early in the morning looking at the ancient town of Espalion, which witnessed both the victory and the defeat of British arms long ere the Maid of Domrémy came to the rescue of the golden lilies. Its capture took place soon after the Battle of Crécy. The lords of Espalion were the Calmont d'Olt, who played an active part in the wars with the English. The town deserves a prominent place among the many picturesque old burgs stamped with mediæval character on the banks of the Lot. One may stand upon its Gothic bridge of the thirteenth century and dream of the past without risk of being hustled by a crowd except on market days. This venerable bridge must have been admirably built to have withstood all the floods which have smote it in the course of six centuries. The great central arch is so much higher than the others that in crossing you go up a hill and then down one. Close by on the river-bank is the sixteenth-century Hôtel de Ville, a castle, partly built on a rock, in the gracefully-ornamental style of the French Renaissance, with turrets, mullioned windows, and a loggia.

Having crossed the river, I went in search of the chief architectural curiosity in or near Espalion— that known as the Church of Pers, or the Chapel of St. Hilarion. It is on the outskirts of the town, and stands in the old cemetery. I had first to find a potter who kept the key, and I discovered him at length in a narrow street in the midst of his clay and the vessels of his handicraft. He gave me the great key, and it was one that some fervent archæologist might press reverentially to his heart, for the smith who forged it must have died centuries ago. Entering the cemetery, I saw, surrounded by a multitude of closely-packed tombs and grave mounds, on which the long grass stood with the late summer flowers, a small Romanesque building that seemed to have sunk far into the soil, like the ancient lichen-covered slabs from which the inscriptions had been washed away by time's inexorable and ever-wearing sea. Perhaps the soil had risen about the walls.

This church of the twelfth century is built of red sandstone, the blocks being laid together without mortar. On entering it such a dimness falls, with such a sacred silence; the air is so heavy with dampness and the odour of mildew, that you feel as if you were already in the vestibule of the Halls of Death, where darkness and stillness have never known the sound of a human voice or the blessed light of the sun. The design of the building is that of a nave with transept and apse. At each end of the transept is some curious cross-vaulting. The columns have all very large capitals in proportion to the diameter and height; some are ornamented with plain acanthus-leaves, others are carved with numerous small figures of men and animals, ideally uncouth and typical of the fantastic medley of Christian symbolism and the barbaric imagination that found a mystical relationship between the monsters of its own creation and the problems of the universe. The exterior of the church is not less interesting than the interior. The charming Romanesque apse, with its three narrow windows, its blind arcade, the capitals ornamented with the acanthus, the row of fantastic modillions above carried all round the building, their sculpture exhibiting the strangest variety of ideas—heads of men, women, beasts, birds, and fabulous monsters; and then the venerable portal, with its elaborate bas-relief of the Last Judgment, furnish much matter for reflection and study. In this 'Judgment' Christ is standing in the midst of the Apostles, and the dead are rising from the tombs below. Fiends are pulling the wicked out of their coffins, and others are throwing the condemned into the wide-opened jaws of a frightful monster. Above are numerous figures separated by various mouldings forming archivolts. The arch of the door is Gothic, but all the other work is Romanesque. The belfry is simply a roofed wall pierced with four arched openings for bells.

Espalion had once its strong fortress on a neighbouring hill—the Castle of Calmont d'Olt. It is now a ruin. I climbed to it, and found the undertaking more tedious than I had supposed. The narrow path winding through the vineyards was bordered with cat-mint, agrimony, vervain, and camomile. Then it passed through a little village, where there were old walnut-trees and mossy walls, and a small church with these words over the door: 'C'est ici la maison de Dieu et la porte du ciel.' After the village, the path was almost lost amidst blocks of sandstone and the *débris* of the fortress, where snakes basking in the sun slid away at my approach, hissing indignantly at the intruder. On the summit there had been in the far-off ages an outpour of basalt, which had crystallized into columnar prisms, and upon this foundation of ancient lava the castle was built. A good deal of wall and the lower part of a rectangular keep remain of this fortress, which dates from the twelfth century. The outer wall was strengthened with semicircular bastions, the ruins of which are seen. Fennel now thrives amongst the fallen stones, which were dumb witnesses of so much that was human.

Returning to the inn, I resisted the temptation held out to stop and lunch, although the preparations in the kitchen were far advanced, and started off on the road to Estaing. I was again following the Lot, which here flows between high vine-clad hills. After walking a few miles, I saw a bush over the door of a roadside cottage, and, entering, found that the only person in charge of this very rustic inn was a pretty girl of about seventeen. She looked a little scared at first; but when I had sat down with the evident intention of making myself at home, she became reconciled to the sight of me, and consented to let me have what there was in the house to eat. This was not much, as she took care to point out. The nearest approach to meat there was eggs, excepting, of course, the fat bacon—quite uneatable in the English fashion—which is the basis of all the soup made throughout a great part of France. Having lighted a fire on the hearth, and fried me some eggs with bits of fat bacon instead of butter, she said she must go and call 'papa,' who was working in the vineyard. So she left me in charge of the inn while she went to fetch her father on the hillside. While I was alone, I looked at the sunny view of green meadows and trees through the open door that faced the shining river, and easily fancied that what I saw was a bit of verdant England. In the room, too, the twittering of a pair of canaries recalled impressions of other days; but the plague of flies was thoroughly French, and it soon brought me back to realities. When the girl returned with her father, she gave me some excellent goat-cheese, and for my dessert some hazelnuts, together with a spirit distilled from plums, similar to the *quertch* of Alsace.

I had not been long in the sunshine again, when I noticed a large house in the midst of the vines not far off the road. On drawing near I found that it was ruinous, and had been long since abandoned. It had been a rather grand house once, and must have belonged to people of importance in the country. There was a finely-carved scutcheon with arms over the Gothic door, and the mullioned windows, which had lost all their glass, had something of the pathos of gentility that, becoming poor and old, has been abandoned to all winds and weathers. The little courtyard was full of high weeds and shrubs, and the wild flags that grow on the rocks had laid their green leaves together to hide the wounds of the old walls. Swallows, sparrows, and bats were now the tenants of this mysterious house, which must have had a troubled history. The picture has since haunted my memory; the mind goes back to it in a strange way, and the sentiment of it, as it was communicated to me, I find perfectly expressed in these lines by Alphonse Karr:

> 'De la solitaire demeure
> Une ombre lourde d'heure en heure,
> Se détache sur le gazon,
> Et cet ombre, couchée et morte
> Est la seule chose qui sorte
> Tout le jour de cette maison.'

Some distance farther I passed another deserted dwelling. It was perched upon rocks, and was overgrown with ivy and clematis. The road led me down beside the Lot, which now began to rush again over rocks as the hills drew closer, and the valley became once more a gorge. On one side were dense woods; on the other vines reached up to the sky.

At length I saw before me a row of houses beside the river in a bright bit of valley hemmed in by high cliffs. On the rocks behind the houses were a church and a castle.

This was Estaing. It is a little place full of originality, and looks as if it had been built to set forth the dream of some old writer of romance. The late-Gothic church is more quaint and odd than beautiful. The architect sported with the laws of symmetry, and revelled in the fanciful. The nave is much wider at one end than the other. The great sundial over the door, bearing the date 1636, is scarcely less useful now than when it was placed there. The castle is a strange pile, all the more picturesque by its incongruity. It stands upon a mass of schistous rock about fifty feet above the river. Most of the visible portion of the building is late Gothic and Renaissance; but this was grafted upon the lower walls and arches of a feudal fortress. Towers rise from towers, mullioned windows have their lines cut in the shadow of beetling machicolations, and higher still are dormer windows with graceful Gothic gables. This castle is now a convent and village school. From the court I could see the Sisters' little garden, where flowers and melons and potherbs were curiously mixed without the gardener's systematic art, which is so often a deadly thing to beauty; and nasturtiums climbing the weedy walls from rough deal boxes were basking in the steady glow of afternoon sun, which seemed to me so intensely brilliant because I was in the dark shadow. A Sister consented to let me go to the top of the highest tower, and she went before me rattling her keys officially. On the way she showed me a fine Renaissance chimney-piece with florid carvings.

After Estaing the valley became wilder, and the river fell over rocks in a series of cascades. Clouds came up and hid the sun; a rainy wind made the willows hoary, and set all the poplar leaves sighing and quivering. The vines had disappeared, and the wooded gorge became very solemn in the fading light. There was one figure in the landscape—that of a peasant woman bending and rolling up into bundles the hemp that had been spread out to dry. It added the human touch of melancholy to the sadness of the picture. More and more gloomy became the scene. Great black precipitous rocks of schist, their hollows filled with sombre foliage, rose in solemn grandeur far above me, and in the bottom the plunging stream foamed and roared. The mad wind caught up the dust from the road and whirled it onward, and then the rain began to fall. Rockier and darker became the way, and louder the roar of the stream. So narrow was the gorge at length that the road ran along a ledge that had been cut in the gneiss.

When I was still some miles from Entraygues (called by the peasants Entrayou), I met a young gendarme. He did not ask me for my papers, for he was a native of the district of Lourdes, and had been brought into contact with so many English people at Pau that he detected at once my Britannic accent, which has not been worn away by many years' residence in France. To him the fact of my being an Englishman was a sufficient assurance that I was respectable. He was a rakish, devil-may-care fellow, who, after being a sub-officer in the army, had lately been moved into the gendarmérie. His heart had been deeply touched by an English governess whom he had met at Pau, and he spoke to me about her with 'tears in his voice.' He talked much about Lourdes, where he said the people were sincerely religious, and not hypocritical. His opinion of the Aveyronnais was somewhat different, but perhaps unjust, for as yet he could not have had much experience of them. Having taken the precaution to tell me that he was anything but a strict Catholic himself, he declared that he was a believer in miracles.

'Why?' I asked.

'Because,' said he, 'my father saw Bernadette go up a rock on her knees—one that no man could climb—and I myself have been a witness of miracles at Lourdes. I have seen at least twenty people cured at the fountain. One was a captain, who was so paralyzed that he had to be carried to the water, and when he came away he walked as if nothing had been the matter with him.'

Thus talking we reached Entraygues. I allowed the gendarme to take me to the inn of his fancy, which he praised with true Southern warmth for its comfort and good cheer. The large kitchen as we entered was only lighted by the flame of the wood-fire on the hearth, in front of which a fowl and a piece of veal were turning on the same spit, moved by clockwork that said 'click-clack, click-clack;' which was as genial an invitation to dinner as any I had ever heard. Presently the lamp was lighted, the table was laid, and I sat down to dinner with the innkeeper and the gendarme from the Basses Pyrénées. The meal was of the substantial kind, such as gives complete satisfaction to the wayfarer at the end of his day's wandering, after putting up with frugal fare on the road. The aubergiste brought out his best wine, and his best cheeses made from goat's milk, and which had been kept carefully wrapped up in vine leaves. These little cheeses, when they have been allowed to mature in a wrapping of vine or plane leaf, are among the best made. The landlord had studied all matters relating to the stomach within the range of his experience. He said that hares were not fit to eat unless they had fed chiefly on thyme, and that a starling had no value in the kitchen until it had been feeding on juniper berries.

This night when I went to bed I had not the frantic crowing of cocks to keep me awake, but the soft murmuring of the flowing river to lull me asleep. The weather being now fair and calm after the troubled evening, I threw the window open, so that I could feel the wafting of the great invisible wings of the summer night, and listen to the soothing song of the water repeating the tales that were told to it by the rocks and the woods on its way down from the Lozère mountains.

I was again on the banks of this beautiful river—at no place more beautiful than at Entraygues—when the rising sun was gilding only the topmost vines of the high western hill that shadows it. The little town of 2,000 inhabitants is close to the spot where the Thuyère falls into the Lot. It lies in the angle

where two lovely valleys meet. The Thuyère
comes down from the Cantal mountains, and as it
reaches Entraygues it spreads out over a broad
smooth bed of pebbles, its water as clear as rock-
crystal; and when the morning sun looks down
upon it over the vine-clad hills, it is like something
that has been seen in the happiest of dreams.
There is a castle at Entraygues, and, as in the case
of the one at Estaing, it is now used as a convent
and school. The archæologist will find perhaps
more to interest him in the two thirteenth-century
bridges which span the Lot and the Thuyère, both
noble specimens of Gothic work.

As I left Entraygues the bells in the church-
tower were ringing—not the monotonous ding-dong
with which French people generally have had to
content themselves since the Revolutionists turned
the old bell-metal into sous, but a blithe and joyous
peal of high silvery tones that seemed to belong to
the blue air, and to be the voices of the little spirits
that flutter about the morning's rosy veil. My
design was to reach the abbey of Conques before
evening, but instead of going directly towards it
over the hills, I preferred to keep as long as possible
in the valley of the Lot, which is here of such
witching loveliness. As there was a road on the
river-bank for many miles, I could follow this fancy,
and yet feel the comfort of walking on good ground.
Although the season was getting late, I found the
valley below Entraygues very rich in flowers.

Agrimony, mint, and marjoram, with a tall inula, and the pretty, sweet-scented white melilot, were in great abundance along the bank. Upon the rocks, which now bordered the road, were the deep red blossoms of the orpine sedum, and a small crimson-flowered stock with very hoary stem. A tall handsome plant about three feet high, with large white flowers, drew me down a bank to where it was growing near the water. I found that it was a very luxuriant specimen of the thorn-apple (*datura*). While I was admiring its poisonous beauty a woman stopped on the road just above me, and, after contemplating me in silent curiosity for a few minutes, said to me first in *patois* and then in French (when I replied to her in this language):

'It is a wicked plant, that! The beasts will not touch it, so you had better leave it alone.'

Although I did not think this association of ideas very complimentary to myself, I thanked her for her good advice. I nevertheless took away as a souvenir a flower and one of the thorny apples, seeing which the peasant trudged on her way, saying no doubt that it was wasting time and words to give advice to lunatics. Again the cliffs drew very close together, and the valley was nothing more than a deep crack in the earth's crust. On one side was unbroken forest; on the other vines were terraced up the rocky steep to the height of seven or eight hundred feet. Even amidst the jutting crags the adventurous vine lifted its sunny leaves; but, alas! here, too, the phylloxera had begun its work of desolation, and I had little doubt that these hills laden with fruit were destined in a few years to become a waste of stones like so many others that I had seen nearer the plains which had once streamed with wine. The cultivated land by the river was only a narrow strip, and the crops were chiefly maize and buckwheat. At length the vine cultivation was only carried on at intervals. Then the long blue line of water lay between high rocky hills covered with box and broom, bracken and heather. A stream came tumbling down a deep ravine over blocks of gneiss to join the Lot, and a little beyond this was a hamlet.

The morning was now far advanced; so, as I was passing a cottage inn, I wavered a minute, and the result of the wavering was that I crossed the threshold. I said to myself: 'Perhaps I may walk on for miles, and not find another chance so good as this.' It was one of the poorest of inns, but it was able to give me a meal of bread and cheese and eggs, which was as much as I could expect hereabouts. There was also a light wine of local growth—sparkling, fragrant, and deliciously cool. What more could I want? Two motherless girls looked after this waterside inn, and also the ferry belonging to it. The boat lay a few feet from the door. When I was ready to leave, the younger of the two girls ferried me to the other side of the river, and a very pretty figure she made for an artist to sketch—the simplicity of childhood in her face, and the strength of a woman in her bare sunburnt arms. As is the case with so many of the peasants in this district, where the old Gaulish stock (the *Ruteni* and the *Cadurci*) has been much less influenced than in the towns by the tumultuous passage of races from the south, the east, and the north, she was fair-haired, and naturally fair-skinned; but exposure to the sun had darkened her by many shades.

I had been walking for some time in the department of the Cantal, but the ferry landed me on the Aveyron side of the river. I had now seriously to consider the shortest way to Conques, separated from me by very rough hill country and an uncertain number of miles. I was on a narrow path skirting the forest and the water, when I met a peasant family dressed in their best clothes, and on their way, as I learnt, to the village of Notre Dame, where the *fête patronale* was being held. The man, who seemed well pleased with himself in his new black blouse, carried the sleeping baby, and his wife held a great coloured umbrella over it. They were followed by a girl of about fourteen, who wore the open-work hand-made white stockings which the young women of these southern villages use on festive occasions as soon as they begin to grow coquettish. I fell into conversation with these people, who told me that, after reaching the village, I must commence the ascent through the forest. Speaking to the man about the trout, which are plentiful in this part of the river, he entertained me with a story of a selfish angler who once came there, and who had a fish on his hook as soon as he threw a fly. The people of the district—who, it seems, know nothing about fly-fishing—watched his success with wonder and admiration, and asked him to explain to them how he managed to catch fish in that way; but he was surly, and refused to give them any lessons. He had imitators, nevertheless; but after spending many hours vainly endeavouring to hook the crafty trout, they lost patience, and gave up the attempt.

Two or three score of houses huddled together at the foot of a rocky cliff, a little above the water, was Notre Dame. The village was all in movement. The space in front of the church was crowded with peasant figures: a bell was swinging backward and forward in the wall-belfry, as though it was trying to turn right over; stall-keepers with cakes, barley-sugar, and other dainties dear to the village child, to whom the opportunity of feasting even his eyes upon such things comes very seldom, were surrounded by eager little faces, and outstretched sunburnt hands, each clutching the sou that offered such a bewildering field for dissipation. In the auberge hard by was a noisy throng of peasants sitting and standing in a cloud of smoke. Serving-women, hired for the occasion, gaily coifed and be-ribboned, holding bottles and glasses elbowed their way to the men who shouted the loudest for drink, and, catching the jest in the air, gave one as good or as bad in exchange. The scene was one for another Teniers to paint, although there were no costumes to give a local colour to the picturesque. Most of the older men wore the ugly short blouse—generally black in this part of France; but ambitious youths of eighteen or twenty showed a preference for the cloth coat which the village tailor had tried to cut according to the Paris fashion.

Leaving the rustic revellers, the queer little church, with its ancient calvary, rudely carved, and resting upon a single column, I was soon in the shadow of the old chestnut forest that covered the steep side of the high cliffs above the Lot. The path was very rocky and toilsome. A young man, who was hastening down from his home on the hills to join the merrymakers, said to me, in allusion to the roughness of the way: 'Le bon Dieu ne passe pas souvent par ici,' thereby expressing the sentiment of the peasant, who associates all that is wild and rugged in nature with the devil. While still in the forest, and not a little puzzled by its paths, I met a woman and a youth, and asked them if the way I was taking led to Conques. '*Apé*' (yes) was the reply. Not a word of French could I draw from them. When the cliffs were at length scaled, and I was on the open tableland, I found the south wind blowing there with great violence, although in the valley there was scarcely breeze enough to ripple the river pools. The sun was falling into the yellow haze of the west as I began to descend towards the valley of the Dourdou. I came upon a tributary of this stream in the bottom of a deep and solemn gorge, whose steep sides were densely wooded except where the rock jutted out and revealed its dark nakedness, and where higher, near the sky, showed here and there a patch of heather-purple waste, on which the brilliant light was softening into evening tones. But in the depth of the gorge, where the redly-running stream was nearly hidden under the tent of leaves, the air was already dim, and the forms of the trees were beginning to blend with their own shadows.

Following the stream in its course, I found the Dourdou, and then turned down the broader valley. I was tramping wearily on my way, which seemed endless, when, clustered on the side of another wild and thickly wooded gorge running up amidst the hills, I saw many houses, and a dark pile of masonry, rising far above their roofs. I knew that this must be Conques; it showed its religious origin so plainly in the choice of the site. This was selected not because Nature was gentle and pitiful to man in the cleft of those savage hills, but because she was stern and solemn, and the veil that hides the supernatural was felt to be thinner there, where the rocks and forest seemed to the mediæval mind to have remained just as the Almighty hand had fashioned them. A monastery arose in the desert, then the abbey church, and gradually a little lay community placed itself under the protection of the religious one.

A long narrow street, steep and stony, leads to the church, which is all that is left of the Benedictine abbey, excepting some massive buttresses, ruinous arches, and a round tower grafted upon the rock — remnants of the ancient monastery which must have been half a fortress. The burg itself was fortified, and one of the gateways of the old wall is still standing. The existing church dates from the eleventh century, but various details point to the conclusion that it was built on the site of a more ancient structure. For example, in the entrance is a holy-water stoup, the basin having been scooped out of the capital of a column which is supposed to have been one of the supports of a very primitive altar. The figure of an emperor is carved on one of the faces, and on another that of a pagan divinity. The architecture of the church is simple and majestic, the only jarring note being the cupola raised about the time of the Renaissance over the intersection of the nave and transept. The barrel-vaulted nave, crossed by plain broad fillets, is in keeping with the early Romanesque severity of the façade. The ornament is nearly confined to the tympan over the portal, the capitals of columns, and to the choir with its seven absidal chapels. The choir itself is cross-vaulted, and the sanctuary, except at its junction with the nave, is enclosed by an arcade of narrow stilted arches, the only ornament of the capitals being acanthus leaves; but those against the wall are elaborately storied with little figures. A moulding of small billets is carried round the apse. The great height of the nave vaulting, obtained by a triforium and clerestory, is very remarkable in a Romanesque church of such early construction. In accordance with the style of the period, the capitals of the nave show a complete absence of uniformity, some being carved with figures, and others with leaves or intricate line ornament. To obtain an adequate impression of all the fantastic imagination expressed in these capitals, and the craftsmanship brought to bear upon the carving, it is necessary to climb to the triforium galleries. The aisle windows are narrow and placed high in the wall. The interest of the exterior is centred upon the bas-relief representing the Last Judgment, which fills the entire tympan of the arch covering the two main doorways. The composition, which contains over a hundred figures, is singularly animated, and although the forms are uncouthly proportioned, and the treatment of the subject in some of the details touches what to the modern mind seems grotesque, it is an exceedingly vivid and faithful reflection of the religious ideas of the age that produced it. What now appears grotesque was then sublime and awful. We smile at the barbaric imagination that placed here, at the door of hell, the head of a vast and hideous monster of the crocodile family, into whose gaping jaws the damned are being thrust by a pantomime devil; but eight centuries ago Christian people had too lively a faith in the materialistic horrors of the infernal kingdom to perceive anything extravagant in this idea of stuffing a scaly monster with condemned sinners. Eight centuries ago!—the peasant of the Aveyron and of Finistère still look upon these Dantesque sculptures with genuine awe. Those who blame the monks for giving the devil a forked tail and a pair of horns, and otherwise exhausting their invention in the endeavour to materialize the terrors of hell, are strangely unphilosophic. The mass of humanity with whom the monks had to deal had the minds of children in regard to metaphysical ideas; only by the pictorial method could they be sufficiently impressed with the joys or horrors of the future life. Bas-reliefs such as this must have had a great influence on the conduct of many generations; nor has their influence yet ceased, although, as popular education spreads, the interest taken in these quaint sculptures by those for whom they were especially intended, so far from being stimulated, is lessened. Inasmuch as the mind needs deep ploughing for the new culture, and the majority can get no more than a superficial raking, the peasant of to-day is often a poorer man intellectually than his father was—poorer by the loss of faith and the confusion of ideas.

The sculptor of this Last Judgment—a Benedictine monk, doubtless, like the architect of the church who has left this personal record, 'Bernardus me fecit,' upon a stone in a dim corner—died centuries ago, and although his bones or their dust may be near, his name will never be known. But how his mind lives in the figures that took life under his hand! With what inspired longing of the soul he must have conceived and felt the majesty of Christ sitting in judgment at the end of time to have expressed so much that is sublime in the holy face and figure with his poor knowledge of art! The right hand is raised to bless the just, and the left repels the unforgiven. Grouped around the central figure are saints and angels. Peter, holding his keys, is followed by a crowd of the elect, headed by an old man on crutches, and a crowned sovereign —said to be Charlemagne—carries a reliquary. In the lower half of the tympan Satan is enthroned, his feet resting upon a writhing and hideously grimacing figure, supposed to be that of Judas. Immediately above, an angel and a fiend are weighing souls in a pair of scales, and the demon is trying to cheat. In this lower division the infernal punishments inflicted upon sinners of different categories are set forth. The sin of Francesca and Paolo is treated less poetically than by Dante, for here two guilty lovers are seen hanging to the same rope. A glutton is being stuffed with flaming viands, sent up from the devil's kitchen. All manner of torture

is being inflicted by jubilant demons upon the souls
that have fallen into their clutches. One has caught
in the net that he has just thrown a mitred abbot
and two other monks. As the dead rise from their
tombs the justiciary angels bar the way of the
wicked who strive to approach the Judge. A
seraphim holds the closed book of life, upon which
these words are carved: 'Hic signatur liber vitæ.'
On various parts of the portal are numerous inscriptions, some of which, like the following, are in
leonine verses:

> 'Casti pacifici mites pietatis amici
> Sic stant gaudentes securi nil metuentes.'

The archæological interest of Conques is not confined to its church. Here, hidden from the world in
this obscure little gorge, far from any railway-station,
is one of the most remarkable collections of ancient
reliquaries in France. The chief treasure is the
very ancient gold statue of St. Foy (Sancta Fides)
virgin and martyr, the patron saint of Conques. It
is a seated figure nearly three feet in height, and
its appearance is thoroughly Byzantine; indeed,
one may go farther, and say that it looks much more
pagan than Christian. There is nothing in the
treatment that indicates a Christian motive; while
the antique engraved gems with which it is studded,
illustrating, as some of them do, workings of the
Greek and Roman mind very far removed from the
Christian idea of what is becoming in morals, make
this astonishing statue an archæological puzzle.

The explanation that these gems were placed upon it to symbolize the victory of Christian purity over the impurity of the ancient religions of Greece and Rome is more ingenious than conclusive. This statue of gold (*repoussé*), with regal crown enriched with precious stones and enamels on which may be distinguished Jupiter, Mars, Apollo and Diana, among the more respectable of the divinities, if it was originally intended to represent the virgin Fides, martyred at Agen, was certainly one of the most fantastic achievements of ecclesiastical art. But whether this was its origin or not, the style of its workmanship is considered by competent judges to be sufficient proof that it is at least nine hundred years old.

In favour of the opinion that the statue was made at Conques, there is the fact that the cult of St. Foy at this place dates from the early Middle Ages. The ancient seal of the abbey bears the motto:

> 'Duc nos quo resides,
> Inclyta Virgo Fides.'

Historians of the abbey state that the relics of the saint were brought from Agen to Conques about the year 874, and that Etienne, Bishop of Clermont, caused a basilica to be raised here in her honour between the years 942 and 984. It was under the direction of Ololric, Abbot of Conques, that the existing church was built between the years 1030 and 1062. Throughout the Middle Ages the relics drew large numbers of pilgrims to the spot. In the dialect of the country they were called *Roumious*, because the pilgrimage to Conques was one of those which enjoyed the privilege of conferring under certain conditions the same advantages as were to be gained by the great pilgrimage to Rome. The pilgrims kept the 'holy vigil'—that is to say, they passed an entire night in prayer before the relics with a lighted taper either fixed at their side or carried in the hand. The pilgrimage and the ancient association of St. Foy were revived in 1874.

The darkness of night drove me to take shelter in an inn which, like everything else here, is dedicated to St. Foy. The pilgrims' money had not made it pretentious, nor the people who kept it dishonest—changes which 'filthy lucre' is very apt to bring about in the holiest places. But the pilgrims who come to Conques are, for the most part, peasants who look well before they leap, and who so contrive matters as never to spend more upon anything than they have set aside for it.

Having completed the next morning my impressions of Conques, noting among other things the curious and richly decorated *enfeux* in the exterior walls of the church, I returned to the bottom of the ravine, and having crossed the old Gothic bridge over the Dourdou, began the ascent of the rocky chestnut forest on the other side of the valley. Small white crosses planted at intervals amidst the broom and heather of the open wood marked the way to St. Foy's Chapel for the guidance of pilgrims. According to the legend, it was near this spot that, the relics of the saint having been set down by those who had carried them from Agen, a fountain of the purest water burst forth from the earth, and has continued to flow ever since. I found the chapel a modern Gothic one, with a statue of St. Foy in Roman dress in the niche over the door under a high rugged rock of schist. There was no one but myself to trouble the solitude of this quiet nook on the wild hillside, all broken up into little gullies and ravines, where the aged chestnuts sheltered the tender moss and fern from the eager sunbeam, and kept the dew upon the bracken until the noonday hours. An exquisitely delicate campanula with minute flowers bloomed with hemp-agrimony and wood-sage along the sides of the rills that scarcely murmured as they slid down the clefts of the impervious rock.

As I went higher, the chestnuts became more scattered, and at length the rough land was covered only by the tufted heather and broom. Here, instead of the light whispering of leaves, was the drowsy song of multitudinous bees. The breeze blew freshly on the plateau, and grew stronger as the sun rose. Could it be a cemetery, that grouping of stones that I saw upon the moorland? No; it was a cottage-garden, surrounded by disconnected slabs of mica-schist, standing like little menhirs. A peasant family lived in the wretched dwelling, exposed to the full force of the howling winds, and striving continually with nature for their black bread and the vegetables that give flavour to the watery soup.

A young man with a *béret* on his head overtook me. He was a Béarnais, who had not been long in the district, and who earned his living by certain services that he rendered at widely-scattered farms. He had to walk a great deal in all winds and weathers; therefore he knew the country well, and could give me useful information. I was crossing the hills with the intention of meeting the Lot again in the great coal basin of the Aveyron, and thus cutting off a wide bend of the river. All went well for some time after the Béarnais left me; but at length I became fairly bewildered by the woods and ravines, the hills and valleys that lay before me in seemingly endless succession. Savage rockiness, sylvan quietude, open solitudes, bare and wind-blown, gave me all the sensations of nature which expand the soul; but the body grumbled for rest and refreshment long before I had crossed this singularly wild tract of country almost abandoned by man I had been wading through bracken up to my neck, or wandering almost at hazard through chestnut-woods for an hour or two, when hope was revived by my meeting a peasant, who told me that I was not far from the village of Firmi. I left the great woods, and reached a district that was new in every sense. Entering a little gorge, to me it seemed that nature had been cursed there ages ago, and still carried the sign of the malediction in the sooty darkness of the rocks—jagged, tormented, baleful—that rose on either hand. Nothing grew upon them save a low wretched turf, and this only in patches. Beyond, the metamorphic rock gave place to red sandstone, and the ground sloped down into the little coal basin of Firmi. What a change of scene was there! The air was thick with smoke, the road was black with coal-dust, most of the houses were new and grimy, nearly all the faces were smutty. There was a confused noise of wheels going round, of invisible iron monsters grinding their teeth, of trollies rattling along upon rails, and of human voices. Nature had no charm; but of beauty combined with fasting I had had enough for awhile, so my prejudices melted before the genial ugliness of this sooty paradise, knowing as I did that prosperity goes with such griminess, and that where there is money there are inns offering creature comforts both to man and beast.

Either the angel or the goblin who goes a wayfaring with me led me this time into a heated little auberge infested by myriads of flies, which, getting into the steam of the *soupe aux choux* in their anxiety to be served first, fell upon their backs in the hot mixture, and made frantic signals to me with their legs to help them out. There was no temptation to linger at the table when the purpose for which I was there had been attained; so I was very soon on the tramp again, making for the valley of the Lot.

Leaving Décazeville a few miles to the west, I took the direction of Cransac, being curious to see the 'Smoking Mountains' in that district. Between the little coal basin of Firmi and the large one at Cransac and Aubin lay a strip of toilsome hill country. I had left the round tower of the ruined castle of Firmi below, and was following a winding path up a steep chestnut wood, when two mounted gendarmes passed me going down. About five minutes later I heard the sound of horses' hoofs coming near again. 'One of the gendarmes is returning,' was my reflection, and, looking round, I saw this was really so. The man was trotting his horse up the wood. Being sure that he was coming after me, I walked slower, and gave myself the most indifferent and loitering air that I could put on. In a few minutes he reined up his horse at my side. He was a young man, and his expression told me that he did not much like the duty that his chief had put upon him. Addressing me, he said:

'Pardon, monsieur, you are a stranger in this country?'

'Yes, I am.'

'Will you please tell me your quality?'

In reply I asked him if he wished to see my papers.

'If it will not vex you,' he said. His manners

were quite charming. If he was a native of the Rouergue, the army had polished him up wonderfully. After looking at the papers and finding them satisfactory, he said: 'Je vous demande pardon, monsieur, mais vous comprenez——'

'Oh yes, I understand perfectly, and I assure you that my feelings are not at all hurt!'

And so we parted on very good terms. A woman standing at a cottage door at a little distance watched the scene with a scared and wondering look in her face. When I was again alone, and she saw me coming towards her, she disappeared with much agility into her fortress and shut the door. She must have thought that, although I had managed to escape arrest that time, I should certainly come to a bad end.

After reaching the top of the hill, white smoke rising continually into the blue air led me to the *Montagnes fumantes*. Coming at length to the spot so named, 'Surely,' I thought, 'my wayfaring has brought me at last to the Phlegraean Fields.' All about me were rocks that had been burnt red, black, or yellow, and on their scorched surface not a shrub, nor a blade of grass, nor even a tuft of spurge, grew. The subterranean fires which had burnt these upper rocks had long since gone out; but a hot and sulphurous vapour still passed over them when the wind blew it in their direction. Continuing down the hillside, I heard a crackling as of stones being split by heat, and presently saw little tongues of flame shooting up from the crevices in the soil almost at my feet, but scarcely perceptible in the brilliant sunshine. From these and other vents, however, came intermittent puffs, or continuous fillets of smoke, and the air was almost overpoweringly hot and sulphurous. To wander by night among these jets of fire must be very stimulating to the imagination, for then the hill is lit up by them; but I thought the spot sufficiently infernal by daylight.

Beds of coal lying underneath this rocky hill, perhaps at a great depth, have been burning for centuries, and the same phenomenon is repeated elsewhere in the district. The popular legend is that the English, when they were compelled to abandon Guyenne, set fire to these coal-measures with the motive of doing all the mischief they could before leaving. Such fables are handed down from generation to generation. All the evil that happened to the region in the dim past is placed to the account of the English. These burning hills in the Aveyron have been turned to one good purpose. The hot air that escapes from crevices where there is neither smoke nor fire is used for heating little cabins which have been constructed for the treatment of persons suffering from rheumatic disorders. There they can obtain a natural vapour-bath that is both cheap and effectual.

At the foot of the cliffs lay Cransac, bristling with tall chimneys and in a cloud of dark coal-smoke that filled the valley. Here, instead of the solemn calm of the barren uplands, the murmurous chanting of rills and shallow rivers, and the mystical voices that speak from the depths of the forest, I heard the fretful buzz of a human beehive. Here was human life intensified and yet lowered in tone by aggregation, by the strain of organized effort that suppresses initiative and makes the value of a man merely a question of dynamics. The number of shops, especially of drinking-shops—sordid *cafés* and flashy *buvettes*, where the enterprising poisoners of the coal-miner stood behind their zinc counters pouring out the corrosive absinthe and the beetroot brandy—told of the prosperity of Cransac. Evidently it was a place in which money could be earned by those prepared to accept the conditions. The women wore better clothes than the wives of the peasants; but low morality, instead of the sad but always honourable stamp of ravaging toil, was impressed on many a female face. Even the children looked as degraded by the social atmosphere as they were blackened by the smoke and ever-falling soot. Hastening along the road towards Aubin, I soon found that the two places, separated according to the map by a considerable distance, had grown together. The long road powdered with coal-dust was now a street lined on each side with houses and hovels. Wooden shanties with sooty bushes of juniper hanging over the door, and the word 'Buvette' painted beneath, competed for the miner's money at distances of twenty or fifty yards. One had a notice such as is rarely seen in France, and which was significant here: 'Ready money for everything sold over the counter.' Close by was the sign of a *sage-femme*, who, under the picture of a woman holding aloft in triumph an unreasonably fat baby, announced that she also bled and vaccinated. Grimy children and grimy pigs that were intended to be white or pink sprawled upon the thresholds or wallowed in the hot dust.

Having left the blissful coal basin, I met the Lot again near the boundary-line of the Aveyron and entered the department named after the river. Thence to Capdenac the valley was a curving line of uninterrupted but ever-changing beauty.

The season was farther advanced when I continued the journey from this point to Cahors.

A person who had contracted the 'morphia habit' would probably find the most effectual cure for it by forced residence at Capdenac, because the town does not boast the luxury of a chemist's shop. Supposing the patient, however, to be a lady of worldly tastes, she might die of *ennui* in twenty-four hours. The Capdenac of which I am speaking is not the utterly unpicturesque collection of houses that has been formed about the well-known railway junction on the line to Toulouse, but old romantic Capdenac, whose dilapidated ramparts, dating from the early Middle Ages, crown the high rocky hill that rises abruptly from the valley on the other side of the Lot, which here separates the department named after it from the Aveyron. The situation of this town is one of the most remarkable. It is perched upon a lofty table of reddish rock of the same calcareous composition as that which prevails throughout the region of the *causses*. Its walls are so escarped that the topmost crags in places overhang the path that winds about their base far below. Only strategical considerations could ever have induced men to build a town on such a site. The Gauls set the example, and their *oppidum* was long supposed to have been Uxellodunum, but the controversy has been settled in favour of the Puy d'Issolu.

I chose the hour of eight in the morning for climbing the rock of Capdenac. The broad winding river was brilliantly blue, like the vault overhead, and although the vine-clad hills, which shut in the valley, and the bare rocks, whose outlines were sharply drawn against the sky, were luminous, the light had the pure and clear sparkle of the morning. Reaching the hill, I took a zigzag stony path that led through terraced vineyards. The vintage had commenced, and men, women, and children were busy picking the purple grapes still wet with dew.

The children only, however, showed any joy in the work, for the bunches hung at such a distance from each other that a vine was very quickly stripped. The *vigneron*, with his mind dwelling upon the bygone fruitful years, when these arid steeps poured forth torrents of wine as surely as

October came round, wore an expression on his face that was not one of thankfulness to Providence. They are a rather surly people, moreover, the inhabitants of this district, and I do not think at any time their hearts could have been very expansive. As I approached a woman who had a great basket of grapes in front of her, she hastily threw a bundle of leaves over them, casting a keenly suspicious glance at me the while. If she meant me to understand that the times were too bad for grapes to be given away, the movement was unnecessary. Where now are the generous sentiments and the poetry traditionally associated with the vintage? Not here, certainly. Men go out into their vineyards by night armed with guns, and the depredators whom they fear most are not dogs that have acquired a taste for grapes. The stony path was bordered by brambles, overclimbed by clematis, whose glistening awns were mingled with blackberries, which not even a child troubled to pick. There was much fleabane—a plant that deserves to be cherished in these parts, if it be really what its name indicates, but it would have to be extensively cultivated to be a match for the fleas. After the vineyards came the dry rock, that held, however, sufficient moisture for the wild fig-tree, wherever it could find a deep crevice.

Passing underneath the perpendicular wall of rock, and the vine-clad ramparts above it, built on the very edge of the precipice, the winding path led me gradually up to the town. A little in front of an arched gateway was a ruined barbican, the inner surface of the walls being green with ferns and moss. Four loopholes were still intact. Had it been night I might have seen ghostly men with crossbows issuing from the gateway, but it being broad daylight, I was met by a troop of young pigs followed by a little hump-backed woman who addressed her youthful swine in the language of the troubadours.

In the narrow street beyond the arch a company of gigantic geese drew themselves up in order of battle, and challenged me in chorus to come on; but their courage was like that of Ancient Pistol. No other living creature did I see until I had walked nearly half through the ancient burg, between houses several centuries old, their stories projecting over the rough pitching and the stunted fig-trees which grew there unmolested. Some of these dwellings were in absolute ruin, with long dry grasses waving on the roofless walls. Nobody seemed to think it worth while to rebuild or repair anything. The town appeared to have been left to itself and to time for at least two hundred years. And yet there really were some inhabitants left. I found another gateway and another ruined barbican, and near to these, on the verge of the precipice, a high rectangular tower, which was the citadel and prison. The lower part was occupied by the schoolmaster of the commune, and he allowed me to ascend the winding staircase, which led to two horrible dungeons, one above the other. Neither was lighted by window or loophole, and but for the candle I should have been in utter darkness. Great chains by which prisoners were fastened to the wall still lay upon the ground, and as I raised them and felt their weight, I thought of the human groans that only the darkness heard in the pitiless ages. In another part of the building was a heavy iron collar that was formerly attached to one of these chains. There were also several old pikes in a corner.

A little beyond the citadel I found the church, a small Romanesque building without character. An eighteenth-century doorway had been added to it, and the tympan of the pediment was quite filled up with hanging plants. Still more suggestive of abandonment was the little cemetery behind, which was bordered by the ramparts. It was a small wilderness. Just inside the entrance, a life-sized figure with outstretched arms lay against a damp wall in a bed of nettles and hemlock. It had become detached from the cross on which it once hung, and had been left upon the ground to be overgrown by weeds. I have seen many a neglected rural cemetery in France, but never one that looked so sadly abandoned as this. It was like the 'sluggard's garden,' where 'the thorn and the thistle grow higher and higher.' Most of the gravestones and crosses were quite hidden by dwarf elder, artemisia, wild carrot, and other plants all tangled together. A grave had just been dug in this wilderness and it was about to have a tenant, for the two bells in the open tower were sounding the *glas*, and a distant murmur of chanting was growing clearer. The priest had gone to 'fetch the body,' and the procession was now on its way. On the top of the earth and stones thrown up on each side of the new grave were a broken skull, a jawbone, several portions of leg and arm bones, besides many smaller fragments of the human framework. I thought the gravedigger might at least have thrown a little earth over these remains out of consideration for the feelings of those who were about to stand around this grave, but concluded that he probably understood the people with whom he had to deal. Presently this functionary—a lantern-jawed, nimble old man, with a dirty nightcap on his head—made his appearance to take a final look at his work. After strutting round the very shallow hole he had dug, in an airy, self-satisfied manner, he concluded that everything was as it should be, and retired for the priest to perform his duty.

The great difficulty with the people of Capdenac in time of war must have been the water supply. When their cisterns were empty, they had the river at the bottom of the valley and a spring that flowed at certain seasons, as it does now, at the foot of the rock on which they had built their little town. When they were besieged, they could not descend to the Lot to draw water; consequently they laid great store by the stream at the base of the rock. A long zigzag flight of steps down the side of the precipice was constructed, and it was covered by a wall that protected those who fetched water from arrows and bolts. Near the spring this wall was built very high and strong, and was pierced with loopholes. It also served as an outwork. The steps and much of the wall still exist. The spring in modern times came to be called Cæsar's Well, because the elder Champollion and others endeavoured to prove that Capdenac was the site of Uxellodunum. The fact, however, that the spring is dry for several months in the year, and could never have been aught else but the drainage of the rock, is in itself a sufficient refutation of the hypothesis; because, according to Cæsar, the fountain at Uxellodunum was so perennially abundant that when he drew off the water by tunnelling, the Gauls recognised in this disaster the intervention of the gods.

Capdenac appears to have given the English a great deal of trouble, which the natural strength of the place fully explains. It must have been a fortress of the first order in the Middle Ages, and would be so to-day, if the French thought it worth while to use it in a military sense; but, happily for the inhabitants of this part of France, their territory now lies far from the theatre of any war that is likely to occur. A charter by Philippe le Long, dated 1320, another by King John, and a third by

Charles VII., recognise the immunity of the people of Capdenac from all public charges on account of the resistance which they constantly opposed to the English. The rock must, nevertheless, have fallen into the hands of a company attached to the British cause, for the Count of Armagnac bought the place in 1381 of a band of so-called English *routiers*. Sully lived there after the death of Henry IV., and the house that he occupied still exists.

According to a local tradition, Capdenac was on the point of being captured by the English, when it was saved from this fate by a stratagem. The defenders were starving, and the besiegers were relying upon famine to reduce them. In order to make the English believe that the place was still well provisioned, a pig was given a very full meal of all the corn that could be scraped together and then pushed over the side of the rock in a cautious manner, so that the animal might appear to be the victim of its own indiscretion. The pig fulfilled expectations by splitting open when it struck the ground, and thus revealed the corn that was in its body. When the English saw this, they said: 'If the men of Capdenac can afford to feed their swine on wheat, they must still have plenty for themselves.' Discouraged by this reflection, they raised the siege. When they went away there was not an ounce of bread left to divide amongst the garrison.

A market was being held at Capdenac—the lower town—as I left it. Bunches of fowls tied together

by the legs were dangling from the hands of a score
or so of peasant women standing in line. The
wretched birds had ceased to complain, and even to
wriggle; but although, with their toes upward and
their beaks downward, life to them could not have
looked particularly rosy, they seemed to watch with
keen interest all that was going on. Only when
they had their breasts well pinched by critical
fingers did they struggle against their fate. The
legs of these fowls are frequently broken, but the
peasants only think of their own possible loss; and
women are every bit as indifferent to the sufferings
of the lower animals as men.

There was a sharp wrangle going on in the
Languedocian dialect over a coin—a Papal franc—
that somebody to whom it had been offered angrily
rejected. Here I may say that one of the small
troubles of my life in this district came from accepting coins which I could not get rid of. As a
rule, the native here turns over a piece of money
several times before he satisfies himself that no
objection can be brought against it; but if, in the
hurry of business, the darkness of night, or the
trustfulness inspired by a little extra worship of
Bacchus, he should happen to take a Papal, Spanish,
Roumanian, or other coin that is unpopular, he puts
it on one side for the first simpleton or stranger
who may have dealings with him. Thus, without
intending it, I came to possess a very interesting numismatical collection, which I most un-

conscientiously, but with little success, tried to scatter.

I made my way down the valley of the Lot, taking the work easily, stopping at one place long enough to digest impressions before pushing on towards a fresh point. This valley is so strangely picturesque, so full of the curiosities of nature and bygone art, that if I had not been a loiterer before, I should have learnt to loiter here.

Keeping on the Aveyron side of the river, I soon reached the village of St. Julien d'Empare, where almost every house had somewhat of a castellated appearance, owing to the dovecot tower which occupied one angle and rose far above the roof. One of these houses had two rows of dormer windows, covered by little gables with very long eaves in the high-pitched roof, whose red tiles were well toned by time. The tower-like pigeon-house, with extinguisher roof, stood at one end upon projecting beams, and the pigeons kept going in and coming out of the holes in their two-storied mansion. One sees dovecots everywhere in this district, and most of them are two or three centuries old. Some are attached to houses, and others are isolated on the hillsides amongst the vines. When in the latter position, they are generally round, and are built on such a scale that they really look like towers.

There were grape-gatherers in the vineyards, but they had to search for the fruit. The wine grown

upon these hills by the Lot has been famous from
the days of the Romans; but there is very little of
it left. There is, however, a consoling side to every
misfortune. A man of Figeac told me that since the
vines had failed in the district the death-rate had
diminished remarkably.

'Why?' I asked.

'Why?' replied he, with a sad smile, 'because in
the happy times everybody drank wine at all hours
of the day; but now, in these miserable times, nearly
everybody drinks water.'

The new state of things would be still more
satisfactory from a teetotal point of view if Nature
were less niggardly of water in these parts. In some
localities it has to be strictly economized, and this is
done in the case of streams by using it first for the
exterior, and afterwards for the interior needs of
man. I, having still some English prejudices, would
rather run all the risks incurred by drinking wine,
than swallow any more than I am obliged of the
rinsings of dirty linen.

Having crossed the Lot by a suspension bridge,
a roadside inn enticed me with its little terrace,
where there were many hanging plants and flowers,
and a wild fig-tree that had climbed up from the
rock below, so that it could look into people's
glasses and listen to their talk in that pleasant
bower. I might have lingered here too long had it
not been for the wasps, which were even a greater
nuisance than the flies.

To reach the village of Frontenac I took a little path leading through maize-fields by the river's side. The maize was ready for the harvest, and the long leaves had lost nearly all their greenness. The lightest breath of air made each plant rustle like a paper scarecrow. The river was fringed with low, twiggy willows and a multitude of herbs, rich in seeds, but poor in flowers. Among those still in bloom were the evening primrose, soapwort, and marjoram. The river was as blue as the heaven, and on each side rose steep hills, wooded or vine-clad, with the yellow or reddish rock upon the ridges glowing against the hot sky. As I was moving south-west I had the afternoon sun full in the face. The lizards that darted across the path, raising little clouds of dust in their hurry, found this glare quite to their taste, but it was too much for me, and when at length I saw a leafy walnut tree I lay down in the shade until the fiery sun began to touch the high woods, the river, and the yellow maize-stalks with the milder tones of evening.

A narrow grassy lane between tall hedgerows sprinkled over with innumerable glistening blackberries led me to Frontenac, a village upon the rocky hillside. Here is a little church partly raised upon the site of a Roman or Gallo-Roman temple. A broken column left standing was included in the wall of the Romanesque apse, upon the lower masonry of which both pagan and Christian hands have worked. The nave has been rebuilt in modern times, but in the open space before the entrance Roman coffins crop up above the rough paving, separated from each other only by a few feet. There is a stone coffin lying right across the doorway, and the *curé*, whom I drew into conversation, confided to me, with a comical smile upon his pale dark face, that he had raised a fragment of the lid to see if anything more enduring than man had been left there, but that he found nothing but very fine dust. Every bone had become powder. This priest was a companionable man, and he must have looked upon me with a less suspicious eye than most people hereabouts, for he invited me into his house to take a *petit verre* with him. But the sun was getting near the end of his journey, and I had to fare on foot to the next village; so I thought it better to decline the offer.

The next village was St. Pierre-Toirac, also built upon the hillside above the Lot. It is a larger place than Frontenac, and must have been of considerable importance in the Middle Ages, to judge from its fortified church, whose high gloomy walls give it the appearance of a veritable stronghold. Some of the inhabitants say that it was built by the English, but the architecture does not indicate that such was the case. The interior is a beautiful example of the Romanesque style. The capitals of the columns are fit to serve as models, so strongly typical are the designs, and so exquisite is their workmanship. It is probable that the walls of the church were raised, and that it was turned into a fortress during the religious wars of the thirteenth century between Catholics and Albigenses, which explain the existence of so many fortified churches in Languedoc and Guyenne, as well as so many ruins.

I had reached this church by an old archway, whose origin was evidently defensive, and crossing the dim and silent square, surrounded by mediæval houses, some half ruinous, and all more or less adorned with pellitory, ivy-linaria, and other wall-plants which had fixed their roots between the gaping stones, I passed through another archway, and stopped at a terrace belonging to a ruined château or country-house. Here I was looking at the valley of the Lot in the warm after-glow of sunset, when an elderly gentleman came up to me and disturbed my contemplative mood by asking me not very courteously if I wanted to see anybody. I was somewhat taken aback to find such an important-looking person in such a dilapidated place. I tried, however, not to appear too much overcome, and explained that it was only with the intention of seeing the picturesque that I had found my way to that ruinous spot. The agreeable person who had questioned me now let me understand that it was his spot, and informed me that nobody was allowed to see it 'sans être presenté.' Then, looking at me very fiercely, he said :

'Are you an Englishman or a German?'

'An Englishman,' I replied, whereupon his

ferocious expression relaxed considerably, but he did not become genial.

I retired from his ruin considerably disgusted with its owner, who contrasted badly with all Frenchmen in his social position whom I had previously met. I asked a woman who he was, and she replied that all she knew about him was that he was an 'espèce de noble.' Her cruelty was unintentional. The next morning I learnt from an old Crimean soldier, who knew I was English because he had drained many a glass with my fellow-countrymen, that the magnates of the village had held a consultation overnight upon the advisability of coming down upon me in a body and asking me for my papers. Nothing came of it, which was well for me, for I had come away without my papers.

There was rain that night, and when morning came it had changed the face of the world. The sun was shining again and warmly, but summer had gone and autumn had come. Upon the rocky slopes the maples were on fire; in the valley the large leaves of the walnut-trees mimicked the sunshine, and by the river-side the tall poplars, as they bowed to the water deities, cast upon the mirror of many tones the image of a trembling golden leaf repeated beyond all power of numbering. A little rain had been enough to produce this magical change. It had opened the great feast of colour that brings the year to its gray, sad close.

But the sky was brilliantly blue when I left

St. Pierre-Toirac. The next village was Laroque-Toirac. The houses were clustered near the foot of an escarped hill, where thinly-scattered pines relieved the glare of the naked limestone. Upon a precipitous rock dominating the village is a castle, the lower works of which belong to the Feudal Ages, the upper to the Renaissance epoch—a combination very frequent in this district. The mullioned windows and the graceful balustrade, carried along a high archway, are in strong contrast to the stern and dark masonry of the feudal stronghold. This picturesque incongruity reaches its climax in the lofty round tower upon which a dovecot has been grafted, whose extinguisher-roof, with long drooping eaves, is quite out of keeping with the machicolations which remain a little below the line of the embattled parapet that has disappeared. The castle is now used for the schools of the commune, and a score or so of little boys and girls whom I met on my way up the rough path stared at me with much astonishment. I climbed to a bastion of the outer works, where a fig-tree, growing from the old wall, and reaching above it, softened the horror of the precipice; for such it really was. The masonry was a continuation of one of those walls of rock which give such a distinctive character to the geological formation of this region. The village lay far below—a broken surface of tiled roofs, sloping rapidly towards the Lot, itself a broad ribbon of many blended colours, winding through the sunlit plain. The castle of Laroque belonged to the Cardaillac family. In 1342 it was stormed and taken by Bertegot Lebret, captain of a strong company of English, who had established their headquarters at Gréalou.

As I approached Montbrun, the next village, the rocks which hemmed in the valley became more boldly escarped. In their lower part the beds of lias were shown with singular regularity. Box and pines and sumach were the chief vegetation upon the stony slopes, where the scattered masses of dark-green foliage gave by contrast a whiter glitter to the stones. Montbrun, like so many of the little towns and villages hereabouts, is built upon rocks immediately below a protecting stronghold, or, rather, what was one centuries ago. The windows of some of the dwellings look out upon the sheer precipice. The vine clambers over ruined houses and old walls built on to the rock, and seemingly a part of it. Of the mediaeval castle little is left besides the keep. The Marquis de Cadaillac, to whom it belonged, strengthened the fortifications with the hope that the stronghold would be able to resist any attack by the English; but it was nevertheless captured by them.

After leaving Montbrun I saw nothing more of civilization until I came near a woman seated on a doorstep, and engaged in the exciting occupation of fleaing a cat. She held the animal upon its back between her knees, and was so engrossed by the pleasures of the chase that she scarcely looked up to answer a question I put to her. The word *café* painted upon a piece of board hung over another door enticed me inside, for it was now nearly midday, and I had been in search of the picturesque since seven o'clock, sustained by nothing more substantial than a bowl of black coffee and a piece of bread. This is the only breakfast that one can expect in a rural auberge of Southern France. If milk is wanted in the coffee it must be asked for over-night, and even then it is very doubtful if the cow will be found in time. To ask for butter with the bread would be looked upon as a sign of eccentric gluttony, but to cap this request with a demand for bacon and eggs at seven in the morning, as a man fresh from England might do with complete unconsciousness of his depravity, would be to openly confess one's self capable of any crime. People who travel should never be slaves to any notions on eating and drinking, for such obstinacy brings its own punishment.

A stout woman with a coloured silk kerchief on her head met me with a good-tempered face, and, after considering what she could do for me in the way of lunch, said, as though a bright idea had suddenly struck her:

'I have just killed some geese; would monsieur like me to cook him some of the blood?'

'Merci!' I replied. 'Please think of something else.'

An Englishman may possibly become reconciled to snails and frogs as food, but never, I should say, to goose's blood. In about twenty minutes a meal was ready for me, composed of soup containing great pieces of bread, lumps of pumpkin and haricots; minced pork that had been boiled with the soup in a goose's neck, then a veal cutlet, covered with a thick layer of chopped garlic. Horace says that this herb is only fit for the stomachs of reapers, but every man who loves garlic in France is not a reaper. Strangers to this region had better reconcile themselves both to its perfume and its flavour without loss of time, for of all the seasoning essences provided by nature for the delight of mankind garlic is most esteemed here. Those who have a horror of it would fare very badly at a *table-d'hôte* at Cahors, for its refined odour rises as soon as the soup is brought in, and does not leave until after the salad. Even then the unconverted say that it is still present. To cultivate a taste for garlic is, therefore, essential to happiness here.

I crossed a toll-bridge over the river just below Cajarc, and again entered the department of the Aveyron, my object being to ascend the valley of a tributary of the Lot, to a spot where it flows out of a pool of unknown depth, called the Gouffre de Lantouy. The road passed under the village of Savagnac, built upon the hillside. A Renaissance castle, with sham machicolations, little chambers with their projecting floors resting on brackets, turrets on *culs de lampe* and with extinguisher roofs, and a high terrace overgrown with vines and fig-trees left to fight their own battle, lorded it over all the other houses, like a sunflower in an onion-bed. But the castle, although it gives itself such aristocratic airs, is, in these days, nothing but a farmhouse, sacks of maize being now stored in rooms where ladies once touched the lute with white fingers, and where gentlemen may have crumpled their frills while swearing eternal love upon their knees. The little cemetery adjoining the château has swallowed up the great and the lowly century after century, and the rank grass, now sprinkled with the lingering flowers of summer, barely covers their mingled bones. The old gravestones, left undisturbed, have sunk into the soil nearly out of sight. Such is the ending of all that is human.

A little beyond this village a peasant woman, whom I met picking up walnuts from the road that was strewn with them, lifted her wide-brimmed straw hat to me as I passed. This was indeed polite. I now left the road, and followed a lane by the stream that flows out of the *gouffre*. This valley is narrow enough to be called a gorge, and the stony hills on either side presented a picture of utter barrenness and desolation. But along the level of the stream the deep-green grass shadowed by the hill was lighted up with the pale-purple death-torches of the poisonous colchicum. After crossing a stubble-field, now overgrown by the violet-coloured pimpernel, I reached the sinister pool, fringed with the flag's sword-like leaves and shadowed by willows and alders. I expected to find the water all in tumult; but no, it had the dark, solemn stillness of the mountain tarn. The two streams that poured out of it to meet a little lower down the valley hardly murmured as they started upon their journey amidst the iris and sedge, although the body of water was strong enough to turn a millwheel.

There is something that troubles the imagination in the appearance of this lonely pool for ever silently overflowing, and so deep that nobody as yet has been able to find the bottom. On the side of the stony hill close by are some ruined walls of a church and convent, said to have been built by St. Mamphaise. The peasants of the district have an extraordinary story with regard to this convent, which is either the cause or the consequence of the superstitious awe in which they hold the Gouffre de Lantouy. This legend is to the effect that the conventual building was once inhabited by women who ate children, and that a certain mother, whose baby they had kidnapped and eaten, cursed them so heartily and to such purpose that the *gouffre* was formed, and their convent, or the greater part of it, was supernaturally carried down the hill and plunged into the bottomless water. The legend also says that those who stand by the pool on St. John's Eve will hear the convent bell ringing. It not being St. John's Eve when I was there I was unable to test the truth of this part of the legend. What I did hear was a raven croaking from the ruin, and the sound harmonized well with the air of mystery and gloom hanging over the spot.

There is some historic reason for believing that the convent at Lantouy was founded by Charlemagne. Very near this spot are the remains of some ancient fortified works, and the locality is known as 'La domaine de Waïffier.' This name is evidently the same as Waïfré. There is reason to believe that the last of the sovereign Dukes of Aquitaine made a stand here when pursued by his implacable enemy Pepin le Bref. The people pronounce the word 'Waïffier' as though it commenced with a 'G.'

Towards evening I recrossed the Lot and entered Cajarc. Passing through the little town, which is not in itself very interesting, I took a path winding up the side of the hill, at the base of which lies the burg. I wished to see a cascade that has a local reputation for beauty. I reached the foot of a high, fantastic rock, from the ledges of which masses of ivy hung woven together like a veritable tapestry of nature. A small stream descended from the uppermost ridge upon a rock covered with moss showing every hue of green, and then into a dark pool below. The hillside above the cascade has been extensively tunnelled for phosphate. An Englishman discovered the value of the site, and dug a fortune out of it. There are several phosphate-mines in this district, all more or less connected with British enterprise. Phosphate inspires respect for Englishmen here, for it has been the means of giving a great deal of employment and rendering petty proprietors, who could barely get a living out of their thankless soil, comparatively rich. The inhabitants, therefore, consider English speculators in the light of public benefactors, and such they have really proved, although the motive that brought them here was scarcely a philanthropic one. Neither the French nor the British public has any conception of the extent to which the mineral resources of France are worked by the English.

Cajarc, although it looks like a village to-day, was once a fortified town of considerable importance in the Quercy. Its inhabitants offered an obstinate resistance to the English on several occasions. In 1290 they refused to swear fealty to the King of England until their lord, the Bishop of Cahors, gave them the order to do so in the name of the King of France. Subsequently in the same and the following century, when the Quercynois were again in arms against the English, various attempts to take the town by surprise failed through the vigilance and courage of the burghers. To punish them, the English, in 1368, destroyed their bridge across the Lot, of which some remnants may still be seen.

After leaving Cajarc in the morning I was soon alone with Nature on the right bank of the river. Autumn was there in a gusty mood, blowing yellow leaves down from the hills upon the water and driving them towards the sea over the rippled, gray surface lit up with cold, steel-like gleams of sunshine struggling through the vapour. The wilderness of herbs and under-shrubs along the banks was no longer aflame with flowers. Dead thistles, whose feathered seeds had drifted far away upon the wind to found new colonies, and a multitude of withered spikes and racemes, told the old story of the summer's life passing into the death or sleep of winter. Yet the river-banks were not without flowers. A rose, very like the 'monthly rose' of English gardens, was still blooming there, together with hawkweed, wild reseda, and a mint with lilac-coloured blossoms which one sees on every bit of waste ground throughout this region.

A rock rising from the river's bank carried the ruin of an ancient chapel. Only the apse was left. It contained one narrow deeply-splayed Romanesque window, and a piscina where the priest washed his hands. The altar-stone lay upon the ground where the altar must have stood, and behind it a rough wooden cross had been piously raised to remind the passer-by that the spot was hallowed.

The road now ran under high red rocks or steep stony slopes, where, on neglected terraces overgrown with weeds, the dead or dying vines repeated the monotonous tale of the phylloxera.

I passed through the village of Lannagol, mostly built upon rocks overlooking the bed of its dried-up stream, and was soon again under the desert hills, where the fiery maple flashed amid the sombre foliage of the box. The next village or hamlet was a very curious one. Rows of little houses, some of them mere huts, were built against the side of the rock under the shelter of huge masses of oolite or lias projecting like the stories of mediæval dwellings. People climbed to their habitations, like goats, up very steep paths winding amongst the rocks. The overleaning walls were blackened to a great height by the smoke from the chimneys.

It was dusk when I crossed a bridge leading to the village of Cénevières, where I intended to pass the night. There was a very fair inn here, less picturesque than many of the auberges of the country, but cleaner, perhaps, for this reason. The aubergiste was suspicious of me at first, as he afterwards admitted, for like others he had turned over in his mind the question, Is he a German spy? Judging from my own experience in this part of France, I should say that a German tourist would not spend a very happy holiday here. The sentiment of the Parisians towards the Teuton is fraternal love compared to that of the Southern French. These people proved themselves to be thorough going haters in the religious wars, and the old character is still strong in them.

Although the Germans in 1870-71 did not show themselves in Guyenne, the resentment of the inhabitants towards them is intense, and it is the vivacity of this feeling that renders them so suspicious of foreigners. I noticed, however, that as I went farther down the Lot the people became more genial, so that the long evenings in the rural inns generally passed very pleasantly. Dinner over, I usually took possession of a chimney-corner, the only place where one can be really warm on autumnal nights, and while satisfying the curiosity of the rustic intelligence concerning the English and their ways I gathered much information that was useful to me respecting local customs and the caverns, castles and legends of the district where I happened to be. By nine o'clock everybody was yawning, and if the village blacksmith, the postman, and the bell-ringer had not left by that time, they were in an unusually dissipated frame of mind. By ten o'clock the great kitchen was dark, and the mice were making up a quadrille upon the hearth, supposing no cat to be looking on.

Early the next morning I was climbing the hill towards the Castle of Cénevières. This building is a most picturesque jumble of the castellated styles of the thirteenth, fifteenth, and sixteenth centuries. The oldest part of the structure—and it is very considerable—is that of a frowning feudal fortress of great strength, built upon a rock, which on the side of the Lot is a perpendicular wall some 200 feet high. The inhabitants agree in saying that the feudal walls are the work of the English, but they are probably in error. The original castle belonged to Waïfré. It afterwards passed to the Gourdon family, who doubtless rebuilt it upon the old foundations. The last descendant of this family was one of the most ardent Huguenots in the Quercy. The late Gothic superstructure, which is still inhabited, has a very high-pitched roof, with dormer windows covered by high gables with elaborate carvings. Very near this castle, in the side of the cliff, is a fortified cavern, which for centuries has gone by the name of La Grotte des Anglais. It must have been in communication with the castle, of which it may have served as an outwork or a place of refuge in the last extremity. I might have passed the whole day trying to find it but for the help of a peasant, who led the way down the rocks, hanging on to bushes of box. The remains of a small tower, pierced with loopholes on one side of the opening, and the other ruined masonry, leave no doubt as to the defensive use to which this cavern was at one time put.

Having left Cénevières, I recrossed the Lot and passed through Saint-Martin, a village of little interest, but the point from which it is most convenient to reach a certain cave where animals of the prehistoric ages were obliging enough to die, so that their skeletons might be preserved for the delight and instruction of the modern scientific bone-hunter. This is not one of the celebrated caves in the department, consequently the visitor with thoughts fixed on bones may carry away a sackful if he has the patience to grub for them. If the cavern were near

Paris it would give rise to a fierce competition between the palæontologist and the *chiffonnier*, but placed where it is the soil has not yet been much disturbed. I went in search of it up a very steep, stony hill, and there had the good fortune to meet an old woman who was coming down over the rocks with surprising nimbleness. She knew at once what I wanted. Although she spoke French with great difficulty, three words out of every five being *patois*, she made me understand that her house was just in front of the cave, and that it was not to be visited without her consent and guidance. She therefore began to reascend the 'mountain,' as she called the hill, making signs to me to follow. There was certainly nothing wrong with the old woman's lungs, for it was as much as I could do to keep pace with her, especially when she led the way up almost naked rock. At length we reached the brow of the hill, where a cottage showed itself in a desert of limestone, but where a little garden, by dint of long labour, had been formed upon a natural terrace on which the sun's rays fell warmly.

The woman left me in the cottage while she went to find her daughter. It was composed of one small room, in which there were two beds, an old worm-eaten walnut buffet, an eight-day clock after the pattern of Sir Humphrey's, a hearth covered with white wood-ashes, a large wheel-shaped loaf of black bread in a rack, onions, grapes, garlic, and balls of twisted hemp hanging from the beams, baskets of maize and chestnuts, and a great copper swing-pot, only a little less imposing than the one out of which the scullion fished the fowls for Sancho Pança. I afterwards learned that two couples slept in the two beds—the old pair and the young pair.

Presently the old woman reappeared, followed by a much younger one, carrying upon her head a copper water-pot, that glowed in the sun like a wind-blown brand. Having set down her pot, the daughter, a rather wild-looking person with sun-baked face and large gleaming eyes, took an old-fashioned brass dish-lamp—a deformed and vulgar descendant of the agate lamp held in the hand of the antique priestess—and, after bringing the wick towards the lip, lighted it. I lit the candle I had brought with me, and, followed by the old woman, we entered the cavern, near the mouth of which was a fig-tree. The entrance was so small that it was almost necessary to crawl for some distance; but it must have been much larger at one time if the story that the younger woman told me about the bones of a mastodon having been discovered inside was well founded. As we proceeded, the roof rose rapidly, so that the rocks overhead could not presently be seen by the light of the candle and lamp. Farther in, the roof became lower, and it was connected with the ground in places by natural columns of vast size, formed in the course of ages by the calcareous deposit of the dropping water.

Near the end of the cavern, at about 100 yards from the entrance, various holes dug in the yellow soil showed where the bone-searchers had been at work. I had ample encouragement, for I had only to stir the earth a little to find bones half turned to stone. I selected two or three teeth with the hope that a scientific friend would say they were a mastodon's or a mammoth's. If I had liked the prospect of carrying a bag of bones on my back down the valley of the Lot, I might have taken away many very large specimens. I called to mind, however, an experience of early days which prevented me from being again a martyr to science. I had found a quantity of bones in a newly-dug gravel-pit, and fully believing that they belonged to some animal that flourished before the flood, I carried them twelve miles with infinite labour and suffering, and then learned that they were part of the anatomy of a very modern cow. Since that adventure I have left bones for those who understand them.

I had ample leisure for studying the river after leaving Saint-Martin, for I stood upon the bank waiting for a ferryman until I lost all the patience I had brought with me. He was taking a couple of oxen harnessed to a cart across the stream, and the strong wind that was blowing sent the great flat boat far out of its course.

Every day I noticed a larger fleet of floating leaves upon the water, hurrying through the ever-

curving valley, drifting over the golden reflections
of other leaves that waited for the gust to cast them
too upon the water ; passing into the deep shadow
of bridges whose arches resounded with mournful
murmurs, riding the white foam of the weirs,
whirling in the dark eddies beyond, gliding in the
brown shade of vine-clad hills and under the beetling
brows of solemn rocks, now mingling with the
imaged dovecot with pigeons perched upon the red-
tiled roof, now with the tracery of Gothic gables
or the grim blackness of feudal walls splashed with
fern and pellitory, now in a warm glow of dying
summer, and now in the melancholy gray of wintry
clouds heavy with rain. Away they went, the
multitudinous leaves—children of the poplar, the
willow, the fig-tree, and vine ; some broad and
clumsy like rafts or barges, others slender and
graceful like little skiffs; all stained with some
brilliant colour of autumn.

I had reckoned upon getting a mid-day meal at a
village called Crégols on the opposite bank, but
when I at length reached it I had another trial.
The only place of public entertainment was an
exceedingly dirty hovel that called itself a *café*,
and the woman who kept it declared that she had
no victuals of any sort in the house. This, of
course, was not true, but it was a polite way of
saying that she did not wish to be bothered with me.
The wayfarer in the little-travelled districts of
France must not expect to find in all his stopping-

places a fowl ready to be placed on the spit for him. Had I obtained a meal at Crégols, I should have looked for some dolmens said to be in the neighbourhood, but failure in one respect spoilt my zeal in the other. I am afraid, moreover, that I only half appreciated the grandeur of some prodigious walls of rock which I passed in my rapid walk to the little town of Saint-Cirq-la-Popie. It is deplorable to think how much the mind is influenced by internal circumstances which ought to have nothing to do with the spirit.

After climbing a steep wood where there were unripe medlars, I came in sight of a small burg, lying high above the Lot in a hollow of the hill. A fortress-like church towered far above the closely-packed red-tiled roofs sprinkled with dormer windows, and upon a still higher rock were the ruined walls of a castle. This was Saint-Cirq-la-Popie, a place no less quaint than its name. I was presently seated in a dimly-lighted back-room of an auberge, whose walls—built apparently for eternity—dated from the Middle Ages. The hostess, who, as I entered, was gossiping with some cronies in the dark doorway, while she pretended to twist the wool that she carried upon the most rustic of distaffs—a common forked stick—laid this down, and, blowing up the embers on the hearth, proceeded to cook some eggs *sur le plat*. This with bread, goat-cheese and walnuts, and an excellent wine of the district—the new vintage—made my lunch. The fact that there was no meat in the auberge reminded me that it was Friday.

Speaking generally, the inhabitants of the Lot are practising Catholics. The churches are well filled, and the clergy are as comfortably off as French priests can expect to be in these days. It is no uncommon thing for a *curé* to keep his trap. I have several times met priests on horseback in the Quercy, but never without thinking that they would look better if they used side-saddles.

The early Gothic Church of Saint-Cirq-la-Popie, to judge by its high massive walls and round tower, was raised more with the idea of defence than ornament. In the interior there is still the feeling of Romanesque repose; nothing of the animation of the Pointed style—no vine-leaf or other foliage breaks the severity of the lines. I ascended the tower with the bell-ringer's boy. In the bell-loft, with other lumber, was an old 'stretcher,' very much less luxurious than the *brancard* that is used in Paris for carrying the sick and wounded. It was composed of two poles, with cross-pieces and a railing down the sides. I ascertained that this piece of village carpentry was used within the memory of people still living for carrying the dead to the cemetery merely wrapped in their shrouds. They were buried without coffins, not because wood was difficult to obtain, but because the four boards had not yet come into fashion at Saint-Cirq-la-Popie. To bury a person in such a manner even there would nowadays cause great scandal, but sixty or seventy years ago it was considered folly to put good wood into a grave. A homespun sheet was thought to be all that was needed to break the harshness of the falling clay. And there are people who call this age that gives coffins even to the poorest dead utilitarian!

Among other curious things I saw in this ancient out-of-the-way burg were two mediæval corn-measures forming part of a heap of stones in a street corner. They had much the appearance of very primitive holy-water stoups, such as are to be seen in some rural churches, for they were blocks of stone rounded and hollowed out with the chisel. Each of these measures, however, had a hole in the side near the bottom for the corn to run through, and irons to which a little flap-door was once affixed in front of this hole. The commune treated these stones as rubbish until some accidental visitor offered 500 francs for them; now it clings to them tightly, hoping, no doubt, that the price will go up. Prowling curiosity-hunters are destined to destroy much of the archæological interest of these old towns. They are doing to them what Lord Elgin did to the Parthenon. Fantastic corbel-heads and other sculptured details disappear every year from the Gothic houses, and find their way into private museums.

As I was taking leave of the bellringer's boy— a lad of about fifteen—he put his hand under his blouse and, pulling out a snuff-box, offered me a pinch. I had met plenty of boys who chewed tobacco—they abound along the coast of Brittany—but never one who carried a snuff-box before.

The castle whose ruins are to be seen on the bluff above the church received Henry IV. as a guest after his memorable exploit at Cahors.

A man who was laying eel-lines across the Lot consented to take me to the other side in his boat, and there I struck the road to Cahors, which closely borders the river all along this valley. In several places it is tunnelled through the rock, where the buttresses of the cliffs could not be conveniently shattered with dynamite. All this has been the work of late years. Previously the passage between the river and the rocks was about as bad as it could be. The English fortified several of the caverns in the cliffs commanding the passage, to which the name of *Le Défilé des Anglais* was consequently given. Now the term is applied by the country people to the caves themselves, wherever these have been walled up for defence.

I soon reached one of these caverns, the embattled wall being a conspicuous object from the road below. Having fallen into ruin, it had lately been repaired at the expense of the commune. To an Englishman the spot could not be otherwise than strangely interesting. I imagined my own language being spoken there five or six centuries ago, and speculated as to whether the accent was Cockney or Lancashire, or West of England.

Several fig-trees grew beside the walled-up cavern, and I was picking the ripest of the fruit when I heard a voice from the road below calling upon me to come down. Peering through the boughs, I saw a man seated in the smallest and most gimcrack of donkey-carts. It was something like a grocer's box on wheels. The owner gave violent smacks to the plank on which he was sitting, to let me understand that there was room for another person. I did not think there could be, but I left the figs and came down the rocks.

'If you are going to Saint-Géry,' said the man, 'I can take you about five kilomètres on the road.'

'But the donkey,' I urged, 'will lie down and roll.'

'What, the little beast! Not he! he will go along like an arrow.'

I accepted the invitation, and away went the donkey, making himself as much like an arrow on the wing as any ass could. My companion, who was a handsome fellow, with a moustache that one would expect to see upon the face of a Sicilian brigand, was a cantonnier, and as he scraped out the ditches and mended the roads, his donkey browsed upon what he could find along the wayside. In summer and winter they were inseparable companions, and had come to thoroughly understand one another. The cantonnier confided to me that he was formerly employed in the phosphate quarries, and that he had closed his experience in this line by working three months without wages for an Englishman whose speculation turned out a failure. Phosphate then lost its charm upon the proprietor of the donkey-cart, for it had caused him to 'eat all his economies,' and he resigned himself to the wages of a road-mender, which were small but sure. It was getting dusk when we parted. My next companion on the road was a poor bent-backed, shambling, idiotic youth, who was driving home two long-tailed sheep and a lamb, and who had just enough intelligence for this work. He kept at my side for a mile or two, flourishing a long stick over the backs of the sheep and uttering melancholy cries. His presence was not cheering, but I had to put up with it, for when I walked fast he ran. He likewise left me at length to continue my way alone, and his wild cries became fainter and fainter. Then, in the deepening dusk, two churches, one on each side of the river, began to sound the angelus. A gleam of yellow light lingered in the western sky between two dark hills, but the clouds above and the river below were of the colour of slate. Suddenly a bright blaze flashed across the dim and misty valley from a cottage hearth where a woman had just thrown on a faggot to boil the evening soup, and the gloom of nature was at once filled with the sentiment of home.

It was quite dark when I reached Saint-Géry. The narrow passage leading to the best inn was illumined by the red glare of a forge, and was rich in odours ancient and modern. Some twenty geese tightly packed in a pen close to the hostelry door announced my arrival with shrieks of derision. They said: 'It's Friday; no goose for you to-night!' Those who suppose that geese cannot laugh have not studied bucolic poetry from nature. The forge was attached to the inn, a very common arrangement here, and one that enables the traveller who has hope of sleep at daybreak—because the fleas are then thinking of rest after labour—to enjoy the melody of the 'Harmonious Blacksmith' without the help of Handel.

I was not cheered by the sight of goose or turkey turning on the spit as I entered the vast smoke-begrimed kitchen, lighted chiefly by the flame of the fire, but the great chain-pot sent forth a perfume that was not offensive, although the soup was *maigre*. There was also fish that had been freshly pulled out of the Lot. The cooking left something to be desired, but the hostess, the wife of the Harmonious Blacksmith, had thrown her best intentions into it. A rosy light wine grown upon the side of a neighbouring hill compensated for the lack of culinary art. It was a rather rough inn, but I had been in many worse. Seated in the chimney-corner after dinner, and sending the smoke of my pipe to join the sparks of the blazing wood up the yawning gulf where the soot hung like stalactites below the calm sky and twinkling stars, I had a long talk with the aubergiste, who told me that he had been taken prisoner at Sedan, and had, in consequence, spent eight months in Germany. He considered that he had been as well treated by the Germans as a prisoner could expect to be. He had always enough to eat, but there was no soup, and, lacking this, he thought it impossible for any civilized stomach to be happy.

Rural inns have charms, especially when they are old and picturesque, and smell of the Middle Ages; but to be kept a prisoner in one of them by rainy weather is apt to plunge a restless wanderer into the Slough of Despond. The chances are that the inn itself becomes at such times a slough, so that Bunyan's expression is then applicable in a real as well as in a figurative sense. There is a constant coming in and going out of peasants with dripping *sabots*, of dogs with wet paws, and draggle-tailed hens with miry feet; geese, and even pigs, not unfrequently venture inside, and have a good walk round before their presence is noticed and they are treated to quotations from Rabelais, enforced with the broomstick. Then the rain beats in at the open door, which nobody troubles to close. Under these circumstances, the rural inn becomes detestable. So I found the auberge at Saint-Géry, where I waited long hours for the weather to change, after having received a soaking while climbing the escarped cliffs which rise so grandly on one side of the little town.

A fortified cavern and a ruined castle tempted me up the rocks. On my way I passed a small Gothic house, dating apparently from the fourteenth or fifteenth century, with pointed arched doorway and window lights separated by slender columns with foliated capitals carved by no clumsy rustic workman. The boy who accompanied me had the key. As I entered I was met on the threshold by the fragrant odour of the tobacco-plant; I perceived that the mediaeval house was used for drying tobacco-leaves —a purpose that could never have been in the imagination of the original owner, for those stones were laid together long before the herb, now so precious to the French Government, was brought to Europe. The stalks with all the leaves attached were hung to strings stretched from wall to wall. There is much tobacco grown hereabouts in the valley of the Lot, but it is considered too strong for smoking purposes, and is therefore made into snuff. When the utmost care has been used in its cultivation and drying the price paid by the Government to the grower does not exceed half a franc the pound. Those who enjoy the privilege of raising it consider the money very hardly earned.

I reached the ruined castle at the foot of the limestone buttresses supporting the plateau above. Enough is left of the wall to show that it must have been a strong place at one time. It is attributed by common consent to the English. Protected on one side by the abrupt rock, it overlooked the valley from a height that to an enemy must have been very difficult of access. The fortified cavern is in the escarped cliff above the castle, with which there was, perhaps, a secret communication. The upper part of the wall is gone, but what remains is about ten feet high and nine feet thick. Swallows build their nests in the roof of the cavern, and the spot is noisy with the harsh cries of countless jackdaws. These sagacious birds can doubtless tell many stories of the English which they received from their ancestors.

When I returned to the auberge wet and shivering, I found no sympathy, the thoughts of the hostess being occupied by a matter that interested her more deeply. The badgers had eaten her maize which she needed for fattening the geese, and her tongue was busily employed in wishing them every misfortune, both in time and eternity. Badgers are very numerous in the district, and they continue to increase and multiply, while the peasants jeopardise their immortal interests by cursing them every time they see a spike of ripening maize pulled down and half stripped of its corn. In the daytime these animals sleep comfortably, digesting their ill-gotten meal in the holes of the rocks, which are so honeycombed that dogs cannot easily get at the hermits. Moreover, it is not every dog that likes the prospect of being bitten nearly in half, the badger being much better known than trusted by the canine race.

Another animal that flourishes here, in spite of the hatred in which it is held by the inhabitants, is the fox, which likewise finds the valley an Elysium on account of the convenient neighbourhood of the rocks pierced with multitudinous holes. Badgers and foxes, with all their vices, are preferable to the hyenas which used to infest this part of France, as is proved by the bones found in the larger caverns. The present inhabitants ought to take comfort from this reflection, but they do not.

While the aubergiste's wife, a little woman who carried about with her the outline of a wine-cask, was breathing maledictions upon the badgers, and venting her fury upon the little boy-of-all-work — who, being used to such outbursts, ate his morning allowance of soup with philosophic indifference — I took up my place again in the chimney-corner, and endeavoured to dry myself on all sides by somewhat imitating the movement of a fowl turning on the spit.

At length the heavy pall of cloud lifted, and when the first yellow gleam of sunshine filtering through vapour was reflected by the puddles and streaming roofs, I walked out of Saint-Géry. When the last houses were out of sight, solitude added to the desolate grandeur of the scenery. It was a relief to be alone with Nature, dripping as she was with recent tears, after the depressing influences of the inn—the dimness, dampness, and dirt, the unreasoning anger of ignorance, the dull routine of human beings whose chief concern was to feed themselves and the animals which helped them to live. As an alterative to the mind, rural life is of real value in the case of those who have been carried round and round in the whirlpool of a great city until they have had more than enough of the sensation ; but, like other useful medicines, rusticity is best when taken in moderate doses, and at judicious intervals. I had stayed at Saint-Géry long enough to feel like a fish that in jumping out of water for the sake of variety had fallen upon the mud.

The sun that changes the face of all things, and warms the ideas no less than the earth, now shone out from a blue sky, spreading fire over the ruddy tops of the chestnut woods, and flashing into the dark caverns of the ancient crags, fringed with box, sumach and juniper. I noticed that one of these caverns had been fortified, but my curiosity was satisfied with the distant view. A yellow chicory, quite leafless, was still blooming on the stony banks, and I also found a white scabious. Green hellebore and wild madder flourished amidst the broken limestone. A forest of brown maize-stalks, from which the golden corn had been gathered, followed the windings of the river, now turgid and tumultuous, and dyed sienna-red by the washings from the hills. Every day the increasing water as it descended the weirs made a wilder tumult. These weirs are a great

beauty to the Lot, for they generally form an angle
or the arc of a circle, and the river tumbles over the
rough blocks like a natural cascade. They are connected with a series of locks, which render the
stream navigable from the sea; but one rarely sees
a barge upon it now, the railway having completely
ruined the water traffic, and caused a most elaborate
and costly piece of engineering to be practically useless.

The valley now widened out, and a village came
into view, together with a ruined castle upon a
mamelon, that rose like a volcanic cone from the
plain. On the castle wall an immense wooden cross
had been set, showing against the sky with an effect
truly grand. The village was Vers, and the castle,
which was built by the English, is called the
Château de Béars.

At Vers I was met by an old man, who insisted
upon showing me another cave fortified by the
English, after taking the precaution of telling me
that he would accept nothing for his trouble. He
was long and lean and brown, and had a 'glittering
eye' like the Ancient Mariner, but his conversation
was much more cheerful than that of the hero who
shot the albatross. He was a born actor, for he
accompanied his talk with magnificent dramatic
gestures, and, after letting his voice drop suddenly
to a tragic whisper, he would raise it again to the
most gusty and blustering heights of sound. He
was a strong type of the Southerner, inasmuch as

all this amazing vehemence and gesticulation was quite uncalled for. It is remarkable, however, how much may be done by mere action and intonation to impress the listener with the idea that the speaker must be a person of uncommon intelligence. But when half a dozen such talkers are engaged in discussion upon some trivial topic, and each employs the same means to enforce his views upon the rest (this occurs nightly in the *cafés* at Cahors), the Northerner is inclined to think that they are all mad.

The wiry old man explained to me, in order to account for the ease and agility with which, notwithstanding his years and his awkward *sabots*, he stepped from block to block in the ascent, that he had been all his life a rock-blaster. At length we reached the cavern. The English, who used it as a refuge, had shown much sagacity in its selection, for the enemy that attacked them there would have been compelled to climb up the face of the rock beneath by following zigzag ledges, while the besieged behind their loopholed wall were raining arrows and bolts upon them. The wall, as it exists, is twenty or thirty feet high. There is a doorway protected by an inner wall. To reach the upper loopholes and parapet the men mounted upon oak beams resting crosswise between the masonry and the rock. One massive beam, crumbling and worm-eaten, as may be supposed after the centuries that it has been there, may still be seen serving as the lintel of a window.

I made a rather long stay at Vers, in order to visit the site of a Celtic town on the *causse;* but I did not start upon this journey until the next day. The inn where I put up was much more comfortable than some others which I had chosen for night-quarters while wandering down the valley. To anybody fresh from London it would have seemed primitive indeed, with its broad hearth and massive iron dogs, its enormous fire built with logs and the roots of trees, and its cosy chimney-corners, where the sitters' heads were from time to time enveloped with wreathing smoke; but I had grown so accustomed to such sights that this hostelry seemed to contain all the blessings and commodities of an advanced state of civilization.

The hostess was a good and sprightly cook, and I watched her proceedings with a keen interest as I sat upon one of the seats in the chimney. Having hitched the pot that contained the soup upon the hook at the end of the sooty chain, she raked out embers from the centre of the burning mass, and made separate fires with them upon the hearth. Others she carried to a range of small charcoal fireplaces on one side of the spacious kitchen, and very soon afterwards she had saucepans and a frying-pan and a gridiron all murmuring or hissing together. There was too much garlic in her cookery, but I had also grown used to that. Although the phylloxera had blighted nearly all the vineyards in this region, the landlord here was able to put upon the table some wine, grown upon his own hillside, not unworthy of the ancient reputation of the Cahors district for its vintage.

After dinner I returned to the chimney-corner which was decidedly the most comfortable place in the inn, in spite of the smoke and the close neighbourhood of soot, and set about obtaining information from the aubergiste and his cronies who had dropped in concerning the exact whereabouts of a Celtic town whose ruined fortifications, I knew, were to be found somewhere among the barren hills to the west of Vers. It was some time before I could make these men understand what I was really in search of, and when they understood they seemed to think I was a little mad, until the idea struck them that I might be a dealer in antiquities, hoping to pick up certain odds and ends that would repay me for the trouble of walking to such a desolate and uninteresting spot.

At length I gathered that the site of the ancient *oppidum* was at Murcens, a hamlet upon a hill, half a day's walk away to the west, and that the best way to reach it was to follow the valley of the Vers. At about seven o'clock the next morning I started, and, having been warned that I should find no inn where I could get a meal, I took with me some provisions.

It was a gray, dreary morning, and at that hour the weather could not have been more November-like had I been upon the banks of the Severn or the Trent, instead of being by one of the rivers of our ancient southern province of Guyenne.

As I turned westward up the valley of the Vers, I passed under detached fragments of the aqueduct built by the Romans to carry water to Cahors. By taking advantage of the rocks which hem in the narrow valley, they saved themselves the trouble of raising arches to the desired height to ensure the flow. The conduit is carried along upon a ledge hewn out of the natural wall, projecting masses of rock being cut through with the hammer and chisel. The masonry is of undressed stone, but so firmly cemented that it is scarcely less solid than the rock itself.

Where an inconvenient buttress projected, a narrow passage was cut through it for the channel, and the marks of the chisel look as fresh as if they had been lately made. Much of this aqueduct was destroyed in quite recent days, when the rocks were blasted to make room for the road to Cahors. The Romans may have thought of many destructive agencies being employed upon their work, but dynamite was certainly not one of them. Box and hellebore, bramble and dogwood, moss and ferns, have been striving for centuries to conceal all trace of the conduit, and those whose foreknowledge did not lead them to look for it might easily pass by without observing it.

The road followed the stream, now a furious torrent that a man on horseback could hardly ford without risk of being carried away. Two or three weeks previously a mere thread of water wound its way amongst the stones in the centre of the channel. It is one of the many streams which in Guyenne gradually disappear in summer, but at the return of winter fill the long-scorched and silent valleys with the sound of roaring waters. On either side of the gorge rose abrupt stony hills thinly wooded, chiefly with stunted oak, or escarped craggy cliffs pierced with yawning caverns. There was no sunshine, but the multitude of lingering leaves lit up all the desert hills with a quiet, solemn flame. Here and there, amidst the pale gold of the maple or the browner, ruddier gold of the oak, glowed darkly the deep crimson fire of a solitary cornel. In steady, unchanging contrast with these colours was the sombre green of the box.

The stream descends in a series of cascades, and there is a mighty roar of waters. For many yards I have for a companion a little wren, that flies from twig to twig through the well-nigh naked hedge along the wayside, now hidden behind a bramble's crimson-spotted leaf, now mingled with a tracery of twigs and thorns. I can almost believe it to be the same wren that kept up with me years ago in English lanes, and since then has travelled with me so many miles in France, vanishing for long periods, but reappearing as if by enchantment in some roadside hedge, its eyes bright with recognition, and every movement friendly. Whimsical little bird, or gentle spirit in disguise, we may travel many a mile together yet.

My thoughts were turned from the wren by a carrier's cart, which the people of the country would term a *diligence*. It was like a great oblong box with one end knocked out, set on wheels. The interior was a black hole, crammed with people and bundles. When I looked for my little feathered friend it was gone, but we shall meet again.

Two or three miles farther up the valley, near a small village or hamlet, I crossed a low bridge over the Vers, and by following the road on the other side, still ascending the course of the stream, I came to a spot where a volume of water that would soon have filled a large reservoir flowed quietly out of a little hollow at the foot of great rocks. It was the Fountain of Polémie which, on account of its abundant flow in all seasons, is supposed to have been the source from which the Romans led their aqueduct to Divona—now called Cahors. The water of this fountain, which derives its name from Polemius, a Roman functionary, is of limpid purity, and its constancy proves that it rises from a great depth. The Romans must have carried the water on arches across the valley, and probably for a considerable distance down it, before they made use of the natural wall of rock in the manner described, but not a trace remains of the arches, or even of the piers.

In order to reach the tableland of Murcens, it

was necessary to cross again the roaring torrent of the Vers, and after several vain attempts to do so, by means of the rocks lying in its bed, I came to a bridge which solved the difficulty. The scene was now sublimely rugged and desolate. On each side the majestic rocks reared their ever-varying fantastic shapes towards the sky.

I knew, from what I had been told, that Murcens lay somewhere above the escarped cliff on my left, and at no great distance, but the difficulty was to reach it. I had heard of a path, but I soon gave up the attempt to find it. As there was not a human being to be seen who could give me any counsel, I commenced climbing the hill in the direction that I wished to take. It was anything but straightforward walking. The lower part of the steep was strewn with loose stones like shingle, that slipped under the feet, so that I had to proceed in zigzag fashion, taking advantage of every bush of juniper and box and root of hellebore as a foothold. But the vegetation grew denser as I ascended, and I had soon plenty of box and dwarf oak to help me.

Before attempting to climb the upper wall of solid limestone, I sat in the mouth of a small cavern to eat the frugal lunch I had brought with me, and to contemplate at my leisure the wild grandeur of the valley. I could not have chosen a better place for feeling in one sense dwindled, in another expanded, by the majesty of the stony solitude. Suddenly, while I gazed, the sun breaking through the clouds made every yellow tree brighten like melting gold, and drew a voice of joy from all the dumb and solemn rocks.

I leave the remnants of my feast for the foxes and magpies to quarrel over, and feel prepared to put forth a vigorous effort to reach the *causse*. I work my way up by the clefts of the rocks, hanging on to the tough box, and getting thoroughly asperged by the dew that has not yet dried upon it. I have not ascended fifty feet in this manner before I am as wet as if I had been walking in a thunderstorm. I creep along ledges, now to the right and now to the left, and presently I am only about twenty-five feet from the top of the rock that prevents me from attaining my object. It is pleasanter to look up than to look down, for, being no climber of mountain peaks, I do not enjoy the sensation of clinging to the side of a precipice like a caterpillar to a leaf. Now comes the real trial. The rest of the rock above me is quite bare of vegetation. By making four or five steps upwards to the left, then to the right, a spot can be reached where the trouble will be over; but some of these steps need a considerable stretch of leg, and the eye cannot measure the distance with certainty. Time is on the wing, and the days are short. I am strongly tempted to make the essay, but doubt holds me back. What if I were to get half-way, and were unable to go on or to retreat? What if I were to slip and roll down the rocks? If I were not killed outright, who would be likely to come to my aid in such a solitude? The ravens would have ample time to pick my bones before those interested in my existence would know what had happened to me. I resolve that I will not give the birds of ill omen a chance of so rare a meal. In descending, the cold showers from the box bushes add to my humiliation and discomfiture.

Keeping on the side of the hill, I went farther up the valley, seeking a place where I could with better chance of success make another attack upon the difficulties of this rocky wall. I found what I wanted at no great distance, the only objection to the spot being the dense growth of shrubs laden with moisture. It was almost like wading through a stream. At length the line of high rocks was passed, and I was upon land that, notwithstanding its steepness and the multitude of stones with which it was strewn, had undergone some cultivation. That wine had not long since been grown here was evident from the numerous stumps of vines which had been killed by the phylloxera. A few lingering flowers of hawkweed relieved the monotony of the dreary waste. But if, while looking before me, the scene was saddening, in looking back there was a sublime and soul-lifting picture which the forces of Nature had been painting unmolested for ages. I can do no more than suggest to the imagination the combined effect of those fantastic rocks rising from the foaming torrent to the drifting, tinted clouds; buttresses and bastions of the ancient earth laid bare in the mysterious night of the inconceivable past, some black and gloomy as the walls of a feudal moat, others yellow like ochre; others, again, sun-bleached almost to whiteness, yet streaked with ruddy veins—all flashed here and there with burning oak and maple, or sprinkled with the purple blood of the dogwood's dying leaves.

Half an hour later I reached Murcens, only inhabited nowadays by a few peasants in two or three scattered hovels, which are nevertheless called farms. I had no difficulty in finding the wall of the Gaulish town. It is broken down completely in places, but the almost circular line is plainly marked. The site of the *oppidum* is a little table-land raised above the surrounding soil by a natural embankment.

The circumvallation in its best preserved places is now from seven to ten feet high. The materials used were such as Cæsar mentions as having been employed by the Gauls in the fortification of their *oppida*, namely, timber and rough stone. I looked for some traces of the wooden uprights, but although there is ample proof that they existed there down to our own time, my search was vain. Many stones measuring several feet in length were set in a perpendicular position to give extra stability to the wall. The ancient rampart is in places completely overgrown with juniper. Within the wall is nothing but level field. No trace remains of any buildings that stood there in the far-off days when the spot was the scene of all passions and vanities, the tragedy and comedy of human life, even as we know it now. The peasant as he ploughs or digs turns up from time to time a bit of worked metal, such as a coin, or a ring, but the hands which held them may or may not be mingled with the soil that supports the buckwheat and enables the peasant to live. The Gaulish city has no history.

I had some talk with a peasant who had been watching my movements wonderingly. He spoke French with difficulty, but his boy—a lad of about twelve, who had been to school—could help him over the stiles. I got the man to speak about the ancient wall, although it was evidently not a subject that interested him so deeply as his pigsty. He told me that all the beams of wood had now rotted (they may have helped to warm him on winter evenings), but that nails a foot long were often found amongst the stones of the wall or in the soil round about it. He had picked up several, but had taken no care of them. When I observed that I should much like to see one, he said he thought there was one somewhere in his house, and, calling to his wife, he asked her in Languedocian to look for it. While she was searching he drew my attention to a circular stone lying upon the top of his rough garden wall. It was about a foot in diameter, and concave on one side.

'What is it?' I asked.

'A millstone,' he replied.

True enough, it was one of the stones of an ancient handmill, such as was used in remote antiquity, chiefly by women, for grinding corn. It must have been as nearly as possible after the pattern of the first implement invented by man for this purpose. The peasant set no value upon it; I could have had it for a trifle—even for nothing, had I been so minded; but whatever liking I may have for antiquities, it did not gird me up to the task of carrying a millstone back to Vers. The nail could not be found, so I was obliged to leave without a souvenir of the Celtic city. Not far from this spot I found another millstone that would have fitted the one I had left and made a complete mill. They are doubtless still lying upon the dreary height of Murcens; but whether they are there or in a museum, they are as dumb as any other stones, although, had they the power to repeat some of the gossip of the women who once bent over them, they might tell us a good deal that Cæsar left out of his Commentaries because he thought it unimportant, but which we should much like to know.

I did not return by the way I came, but kept upon the plateau, going southward, then, dropping down into another valley at the bottom of which ran a tributary of the Vers, I crossed the stream and rose upon the opposite hill, making somewhat at random towards the village of Cours. On my way I started numerous coveys of red partridges from juniper and box and other low shrubs. Had I been a sportsman carrying a gun I could have made a splendid ' bag,' but these chances generally fall to those who cannot profit by them. I wondered, however, at the lack of poaching enterprise in a district so near to Cahors. It is not often that one meets even in the least populous parts of France so many partridges in an absolutely wild state. Immense flocks of larks were likewise feeding upon the moorland, and the beating of their countless wings as they rose made a mighty sound when it suddenly broke the silence of the hills. I met a small peasant girl with a face as dark as a Moorish child's, and eyes wonderfully large and lustrous. She was a beautiful little creature of a far Southern or Arabian type. At Cours I talked to a woman who was a pure type of the red-haired Celt. How strange it is that with all the intermixture of blood in the course of many centuries the old racial characteristics return when they are deeply ingrained in a people!

I took shelter at Cours from a sharp storm. It was a wretched little village upon a dreary height, and the inhabitants, to whom French was a foreign language, stared at me as if I had been a gorilla. An overhanging ' bush ' of juniper led me to a very small inn that bore the familiar signs of antiquity, dirt and poverty. I knocked at the old oak door studded with nail-heads, and it presently creaked upon its rusty hinges. It was opened by a poor woman whose manners were wofully uncouth; but this was no fault of hers. She was honest, as such rough people generally are. Although she must have wanted money, it did not occur to her to extract a sou from the stranger beyond the just price. When I had had enough of her wine and bread and cheese, and asked her to tell me what I owed her, she carefully measured with her eye how much wine was left in the bottle, how much bread and cheese I had taken, and when her severe calculation was finished she replied, in a harsh, firm voice, which meant that the reckoning being made she intended to stand by it: 'Eleven sous.'

When I met the valley of the Vers again the storm had passed far away; the evening rose was in the calm heaven, and the topmost oaks along the rocky ridge burnt like tapers upon a high altar of the vast temple whose roof is the vaulted sky. Already the deep aisles were dim with gathering shadows. When I reached the inn at Vers it was nearly dark, and after my day's tramp I was very glad to exchange the outer gloom for the brightness of the cheery fireside and the warmth of the chimney-corner beside the redly glowing logs.

The next day brought me to the end of my long journey down the valley of the Lot, for I had decided to leave the country below Cahors until some future day. I reached the city of Divona when the yellow glow of the autumnal rainy sunset was stealing up the ancient walls.

It is always with a certain dread that I say anything about history, because when I am once upon such high stilts I do not know when I shall be able to get down again. Moreover, when one is so mounted, one has to step very judiciously, especially in a region like this, where the roads to knowledge are so roughly paved. Nothing would be easier, however, than to fill a book with the history of Cahors, for the place, since the days of the Romans, has gone through such vicissitudes, and witnessed such stirring events, that those who wish to turn over the leaves of its past have abundant facilities for doing so; but it will be better for me to speak rather of what I have seen than what I have read. Nevertheless, my impressions of this old town at the present day would be like salad without salt if no flavour of the past were put into them.

When, a mud-bespattered tramp, I came down the road by the winding Lot, and saw the pale golden light rising upon the walls of churches and towers high above me, I could not but think of some of the terrible scenes which, in the course of 2,000 years, were witnessed by the inhabitants of Cahors. In the fast-falling twilight I saw the ghosts of the Vandals and Visigoths who helped to destroy the works of the Cæsars, and passed onward to the unknown; of the Franks who burnt Cahors in the sixth century; of the Arab hordes, dabbled with blood, who afterwards came up from the South slaying, violating, plundering; of the English troops under Henry II. besieging and taking the town, accompanied by the Chancellor, Thomas-à-Becket; of the Albigenses and Catholics, who cut one another's throats for the good of their souls; of the Huguenots and Catholics, who repeated these horrors in the sixteenth century for the same excellent reason; but of all these shadows, the most interesting and the most dramatic was that of Henry IV. He was then Henry of Navarre, and the hope of the Protestants in the South, while Cahors was one of the strongholds of Catholicism. What a feat of war was that capture of Cahors by Henry with only 1,400 men, after almost incessant fighting in the streets for five days and nights! How red the paving-stones must have been on the sixth day, when it was all over, and the surviving Navarrese, smarting from the recollection of the tiles and stones that were hurled at them from the roofs by women, children, and old men, had given the final draught of blood to their vengeful swords! Never was so much courage so uselessly squandered. After the lapse of three centuries Henry's figure is still full of heroic life, as, with back set against a shop-window, and sword in hand, he shouted to those who urged upon him the hopelessness of his enterprise: 'My retreat from this town will be that of my soul from my body!'

It is really wonderful how certain buildings at Cahors have been preserved to the present day through all the storms of the tempestuous Middle

Ages, the furious hurricane of religious hatred that brought those centuries to a close, and that other one, the Revolution, which ushered in the new epoch of liberty and well-dressed poverty. Of these buildings, the cathedral has the right to be named first. As a whole it cannot be called a beautiful structure, for its form is graceless ; but what a charm there is in its details! Even its incongruity has a singular fascination. This most evident incongruity arises from the combination that it expresses of the Gothic and Byzantine styles. The façade is very early Gothic (about the year 1200), still full of Romanesque feeling, but the church having been much pulled about in the thirteenth century, it came to have a semi-Byzantine choir and two depressed domes, quite Byzantine, over the nave. The façade, with its squat towers, exhibits no lofty aim, but when one looks at the tabernacle-work in the tympan of the divided portal, the capitals in the jambs and the mouldings of the archivolts, the elegant arcade above and the tracery of the great rose window, one feels that although the Pointed style could not yet embody its dream of beauty by means of the tower and spire, it was moving towards it through a maze of glorious ideas destined to become inseparable from the spirit of the perfect whole. Still more interesting than this façade is that of the north portal (twelfth century). It is Gothic, but the general treatment has much of that Byzantine-Romanesque which produced some very remarkable buildings in Southern

France. The portal is very wide and deeply recessed, and the tympan is crowded with bas-reliefs, the sculpture of which, rude yet expressive, is of a striking originality. There is a broad arabesque moulding in the doorway suggesting Eastern influence, and the closed arcade of the façade, with corbel-table above and its row of uncouth monstrous heads, presents a highly curious effect of struggling motives in early Gothic art.

The nave is much below the level of the soil, and is reached by a flight of steps from the main entrance. These steps at the Sunday services are crowded by the poorer class of churchgoers, sitting, kneeling, and standing, and, like the catechumens in the narthex of the early Christian basilica, they look as if they were separated from the rest of the faithful on account of their not being as yet full-fledged members of the Church. It may well be that they are the most faithful of the faithful, for stone is a hard thing to kneel upon, and when it is used for this purpose without ostentation, it is a pretty safe test of sincerity in religion. The grouping of the people here would interest at once an artistic eye, the more so because many of the women of Cahors wear upon their heads kerchiefs of brilliant-coloured silk folded in a peculiarly graceful and picturesque manner, resembling the Bordelaise coiffure, but yet distinct.

The nave of the cathedral is cold and tasteless, the whole effect being centred upon the choir, the richness of which is quite dazzling. The vault is a semi-dome, and the apse-like polygonal termination is pierced with several lofty Gothic windows, so that the eye rests upon the harmonious lines of the tracery and a subdued blaze of many-coloured glass. Then the columns, walls and vaulting of the choir are elaborately decorated in the Byzantine style, and, all the tones being kept in æsthetic harmony, the result is a general effect more beautiful than gorgeous. I observed it under most favoured circumstances. I entered the church for the first time during the pontifical High Mass. The vestments of the mitred bishop under his canopy, of the officiating priest and deacons, of the canons in their stalls, together with the white surplices and scarlet cassocks of the many choir-boys distributed over the vast sanctuary, and the sunbeams stained with the hues of purple, crimson, azure and green by the windows that reached towards the sky, falling upon all these figures, realized with a splendour more Oriental than Western a grand conception of colour in relation to a religious ideal.

After leaving the cathedral I changed my ideas by looking for the Gambetta grocery. It happened to be close by. The name is still over the door, but the shop no longer looks democratic. Its plateglass, its fresh paint and gilding, and the specimens of ceramic art which fill the window, give it somewhat the air of one of those London shops kept by ladies of title. Sugar, coffee, and candles now hide themselves in the far background, as though they were ashamed of their own celebrity.

Much more interesting than this shop is the old house where Gambetta spent his childhood. His parents did not live on the premises where they carried on their business. Therefore the odour of honey and vinegar had not, after all, so much to do with the formation of the clever boy's character. I found the house down a dark passage. The rooms occupied by the Gambetta family are now those of a small *restaurateur* for the working class. After ascending some steps, I entered a greasy, grimy, dimly-lighted room, the floor of which had never felt water save what had been sprinkled upon it to lay the dust. It had the old-fashioned hearth and firedogs and gaping sooty chimney, a bare table or so for the customers, a shelf with bottles, and the ordinary furniture and utensils of the provincial kitchen. Here I had some white wine with the present occupier as a reason for being in a place that must have often resounded with the infantile screams of Léon Gambetta. I ascertained that he was not born in this house, but that he was brought to it when about three months old, and that he passed his childhood here. I was shown an adjoining room, darker, dingier, less persecuted by soap, if possible, than the other. It was here that Gambetta slept in those early years. Did he ever dream here of a great room in a palace, draped with black and silver, of a catafalque fit for a prince, of a coffin heaped with flowers?

Again I changed my ideas by crossing the Lot and searching for the Fountain of Divona, now called the Fontaine des Chartreux. The old name is Celtic, and as it charmed the Romans they preserved it. Following the river downward, I came to a spot where a great stream flowed silently and mysteriously out of a cavity at the foot of lofty rocks overgrown by herbage and low shrubs that seemed to have been left untouched by the hand of Autumn, that burns and beautifies. The water came out of the hill like a broad sheet of green glass, giving scarcely any sign of movement until it reached a low weir, where it turned to the whiteness of snow. The Romans held this beautiful fountain in high esteem, and if they had known how to raise the water to the level of the town on the opposite bank of the river, they need not have taken the trouble to carry an aqueduct some twenty miles from the valley of the Vers. Nowadays it is the Fountain of Divona that supplies Cahors with water.

Still following the river, I came to that famous bridge, the Pont Valentré, which is one of the most interesting specimens of the defensive architecture of the Middle Ages. It is probably the most curious example of a fortified bridge in existence. In addition to its embattled parapet, it is protected by three high slender towers, machicolated, crenellated, and loopholed. The archway of each spans the road over the bridge, so that an enemy who forced the portcullis of the first, and ran the gauntlet of the hot lead from the machicolations, would have to repeat the same performance twice before reaching the bank on which the town is built. This bridge was raised at the commencement of the fourteenth century. By what wonderful chance was it preserved intact, together with its towers, after the invention of gunpowder? The people of Cahors call it the Pont du Diable. When a certain stone was placed in one of the towers, the devil always pulled it out, or did so until lately.

THE END.

www.ingramcontent.com/pod-product-compliance
Lightning Source LLC
Chambersburg PA
CBHW030558300426
44111CB00009B/1028